THE
NATIONS
WITHIN

The Past
and
Future
of American
Indian
Sovereignty

THE nations WITHIN

Vine Deloria, Jr.
Clifford M. Lytle

University of Texas Press, Austin

Preface copyright © 1998 by University of Texas Press
First University of Texas Press edition, 1998
Reprinted by arrangement with Pantheon Books, a division of Random House, Inc.

⊗ The paper used in this publication meets the minimum requirements of American National Standard for Information Sciences—Permanence of Paper for Printed Library Materials, ANSI Z39.48-1984.

Library of Congress Cataloging-in-Publication Data

Deloria, Vine.
    The nations within : the past and future of American Indian sovereignty / Vine Deloria, Jr., Clifford M. Lytle.
        p.   cm.
    Originally published: New York : Pantheon Books, c1984.
    Includes bibliographical references and index.
    ISBN 0-292-71598-6 (pbk. : alk. paper)
    1. Indians of North America—Politics and government.   2. Indians of North America—Government relations.—1934–   3. Indians of North America—Civil rights.   I. Lytle, Clifford M.   II. Title.
E98.T77D44   1998
323.1'197073—dc21   97-33718

Contents

Preface to the Second Edition   *vii*

1   A Status Higher Than States   *1*

2   Domestic Dependent Nations   *16*

3   The Organization of the Reservations   *28*

4   The Movement for Reform   *37*

5   The Vision of the Red Atlantis   *55*

6   The Collier Bill   *66*

7   The House Hearings   *80*

8   The Indian Congresses   *101*

9   Political Conflict in the Upper House   *122*

10   The Indian Reorganization Act of 1934 and the Collier Bill: A Comparison   *140*

CONTENTS

11   *Bringing the Law to Life*   *154*

12   *Ratification and Its Aftermath*   *171*

13   *The Barren Years*   *183*

14   *The Indian Civil Rights Act*   *200*

15   *The Cry for Self-Determination*   *215*

16   *The Emergence of Indian Nationalism*   *232*

17   *The Future of Indian Nations*   *244*

Appendix: A Comparison of the Wheeler–Howard Act and the Original Collier Bill   *269*

Notes   *275*

Bibliography   *286*

Index   *289*

Preface to the
Second Edition

When the first edition of this book was released in 1984, feelings still ran high against tribal governments organized under the Wheeler-Howard, or Indian Reorganization, Act (IRA). The question then, as now, revolved about the authority granted by federal law to these governments and the role of IRA governments in eclipsing traditional ways of doing things. A great deal of anger still can be found, but the intervening thirteen years have shown that traditional practices always show up in the way Indians act. Today we have a new generation of people in tribal government who make every effort to observe traditional values.

There has been movement toward international recognition of some kind by the United Nations and other countries. While this development seems rather abstract, it is essential to tribal survival now to recognize that the world economy has become one gigantic network of interests. Whether any Indian tribes will receive status among the nations of the world is less important than the fact that Indians are now seeing themselves in a global perspective and are becoming aware of the economic forces shaping the human future. Awareness of the effects of international events and of the importance of establishing links to international organizations and movements places a new responsibility on tribal leaders. Interpreting these abstract relationships to reservation residents is a difficult but worthwhile task. Hopefully the art of politics and governing will be seen in a new light, and

Indians will see new ways to reconcile the old traditions with the IRA governments.

Gaming has become a major industry for many tribes since the first edition of this book, and although we have added a sketch of the nature of this change, developments are proceeding at such a rapid pace that it is difficult to evaluate just how gaming income will affect tribal perceptions of Indians. Some tribes have become enormously wealthy, while the majority, because they are located far from population centers, have virtually no resources to speak of. At some point the wealthier tribes should begin investing in the fortunes of those without gaming resources. A sudden shift in the federal policy defining the status of Indians may well return the pendulum of survival back toward those tribes who own significant land areas.

Tribal governments, like cities and counties, are facing a time when radical changes in the structure of government must take place. The town square, main street, and agency headquarters have all become vestiges of the past. New ways of providing services, and indeed new services, are required. Citizens and tribal members often chafe at regulations and restrictions, not realizing that the burgeoning population has created a need for government to service large numbers of people in a rather impersonal way. Some means must be found to humanize social and political institutions once again. Here traditional Indian customs, if properly incorporated into the functions and mission of government, can prove effective and important. While tribes have continuing problems, the future looks brighter than it has in decades.

With the advent of the Carter, Reagan, Bush, and Clinton administrations, Indian tribes shifted their attention to more practical programmatic considerations. Declining federal budgets for domestic social programs meant a drastic cutback in funds available to operate reservation programs, and unemployment rose swiftly on most reservations, which had depended on an expanding number of federal programs for meeting the employment needs of the tribe. Neither Carter nor Reagan disturbed the status of tribal governments with new policy considerations. They were content to admonish the tribes to enter the world of private enterprise and reduce their dependence on federal largess.

Recent federal policy has featured the slogan of a "government-to-government relationship," which is intended to represent the older idea that tribes have a special political status with respect to the United States. Few Indians or bureaucrats know exactly what this recent phrase is supposed to represent. Since tribes are very much dependent upon the federal government for their operating funds and for permission to exploit the natural resources present on their reservations, the idea of two governments meeting in some kind of contemporary contractual arrangement on anything approaching an equal bargaining position itself seems ludicrous. Nevertheless, the Indian leadership has insisted that this description of the federal-tribal relationship is accurate and describes precisely the framework they believe exists. It is no mistake, in view of the accommodations the tribes and the United States have worked out, that many tribes have erected signs proclaiming their nationhood, that traditional Indians believe themselves to be sovereign entities endowed with almost mystical political powers, and that groups of Indians have recently appeared on the world scene demanding some form of representation in the United Nations.

When we look back at the treaty negotiations between the United States and the respective Indian tribes, there is little mention of the complex of ideas that constitutes nationhood. Indeed, we find very little awareness in either the Indians or the American treaty commissioners that an important status was being changed by the agreement that people were then making. During the 1868 treaty negotiations with the Sioux and Arapaho, at times the American commissioners speak of the Sioux as a small nation that can be totally destroyed by the kind of warfare the United States was willing to wage were peace not forthcoming from the talks. Strangely, the Indians were not cowed by the threats of the treaty commissioners; they knew so little about the white man that they believed they could prevail if the whites wished to make war on them. So finally the United States signed the treaty and agreed to one of the most humiliating provisions it ever accepted. The forts on the Bozeman Trail were abandoned at the demand of Red Cloud that the Sioux hunting lands be kept inviolate, and as the soldiers departed, the Indians rushed into the stockades and burned them to the ground.

In almost every treaty, however, the concern of the Indians was the preservation of the people, and it is in this concept of the people that we find both the psychological and the political keys that unlock the puzzling dilemma of the present and enable us to understand why American Indians view the world as they do today. When we understand the idea of the people, we can also learn how the idea of the treaty became so sacred to Indians that even today, more than a century after most of the treaties were made, Indians still refer to the provisions as if the agreement were made last week. The treaty, for most tribes, was a sacred pledge made by one people to another and required no more than the integrity of each party for enforcement. That the United States quickly insisted that the treaties should be interpreted rigidly as strictly legal documents has galled succeeding generations of Indians and made permanent peace between Indians and the federal government impossible.

The idea of the people is primarily a religious conception, and with most American Indian tribes it begins somewhere in the primordial mists. In that time the people were gathered together but did not yet see themselves as a distinct people. A holy man had a dream or a vision; quasi-mythological figures of cosmic importance revealed themselves, or in some other manner the people were instructed. They were given ceremonies and rituals that enabled them to find their place on the continent. Quite often they were given prophecies that informed them of the historical journey ahead. In some instances the people were told to migrate until a special place was revealed; in the interim, as with the Hebrews wandering in the deserts of Sinai, the older generation, which had lost faith, and the cynics and skeptics in the group would be eliminated until the people were strong enough to receive the message.

Tribal names generally reflect the basic idea that these particular people have been chosen from among the various peoples of the universe—including mammals, birds, and reptiles, as well as other humans,—to hold a special relationship with the higher powers. Thus, most tribal names can be interpreted simply to mean "the people." There are, of course, some variations that have arisen in the course of the Indian historical journey. The people who pierced their noses have now become the Nez Perce; the prosperous people have become the Gros Ventres; the allies, or friends, have become the Sioux; and some tribes have called themselves after the holy location where they finally came to rest—they are now the people who live at the lake, on the river, and so forth.

Because the tribes understood their place in the universe as one given specifically to them, they had no need to evolve special political institutions to shape and order their society. A council at which everyone could speak, a council to remind the people of their sacred obligations to the cosmos and to themselves, was sufficient for most purposes. The tribes needed no other form of government except the gentle reminder by elders of the tribe when the people were assembled to maintain their institutions. Indians had a good idea of nationhood, but they had no knowledge of the other attributes of political existence that other people saw as important. Most of all, Indians had no awareness of the complexity that plagued the lives of other peoples, in particular the Europeans.

First contact with Europeans shocked both the Indians and the explorers. The Indians watched without understanding as the residents in the European settlements bowed before arbitrary authority with a meekness that the Indians loathed. They believed that the whites had surrendered all moral substance in exchange for security in the anonymity of institutional life. Many Indian nicknames spoke derisively of the whites as "people who take orders," or "people who march in a straight line." And most Indians had little respect for white military leaders who commanded their soldiers to go to war while remaining safely in the rear. They might fear a white general, but they respected very few of them.

To the Europeans, Indians appeared as the lowest form of man. No formal institutions were apparent. Leaders seemed to come and go almost whimsically. One might be negotiating with one chief on one occasion and be faced with a different person for no apparent reason except that the Indian council had designated the new man to speak for them. In tracing the source of political authority, whites were really baffled. No one seemed to be in charge of anything. A promise need not even be written down, and there seemed to be no appeal to any formal authority when things went wrong. In frustration, an early painter designated the Iroquois chiefs "kings," because there seemed no way to describe their status within the tribe except through the medium of familiar English feudal terminology.

It was difficult for whites not to conclude that chiefs had some mystical but absolute power over other members of the tribe. Most important social/political positions of leadership in tribes depended upon the personal prestige and charisma of the individual. Even where a position as chief was a lifetime office, qualifications for filling the post were primarily those of personal integrity and honesty, so that respect rather than popularity was the criterion by which Indians selected who would lead them. When whites faced an Indian war party, they would note that the Indians fought with great vigor until their leader was killed. More often than not, the Indian spirit for the fight declined swiftly upon the death of the war chief, and the whites would win the day. This kind of behavior suggested an influence far beyond that of the hereditary European monarchs over their subjects.

The truth, not surprisingly, was somewhat less mysterious. Indian war parties most often were composed of individuals who had volunteered upon hearing the announcement, made by the village crier, that a certain warrior was thinking about leading a war party. No one had to go; there was never a draft in Indian society. But if the warrior had a good reputation and the adventure promised others a chance to distinguish themselves, and if they had confidence in the warrior, then a lot of men, particularly younger warriors, would clamor to be a part of the expedition. It is not difficult to imagine the trauma of seeing the leader of the war party, a man in whom the rest of the party had placed implicit trust, killed in a skirmish. Having lost their leader, the chances were that the Indians would quickly leave the field of combat, disheartened at the turn of events. Whites interpreted this kind of Indian behavior as a political/military defeat rather than the personal loss to the members of the war party that it really represented.

This kind of leadership and these kinds of informal governing institutions existed long ago, when Indian tribes were free to live as they wished. The substance of those days remained in Indian memories, but the political institutions and social customs changed quite rapidly as more contact with whites occurred, so that we can speak of these things now as the spiritual but not the practical heritage of Indians. The important thing is that there was no doubt in the minds of most Indians that, whatever the Europeans might say or do, they were still a free people, that they controlled certain lands and territories, and that they had the capability of punishing their enemies for any transgressions they might suffer. With respect to the lands they lived on, many Indians felt a strong religious duty to protect their territory. Future generations would need the lands to live on, many previous generations had migrated long distances to arrive finally at the place where the people were intended to live. One could sell neither the future nor the past, and land cessions represented the loss of both future and past to most Indians.

The expanding white population did not see it the same way, however, and when faced with the unpleasant choice of ceding their lands or drowning in the tidal wave of settlers who stood poised on their borders, the Indians wisely surrendered their lands and reluctantly moved west, hoping to escape white civilization by staying away from it. The course of American history demonstrated that even this faint hope was illusory, and the result of constant moves and land cessions is our scattered bits and pieces of reservation land that dot the maps of western states today.

Although Indians surrendered the physical occupation and ownership of their ancestral lands, they did not abandon the spiritual possession that had been a part of them. Even today most Indians regard their homeland as the area where their tribe originally lived. The Cherokees recently filed suit to prevent the flooding of a part of the Little Tennessee River where the old Cherokee town of Tellico once stood. To most Americans, and certainly to the federal courts who heard the case, the claim of the Indians was remote, if it existed at all, geographical proximity being more tangible and comprehensible than spiritual beliefs. To the Cherokees who opposed the flooding of the area, however, there was no responsible course except to fight as best they were able to prevent the destruction of their town site.

Today a terrible divisiveness exists in many Indian tribes. After almost a century of regarding their reservations as a place to live, Indians are discovering that they are being prodded into leasing large portions of their lands so that others can exploit the mineral wealth that lies underneath the ground. Sometimes it is coal deposits, often oil or natural gas, and occasionally uranium and molybdenum. All of these resources bring immense wealth, and their removal always leaves some desolation that cannot easily be corrected. Sacredness and utility confront each other within the tribal psyche, and it is not at all certain how Indians will decide the issue. Most Indians are so desperately poor that any kind of income seems a godsend. On the other hand, ancient teachings inform Indians that the true mark of a civilization is its ability to live in a location with a minimum disruption of its features.

Strangely, in the old prophecies in many tribes the conditions of today are accurately forecast. "A time will come," these prophecies begin, and they speak of the total desolation of the land and the abandonment of ceremonials and rituals. Religious gifts of power seem not to be eternal but only to be used within this particular segment of cosmic time. As this cycle of planetary history ends, the culture and traditions that enabled the people to live are changed, distorted, and worn out. When all resources are exhausted, there will be tremendous cosmic upheaval and a new heaven and earth will be created. The survivors of the catastrophe will then receive new prophecies and ceremonies that will enable the people to prosper in the radically changed world that has come to pass. While traditional Indians mourn each step of dissolution, they are also comforted with the thought that a completely new world is in the process of being created. The fact remains, however, that the experience of this generation is one of transformation, heartbreak, and confusion.

The idea of peoplehood, of nationality, has gradually been transformed over the past two centuries into a new idea, one derived primarily from the European heritage, and with a singular focus distinct from the old Indian culture and traditions. It is also important to understand the primacy of land in the Indian psychological makeup, because, as land is alienated, all other forms of social cohesion also begin to erode, land having been the context in which the other forms have been created. In such ideas lie the conceptual keys to understanding how the Indian experiences the world today.

With such understanding, we can see that the occupation of Wounded Knee in 1973 was far more traumatic for Indians than it was for whites, who might have felt a little disturbed at the idea of Indian militants taking up arms against the United States. Wounded Knee is symbolic of the conflict that is raging in Indian hearts everywhere. It arose basically over the question of how the Sioux, and by extension other Indians, should deal with the untenable situation created by the federal government in their communities. The tribes faced seemingly insoluble problems involving the form of tribal government; the claims filed against the United States that were not moving toward resolution; the use of land, tribal and individual, on the reservation; and the nature of education that Indians were receiving. Above all was the perennial dilemma of how Indians could pursue their own religious traditions in a world that refused to recognize the essential spiritual nature of life.

Politically the Wounded Knee occupation pitted traditional Indians and militants against the established tribal government, which had adopted a constitution and bylaws during the New Deal under somewhat less than promising circumstances. The traditional Sioux had always been suspicious of the new tribal government and frequently voiced their opposition to it. But since the tribal government was the only form of political participation that the United States government would recognize and deal with, the traditionals had little choice except to boycott the tribal government and then hope that some crumbs would fall from the table of government largess, which had become available because of

the state statute. In July 1831 they were arrested and in September of that year convicted and sentenced to four years' hard labor. Their appeal reached the Supreme Court in October, and a writ of error was issued to the judges of the state of Georgia by the chief justice. The controversy, now squarely before the high tribunal, was resolved in a decision upholding the right of the missionaries to live and work within the Cherokee lands in conformity to the Cherokee laws and under the Cherokee treaties with the United States.

In this second effort to define the status of Indian tribes, Chief Justice Marshall elaborated on his vague characterization of the Cherokees as "domestic dependent nations."[2] He stated that the "Indian nations had always been considered as distinct, independent political communities, retaining their original natural rights, as the undisputed possessors of the soil, from time immemorial, with the single exception imposed by irresistible power, which excluded them from intercourse with any other European potentate than the first discoverer of the coast of the particular region claimed. . . ."[3] Marshall concluded that "a weak state, in order to provide for its safety, may place itself under the protection of one more powerful, without stripping itself of the right of government, and ceasing to be a state."[4] A good deal of the subsequent history of conflict between the United States and the Indian tribes has revolved around the question of preserving the right to self-government and the attributes of Indian sovereignty as suggested in Marshall's decision.

The Europeans have had an extraordinarily difficult time in understanding the structure, substance, and procedures of the Indian manner of governing their societies. Some non-Indian observers have regarded the Indian propensity to hold land in common as the principle that distinguishes Indians from the European political traditions. Others have suggested that religious beliefs and cultural patterns have prevented Indians from organizing themselves socially or politically in a fashion familiar and acceptable to European minds. A bit of truth exists in every explanation, because the two traditions, European and North American Indian, seem to be diametrically opposed at almost every point at which they could or should be tangent and parallel.

The most profound and persistent element that distinguishes Indian ways of governing from European-American forms is the very simple fact that non-Indians have tended to write down and record all the principles and procedures that they believe essential to the formation and operation of a government. The Indians, on the other hand, benefiting from a religious, cultural, social, and economic homogeneity in their tribal societies, have not found it necessary to formalize their political institutions by describing them in a document. In addition, at least with the American experience, citizenship has been a means by which diverse peoples were brought into a relatively homogeneous social whole, and in order to ensure good citizenship, the principles of government have been taught so that newcomers to society can adapt themselves to the rules and regulations under which everyone has agreed to live. Within an Indian tribal society, on the other hand, the simple fact of being born establishes both citizenship and, as the individual grows, a homogeneity of purpose and outlook. Customs, rituals, and traditions are a natural part of life, and individuals grow into an acceptance of them, eliminating the need for formal articulation of the rules of Indian tribal society.

Violation of these customs did involve action by the community to enforce its rules. The tribe, meeting in council, discussed the violation and called upon its knowledge of precedents in community history which were factually close to the incident under consideration. Great discussions ensued as the community attempted to decide whether or not the current incident was sufficiently similar to warrant the same solution. Although tribes used precedent for making their decisions, punishment was often devised to reflect the best solution for the community at that time and was not always dependent upon following the former resolution of the problem. Because of this great flexibility, there was no need to formulate a rigid set of laws and there was little inclination to make precedents absolute in the same way that the Anglo-Saxon legal tradition found necessary.

The forms of government that Indians have experienced during their contact with the United States have been a mixture of the two traditions. Washington has considered the tribes to be political entities capable of determining their own membership and, in some cases, citizenship as well when there was a distinction between the two ideas. Self-government, consequently, has come to mean those forms of government that the federal government deems acceptable and legitimate exercises of political power and that are recognizable by the executive and legislative branches. This modern conception of self-government dates from the New Deal era, when John Collier, as Commissioner of Indian Affairs, was able to replace the existing policy of assimilation with a new program, which advocated the preservation of tribal cultures and the promotion of federally recognized governments on the reservations. It is crucial to realize at the start that these have not necessarily been the forms of government that the Indian people themselves have demanded or appreciated and are certainly not the kind of government that most Indians, given a truly free choice in the matter, would have adopted by themselves. Traditional Indians see that the task of governing themselves requires the perpetuation of customs, beliefs, and practices whose origin can be traced to precontact times. At the same time, it is important to recognize that, given the decades of erosion traditional cultures have suffered and the sparsity of viable alternatives available in the twentieth century, the present organization of tribal governments is not necessarily an unreasonable compromise between what might have been and what was possible to accept. Let us be very clear, however: self-government is not and cannot be the same as self-determination so long as it exists at the whim of the controlling federal government.

Attempts to regulate the Indian tribes through the guise of an institution having some powers of self-government, although acting as a caretaker of the interests of the non-Indian, appear long before the New Deal. Since some of these institutions allowed a measure of freedom to the people, and did not involve rapid erosion of traditional social patterns, they were not rejected by the tribes.

The first adaptation of traditional forms of government to an institutional structure more compatible with European ideas of government was probably made by the Pueblo Indians of New Mexico shortly after the Spanish established military control over the New Mexico area. The original Pueblo government was a theocracy of priests who filled offices derived from supernatural or religious sources. A council of priests represented the Pueblo in its internal self-governing aspect, and their function was what we would today describe as judicial—the interpretation of tradition, the articulation of custom, and the application of existing beliefs in new situations.[5]

With the coming of the Spanish in the 1600s, the Pueblos discovered that they had to deal with a powerful and continuing political force external to their villages. The Spanish themselves insisted that the Pueblos add certain offices that could perform secular functions and assume responsiblity for relationships between the Pueblo and the governing authorities, secular and religious, in the Spanish colonial structure. Thus, the Pueblos were encouraged to add, and did add, a governor, a lieutenant governor, six captains, and seven *bickari,* who were responsible primarily to the religious authorities of the Catholic Church.[6] With some variations each Pueblo, except the Hopi of Arizona, adopted a secular government, which thereafter had a certain status in the eyes of Spanish and later Mexican governmental officials and protected the people from further intrusions by the Spanish. It was this secular government that received land grants and confirmation of water rights as both property and political privileges for the Pueblo. The antagonism between the traditional Pueblo priests and the Catholic missionaries made Spanish recognition of the preconquest Pueblo government an historical impossibility, and neither the Spanish nor the Mexican government would probably have been moved to recognize either political or property rights in the theocratic council.

The theocratic council, nevertheless, continued to govern the internal relationships of the Pueblos and to determine the important ceremonial year, which is the heart of Pueblo communal existence. The Pueblos have continued to govern themselves for nearly three centuries under this modified form of secular/religious government, and its presence for such a prolonged period of time suggests clearly that the modified compromise form established by the Spanish has indeed become the traditional government of the Pueblos. It is interesting to note that the compromise achieved by the Pueblos allowed them to adjust to the presence of European forms of government attempting to direct their lives on a larger geographical scale with a minimum of conflict and dissension.

Other tribes made similar adaptations in order to survive during the early decades of contact with Europeans. The tribes most affected by European contact, when measured in terms of adaptations made in their forms of government, were probably the Five Civilized Tribes of the South (now of Oklahoma)—the Cherokee, Creek, Choctaw, Chickasaw, and Seminole. Since the degree of adaptation is most clearly visible in the Creek, or Muskogee, confederacy, these people provide a good example of the Indian ability to change, gradually accommodating both traditional and progressive segments of their community.

The Creek confederacy was originally organized on a town basis. Towns were communities that controlled certain areas of land and were comparable with what we have later called tribes when dealing with the Indians of the western United States. In the century before white contact, the Creek confederacy contained between fifty and eighty towns so diverse they represented six different languages: Muskogee, Hitchiti, Koasati, Euchee, Natchez, and Shawnee. The confederacy was thus political in nature first, with some common cultural and linguistic similarities and roots. The towns were divided into "red," or war, and "white," or peace, towns. Red towns declared and conducted wars, planned military expeditions, and conducted foreign relations, first with other tribes and confederacies and later with European colonial officials. White towns held all the councils, conducted adoption ceremonies, enacted laws, and regulated all the internal affairs of the confederacy. White towns were comparable with sanctuaries in older European traditions—no blood was to be shed there. Generally these were towns that had been adopted or recently admitted to the confederacy, and their designation as white towns encouraged them to keep the peace, which they had probably purchased at a bitter price prior to their admission to the confederacy.

Each town was governed by a *micco,* who was appointed for life pending continued good behavior. He had an assistant, a *micco apotka,* and a council of lesser *micco*s to counsel with and advise him. The towns all had a council of older men, designated as "the beloved men," which was composed of distinguished older men too old for active political and religious leadership, an honorary group whose reflections on the meaning of life were never ignored. In addition to these officials, each *micco* had a *heneha,* who directed public works in the town and served as the *micco*'s spokesman to announce decisions to the community.

The war officials of the towns were similarly graded in status. The highest grade of warrior was the *thlocco,* and this person was generally a leader of war parties and military expeditions. *Imala lakalgi*s came next in ranking and were generally adult warriors who had not been raised to any position of leadership in the war towns. Finally the rank–and–file adult males constituted the *imala labotskalgi*s, the little warriors who constituted the bulk of the confederacy's fighting force and may be compared with the enlisted men in a non-Indian military organization. There were, of course, many ceremonial and political duties incumbent upon people in each grade of leadership in the Creek towns, but this basic structure—with some variations according to the traditions and religious histories of individual towns—characterized all the Creek groups.

During the American Revolution, when frontier conflicts between the Americans and the Creek, who were pro-British, escalated, a significant change was introduced into the political organization of the Creeks. Alexander McGillivray, a mixed-blood chief, happened to occupy both the head chief and the head warrior position of the Creek towns that suffered the brunt of the fighting. McGillivray elevated the status of war chiefs above the peace chiefs, who never again regained their powers or influence in the confederacy. Prolonged conflict with the Americans, intrusions by the Spanish into Creek territory, and the intrigues of the British kept the Creeks in turmoil, and the number of war chiefs was significantly expanded to meet the continuing threats on the Creek frontiers. A different government was forced to evolve because of the hostility of the European colonists. Two principal chiefs from the two basic divisions of the Creeks—the upper and lower towns—

were recognized; other major chiefs, primarily war chiefs who had the capability of moving throughout the Creek territory to help repel invaders, were also made a permanent part of the confederacy. And a new confederate council, which included the kings, or *miccos*, evolved from the old confederate structure; it was primarily legislative in nature, as distinguished from the older ceremonial and judicial functions of the council.

With the ascendancy of the United States as the chief nation confronting the Creeks, additional chiefs were added. The Americans tended to spread their gifts more generously than the British and Spanish had done, and the pressure to add chiefs who could sign the treaties and receive special personal presents for their consent was irresistible. Consequently, the Creek confederacy shifted toward a perceptible federal structure and away from the older, more democratic organization of precontact days. By the 1830s, when the Creeks were removed from Alabama to Oklahoma, the tribal government was moving toward a recognizable two-house legislative government with an appointed set of executive officers.

In 1860, after the Creeks had established themselves in the West, substantial reforms were made. The old distinction between the upper and lower Creek towns was eliminated, and the whole tribe became simply the Muskogee nation. Two offices, one principal chief and a second chief, were made a permanent executive branch of government. The nation was divided into four judicial districts, with a judge in each district. Five supreme judges were named, who formed the supreme court of the Muskogee nation. A national police force, known as the "Light Horse," was authorized, consisting of people formerly from the second-ranking warrior class, and the legislative body consisted of a general council representing the influential men of each town. In 1867, as part of the reforms demanded by the United States following the Civil War, the legislature was made a two-house body, with the House of Kings, or former *miccos*, and the House of Warriors—thus bringing together the formerly distinct functions of the white and red towns.

This sketch of the evolution of the Creek confederacy from a completely indigenous and traditional organization to a comparatively modernized European-style government with laws, offices, courts, and police is obviously substantially compressed to illustrate the structural and functional changes experienced by the Creeks. Most of the modifications occurred over a period of time, as people saw the necessity of adapting old forms to fit new situations. Yet even this sketch demonstrates that the Creeks did not throw away their old government, nor

did they eagerly adopt any suggestions of the federal government to develop a government that incorporated certain democratic principles if they did not reflect a discernible and compatible tradition with their own. From 1860 until Congress basically removed all governing powers when Oklahoma was admitted as a state, the legitimacy of the Creek government was its relationship to the past and the traditions of the people—not its adoption of the structure and procedures that the federal government wanted.

Unquestionably the Creeks would not have built this kind of political structure without the constant pressure by the United States to reform their government in ways that would make it easier for the whites to deal with the Creeks. At the same time the innovations and changes were initiated by the Creeks themselves and were not dictated by the federal government to force political compatibility. Hence, we can say that the tribal governments of the Five Civilized Tribes prior to their submersion in 1906 were true political expressions of Indians in transition. Self-government was not "given" to these Indians; they preserved their own version of self-government by innovation. This point is important because all subsequent discussions of self-government by both federal officials and Indians involved facing the question of organizing the tribes and reservations to enable them to carry out certain functions that the federal government wanted performed in a predetermined manner. For a majority of the other tribes in the United States, then, self-government was something "given" to the tribes after they had been reduced significantly in stature, after their ceremonies had been prohibited by the government, and after the patriot leadership had largely been slain in battle or assassinated by government officials or progovernment Indians.

The first real indication that self-government would be a national policy of the federal government came in the punitive treaties forced upon the Five Civilized Tribes following the Civil War. In the 1830s these tribes had been forcibly removed from the South to Oklahoma under treaties that guaranteed them fee simple (or complete) title to their lands and permanent political existence apart from state boundaries and jurisdiction. During the Civil War the Five Civilized Tribes attempted to keep their promises contained in the removal treaties and either serve with the Union forces or maintain a studied neutrality. But there were a great many Southern sympathizers in the ranks of leadership in these tribes; many of them had slaves and lived like other Southern planters. When the federal government refused the services of the Five Civilized Tribes, on the excuse that using Indians in battle against their Southern

white brothers would be a form of savage and uncivilized warfare, the Southern sympathizers broke ranks and signed treaties with the Confederate states.

The Confederate treaties were probably the most favorable treaties any Indian tribes ever signed with a foreign, non-Indian government. They consisted of precise articles outlining the rights of the tribes, allowing participation in the Confederate congress for tribal officials, guaranteeing title to Indian lands and containing the famous promise that the provisions would be good "as long as the waters flow and the grass grows," a phrase many people believe is contained in United States treaties but that exists only in the Confederate treaties with segments of these tribes. Unfortunately the Southern supporters chose the wrong side in this struggle and, when the war ended, Congress was determined to punish the tribes for their participation in the rebellion. As 1866 began, the United States signed a series of treaties with the representatives of the Five Civilized Tribes, which included a provision that the representatives of these Indian nations meet at an annual general assembly, which looked forward to the organization of their lands as a territory of the United States.[7]

Congress appropriated funds to underwrite this experiment in political organization, and the grand council of the Indian Territory met annually until 1874 in an effort to adopt an organic document that would preserve the tribal rights and cultural traditions of the tribes while enabling the territory as a whole to move toward statehood. The prospect of a completely Indian state did not please many of the Indians, but they saw statehood as a vehicle for protecting themselves from any future white intrusions on their land and from their removal further west. The tribes submitted a series of proposed constitutions over the years, which had sophisticated formulas for representing the various tribes of the Indian Territory. Tribal delegates insisted that no existing treaty provisions of any of the tribes of the Indian Territory be affected, and since there were a number of small tribes that had once resided in the Ohio Valley and had a number of complicated treaties, finding the proper formula for representation was no easy task. Nevertheless, the tribal delegates were able to hammer out agreements that admitted the power and population of the larger tribes and yet preserved a semblance of political integrity for the smaller tribes.

Congress and a succession of presidents and secretaries of the interior rejected the Indian efforts to create a suitable constitution for the Indian Territory because no provision was made for the allotment of tribal lands following admission to the Union. It was inconceivable to the federal officials that a state could be admitted to the Union that did

not provide for free commerce with other states, and the communal holding of land struck directly at the personal land tenure system already entrenched in the other states. If an Indian could not sell a tract of land within a state, how could the other states have equal status with the newly admitted Indian state and how could commerce proceed when the best that white citizens might ever achieve within the new Indian state might be the leasing of lands? Property rights, rather than political rights, doomed the Indian state that the Congress had demanded the Indians form; statehood was postponed until such time as the Indians of Indian Territory might agree to hold their tribal property in the form of individual land tenure.

The proprietary aspect of Indian sovereignty was resolved by the General Allotment Act of 1887,[8] when the president was given direction by Congress to negotiate the allotment of the reservations and the sale of the surplus lands to the United States for opening to settlement by homesteaders. The Five Civilized Tribes escaped this statute temporarily, but in 1898 Congress passed the Curtis Act,[9] which gave the Indians a date by which they were to have negotiated an agreement with a special commission to allot their lands. Failing to meet this deadline automatically empowered the commission to move forward with the allotment and the dissolution of the tribal governments. By 1907, when Oklahoma entered the Union,[10] the governments of the Five Civilized Tribes existed by congressional resolution,[11] which contemplated their continuance only until they had concluded the disposal of tribal properties and assets then held in common.

In the dissolution of the governments of the Five Civilized Tribes, the first and best effort by the Indians to adopt forms of government acceptable to the federal government, particularly to Congress, was aborted. Following their removal from the South to Oklahoma, the tribes had adopted constitutions and bylaws that incorporated traditional political forms, historical interests of the respective Indian communities, and the newer tripartite form of government that federal officials felt represented the highest form of democratic government. There is no question that the tribal governments had great difficulty in mediating between the customs and traditions that their people cherished and the need to present to the larger American society a form of political organization that seemed clear, reasonable, and within the established political tradition of the larger society. More remarkable than the rapid adoption of new and sometimes onerous forms of government by these Indians was their ability to preserve within their own communities the respect for law that had characterized their earlier and more familiar way of regulating themselves.

In the half century following the Civil War, every effort was made by the United States to bring Indians within the constitutional framework. Most commentators on this period of American history have objected to the highhanded methods used by the Bureau of Indian Affairs to force the Indians into a preconceived mold within which people believed an automatic progression to a more civilized state could begin. Certainly significant and substantial pressure was brought upon the Indians to forsake their own form of government and demonstrate to the larger society their potential as ordinary citizens. Many people within the tribes held tenaciously to their old customs, and although the older forms of government were badly eroded, they did not completely disappear. More accurately, Indians continued to relate to one another in the traditional behavior patterns that had once completely regulated their own forms of government, but they did so within increasingly new and widely differing political structures allowed them by their agents and superintendents.

Since the common perception of Indian tribes depended in large measure upon the philosophical perspective of the people viewing them, most non-Indians dealing with the tribes during the last half of the nineteenth century assumed without any basis whatsoever that the Indians had no government and were in desperate need to learn some elementary kinds of organization for their own good. An indication of this blindness can be illustrated by citing the language of the Supreme Court in the celebrated *Crow Dog* case (see Chapter 1).

In the Supreme Court opinion, Justice Matthews explained that the morality of the case was nearly as strong as the legal theory supporting the decision. To invoke federal law on an unsuspecting people, he suggested,

> tries them, not by their peers, nor by the customs of their people, nor the law of their land, but by superiors of a different race, according to the law of a social state of which they have an imperfect conception, and which is opposed to the traditions of their history, to the habits of their lives, to the strongest prejudices of their savage nature; *one which measures the red man's revenge by the maxims of the white man's morality.*[12]

Reflection on this statement reveals the degree to which common assumptions regarding the nature of the Indian viewpoint prohibited whites from understanding the Indian idea of self-government. The Indian solution to this murder was to insist upon compensation by the family of the murderer to the family of the slain chief. The two families were reconciled with minimal disruption to the tribal community. In

contrast, the white man's morality demanded that society take revenge on behalf of itself and the injured family; the whites applied the Old Testament rule of *lex talionis,* the shedding of blood for the loss of blood. It was impossible, then, because of cultural blindness, for whites to perceive the foundations of Indian communal life and give the Indians credit for following a higher and more sophisticated understanding of the mechanics of human social interaction.

The effort by the tribes of the Indian Territory to establish an Indian state, then, was the last major effort by Indians to accommodate themselves and their institutions to the demands of the larger society. Although they were willing to adopt some of the white man's political institutions, they could not bring themselves to surrender the idea of peoplehood that each tribe represented, nor could they accept the white man's idea of private property as applied to their lands. When the federal government rejected this Indian overture, it severed an important emotional and conceptual link with the Indian past and made inevitable the necessity for it to sponsor some form of government on the reservations, a form acceptable to its own ideas of government, which would enable it to control the Indians. Both public morality and the remaining military capability of the Indians to resist federal overtures with violence prohibited the immediate forced assimilation of Indians into the American mainstream. Sporadic outbreaks by little groups of traditional diehards on different reservations kept the United States nervous about Indians until the opening of the First World War. By then a new generation of Indians had become accustomed to living on the reservation and accepted the rule of the Bureau of Indian Affairs as a fact of life.

The Organization
of the Reservations

Evolving federal policy in the 1880s was designed to strengthen the government's control over the Indian tribes as they settled on the western reservations. Agents assigned to the various western reservations saw it as part of their duty to help Indians organize a government through which they could be governed. Many agents entered upon this work with a great enthusiasm, and their reports are touchingly naive in recording the progress they were making in teaching the Indians democratic forms of government. The agent for the Blackfeet reservation in Montana, reporting his progress in 1875, is typical in his bewilderment at the ability of the Indians to grasp the principles of government so easily. After giving a clear and concise explanation of the traditional political organization of the Blackfeet bands, he then described his activities in helping the Indians to organize themselves:

My first object was to call the Indians together, nearly all of whom were scattered at long distances from here. After considerable exertion I had the satisfaction of seeing them coming in little by little, until I had over five thousand, embracing bands belonging to the different tribes. I immediately commenced counseling them to organize, elect head-chiefs, and pass laws for their government. . . . Five days were passed in preliminary talks between the different bands, at the end of which I had the pleasure of convening them in council for the purpose of electing three head-chiefs and passing a code of laws. Little Plume, White Calf, and Generous Woman were the chiefs elected, and a code of laws was adopted, a copy of which was forwarded to your office April last . . . .

Although hopefully impressed by the manner in which the laws were passed, *I was unprepared to find them so rigidly maintained and observed, and also to see the strict sobriety and exemplary conduct of these people here.*[1]

Expecting complete ignorance, he encountered a body of people who took laws seriously and obeyed them rigorously.

Although some reservations seem to have been organized as a matter of convenience for the agent to make it easier for him to deal with the tribes and bands over which he had charge, the overall organization of reservation councils seems to have occurred in conjunction with the establishment of the courts of Indian offenses by the Bureau of Indian Affairs. The event that triggered this administrative development was the *Crow Dog* case, which upheld the preservation of tribal law in those areas that had been reserved by the Indians in a prior treaty. The congressional response to the *Crow Dog* decision was to pass the Seven Major Crimes Act of 1885.[2] This statute extended federal court jurisdiction over the serious crimes of murder, manslaughter, rape, burglary, larceny, assault with intent to kill, and arson committed by one Indian against another Indian.

The administrative response to *Crow Dog* was the creation of the courts of Indian offenses. In 1883 Commissioner Hiram Price issued regulations calling for the establishment on each reservation of a "court of Indian offenses."[3] Under this regulation three Indians were to be selected by the agent, with the approval of the commissioner, to act as judges in a quasi-judicial forum to be supervised by the agent for offenses against the peace of the reservation. Generally this court was designed to deal with a class of disturbances that we might today call a public nuisance or minor misdemeanor. By 1885 the movement to develop these courts was in full swing. Congress seemed to approve this movement by appropriating funds to support the Indian police and these courts.

"Soon after taking charge of this agency," reported R. H. Milroy, of the Yakima Reservation in south-central Washington State,

I discontinued the ancient barbaric system of rude government by chiefs, divided this reservation into five districts, and had the Indians elect a justice of the peace in each district; carefully instructed, commissioned, and swore each into office, taking the territorial statutes as a general guide in these matters. The Indian policeman in each district performs the duties of constable for the justice of the peace in each district. I instituted a reservation court of three judges with original jurisdiction in higher criminal and civil cases and appellate jurisdiction in appeals from justices of the peace; reserving to myself the duties of a supreme court. I appointed the three reservation judges during the first two years but at a general election last fall, three reservation judges, together with three reservation commissioners (to perform the duties of boards of county commissioners), were elected.[4]

The commissioner's instructions were simply to organize a court, but Milroy soon found that without complementing and supporting institutions the courts did not make sense. Consequently, he began to organize the whole set of municipal institutions that generally provide those services and give that guidance that courts do not and cannot give. Milroy continued:

I divided the reservation into three divisions and appointed a commissioner in each to form the reservation board. Last fall, as stated, I had these commissioners elected. This board, like boards of county commissioners, has four terms a year. The clerk of the court is *ex officio* clerk and auditor of the board of commissioners. I had the board to lay off the reservation into seven road districts, and to appoint a road supervisor in each, whom I instructed in their duties in relation to warning out the able-bodied men of their districts, opening and constructing roads and bridges, keeping the same in repair, &c. I also appointed a reservation treasurer, to take charge of all fines and taxes and pay out the same on orders of the board. A poll tax of $1 was assessed upon all able-bodied male residents of the reservation under 50 and over 20 years old. The judges, commissioners, and road supervisors (for extra services) and cost of bridges are paid from fines and taxes. Thus the autonomy of this reservation is in good running order, the territorial statutes, as stated, being my general guide.[5]

Agents on other reservations did not have such successes. At Pine Ridge, South Dakota, where agent McGillycuddy was fighting continually with Red Cloud and the other traditional chiefs of the Oglala Sioux, a different situation prevailed. The court of Indian offenses failed because

reliable Indians could not be found to act as judges without pay, Congress having failed to provide funds for the purpose, and the alternative of making use of the three senior officers of the police to act in that capacity was wrong in principle and law. The sentencing power should not be placed in the hands of the police officer who is to carry out the order of the court.

So, agent McGillycuddy reported,

> in the absence of the above court the agency board of councilmen is doing good service composed, as it is, of about one hundred delegates, from our more progressive Indians, with a duly elected president, vice-president, clerk, advocate, and other officers. The board does not meet the approval of many of our superannuated chiefs, but is, nevertheless, doing good work in trying and punishing offenders, and it is to be hoped that they may be ere long sustained and encouraged in their efforts toward civilization by receiving the recognition and approval of the Department.[6]

McGillycuddy's approach of creating a reservation judicial system from an already existing reservation council is the reverse of Milroy's effort to derive a board of councilmen or commissioners from the establishment of a court of Indian offenses, but the result is basically the same. First, we have a system in which efforts are made to circumvent the existing customs and leadership patterns of the reservation people; the system becomes exclusionary very quickly. The administrative creation of institutions does not really supplant the old institutions but simply creates a very powerful competitor for them. Second, there is the basic fact that these boards of commissioners or reservation councils are not really recognized by the Department of the Interior, and they are certainly not recognized by Congress. These institutions are primarily the creature of the agent, and with the constant change of agents in the Bureau of Indian Affairs and the profound ignorance of Indians that the agents generally had, the reservation council was destined to erode very quickly as an institution instead of growing to take on additional responsibilities.

It was not long after the creation of these agent-dominated courts and councils that complaints began to come in regarding the arbitrary actions of the agents. In the minds of the agents, their actions had the approval of the influential Indians on the reservations and so had a measure of justification. No one ever seemed to realize that if certain Indians were vested with powers and benefits *because* they cooperated with the agents, that their control and influence was illusory when they endorsed actions that had no support from the rank and file of reservation Indians.

As complaints about agents continued to grow, private organizations began to take an interest in resolving some of the worst abuses committed by the agents against the Indians. The Indian Bureau at that time was wholly a patronage institution, and although the churches continued to have some influence in appointing agents, political parties had even more influence, and local politicians, especially territorial politicians, had to be satisfied that local representatives of the Bureau of Indian Affairs were acting consonantly with the best interests of the local whites. The Indian Rights Association (IRA), the largest and most aggressive national group concerned with the welfare of Indians, composed of concerned non-Indians in the eastern states, felt that making bureau employees subject to Civil Service regulations would resolve most of the problems that were created by these employees' constant shifting to meet the demands of political parties. After lobbying for several years, the IRA in 1894 was able to get President Cleveland to order all bureau employees placed under the Civil Service regulations. This reform made some improvements but not the substantial reform that the IRA hoped it would make.

The early reservation councils do not seem to have reached any kind of political maturity. Most complaints about reservation conditions center on the actions of the agents, not the council that was supposed to represent the people to the government. If the councils had been effective, a good many of the complaints would have been directed at them rather than the agent. Hence we can regard the reservation councils in most instances as representing the agent's wishes. Opposed to these councils were two distinct groups of Indians—the old traditional chiefs, who still managed to maintain their dignity and influence in spite of agent efforts to undermine them, and the growing number of Indians who completely accepted assimilation as a way of life and counseled tribal members to abandon everything connected with the reservation and seek their fortunes in the white man's world. The councils, caught between past and present, probably did their best to reach some kind of accommodation that would allow the reservation people some freedom.

By the second decade of this century complaints against the agents reached a crescendo, and Congress determined to step into the picture and find a way to bring the agents under Indian control, hoping that by giving Indians some voice the the management of their own affairs, peace and stability could be brought to the reservations. In 1912, Representative John Stephens of Texas introduced H. R. 25242 in the Sixty-second Congress, entitled "a bill conferring upon tribes or bands of Indians the right of nomination of their agent or superintendent, to inspire them to interest themselves in their own affairs, etc." Whether Stephens used this device simply to put the bureau on notice that Congress was watching it or whether he actually believed that his bill would resolve the question of arbitrary action by the agents, the corpus of this proposal was radically different from anything previously proposed for the reservations.

The bill provided that when 20 percent of the adult Indians residing on a reservation or at an agency petitioned their agent or superintendent, he was instructed to assist them in creating an election board to hold an election to select another agent or superintendent. The proposal to select another agent had to be approved by two thirds of the Indians voting, and when the results of the vote were certified to the secretary of the interior, he would be obligated by law to act in accordance with the Indians' wishes. The tribe or reservation could similarly prevent the transfer or dismissal of an agent or superintendent if the people voted to retain him.

There was, of course, a catch in the proposal. The bureau had to certify that the tribes who attempted to use the provisions of this act were "competent of organization in conformity to this act and with ordinary preliminary practices in the performance and maintenance of their organization as herein contemplated."[7] Anyone familiar with the bureaucratic mind would immediately realize that only those reservations where the bureau could control the results of the election would be certified as competent to hold elections. Hence the control that Stephens wished to give to the Indians depended upon an entirely neutral and disinterested bureaucracy for certification, and this possibility was exceedingly remote.

More interesting, however, was section 7 of the bill which the Congressman hoped would interest Indians in their own affairs, which provided that the election board would serve also as a reservation business committee to act on behalf of the people between elections. Presumably if the people chose the right agent and elections committee, the two could then properly administer the affairs of the reservation, since the approval of the people had been obtained. This provision was a step above the informal elections that had been held during the early days of the reservation, but it meant that people would have to judge candidates for office using two different sets of criteria: Would the person be a good election judge and would the person be capable of conducting the business of the reservation?

Succeeding sections of the bill elaborated on the business aspect of the election board. Section 8 declared that no tribal funds could be used without the permission of the election-business council. It was a vague thrust toward Indian self-government. Stephens began to articulate certain functions that Indians should perform, but he had no sense of how to create a workable set of institutions for the reservations. No authority was given to draft a tribal budget, certainly an essential part of authorizing any expenditure of tribal funds. Nor did the bill suggest that the election-business council exercise any municipal powers of self-

framework for improving conditions on the reservation were defeated by the simple inability of members of Congress to understand what they themselves wanted. No political sovereignty of the tribe was presumed to exist; a form of government possessing a wide range of municipal powers was not considered. The proposals could not seem to distinguish between an election committee, which performed a certain and specified function, and a business committee, which would approve expenditures from tribal funds by the agent. Self-government itself was of but peripheral interest to Congress. Nothing really changed.

The Movement
for Reform

Reform is always afoot in the field of Indian affairs. Conditions under which Indians live and the perception of those conditions by policy makers in Washington rarely coincide. Any substantial evidence of mistreatment of Indians will generate a public outcry that must eventually produce an effort to improve the situation. Often the demand for reform is turned aside by cosmetic changes in the image of the Bureau of Indian Affairs, which by avoiding the basic issue only produces worse conditions—and more profound calls for reform. Such was the context in which the *idea* of Indian self-government slowly took shape.

The period of active reform began with the demand for Civil Service status for bureau employees in the early 1890s. Earlier efforts were directed solely at discovering a means whereby the Indians could be brought into the body politic as equal citizens. Christian agents were appointed, off-reservation boarding schools were established, and finally the reservations were allotted. Each remedy in its turn created unanticipated problems that only served to confuse the status of Indians and call forth additional ideas that people hoped would lead Indians to civilization and cure the defects in the system that earlier proposals had produced. The importance of the demand to place Indians under the

Civil Service was to protect the good agents who worked for the bureau and to ensure that bad agents were not given political appointments in the Indian Service. This change signified a willingness of people to listen to the Indian side of the story of what was happening on the reservations and demonstrated an effort to bend the Indian Service to meet their needs.

Francis Leupp, commissioner of Indian affairs from 1904 to 1909, wrote in the preface of his 1910 book *The Indian and His Problem,* that

> the Indian problem has now reached a stage where its solution is almost wholly a matter of administration. Mere sentiment has spent its day; the moral questions involved have pretty well settled themselves. What is most needed from this time forth is the guidance of affairs by an independent mind, active sympathies free from mawkishness, an elastic patience and a steady hand.[1]

This attitude was no doubt bolstered by the passage of the Omnibus Act of 1910,[2] which attempted to bring forward and make consistent all the revisions and amendments of the General Allotment Act, which had been made on a piecemeal basis during the thirty-three years since its passage. The Omnibus Act dealt with the administration of the estates of allottees, the making of leases and timber contracts on allotted lands, and the cancelation of trust patents. Everyone involved with the legislation believed that it placed in the hands of the Interior Department the tools necessary to bring Indian matters to a successful conclusion. It would be only a matter of time before the Bureau of Indian Affairs would work its way out of its historic mission and Indians would become full-fledged American citizens.

In 1912, however, the Supreme Court, in *Choate* v. *Trapp,*[3] thwarted the plans of the state of Oklahoma to tax the allotments of the Choctaws and Chickasaws and called into question the status of the Five Civilized Tribes of that state. The following year another body blow to the tranquillity of Indian affairs was delivered when the court announced in *United States* v. *Sandoval*[4] that the Pueblo Indians of New Mexico were wards of the national government in the same manner as were other Indians. Together these decisions showed an interested nation that the Indians did have some legal rights that the Supreme Court would not allow to be trampled.

Almost as if the federal establishment intended to forge the diverse elements of Indian sympathy into one concentrated force, a series of events then took place that stirred up Indian affairs as never before. In 1916, after several years of agitation beginning with the mention of peyote at the Lake Mohonk Conference in 1914, a bill was introduced in the House of Representatives—the Gandy Bill, H.R. 10669—which sought the suppression of peyote, a hallucinogenic cactus used in services of the Native American Church. The Bureau of Indian Affairs and some church bodies worked hard to banish this substance on the reservations but, as the Reverend Dr. Edward Ashley had warned the Lake Mohonk delegates, "it is a religious institution and comes within the Constitution of the United States".[5] In 1918 Representative Carl Hayden of Arizona introduced a bill amending the laws dealing with liquor to include peyote.[6]

When hearings were held on the Hayden Bill, two points of view were evident. The private Indian interest groups including the Indian Rights Association, the National Women's Christian Temperance Union, the National Congress of Mothers and Parent-Teachers Associations, the Bureau of Catholic Missions, and the Anti-Saloon League of America all supported the legislation, reciting outrageous and generally fictitious descriptions of debauchery on the reservations because of this substance. Opposing them were the members of the Society of American Indians, the first national Indian organization; some scientists; and some prominent ethnologists. The bill was defeated and the threat to Indian religious freedom turned aside. The hearings had an importance far beyond the immediate subject, however, since those organizations objecting to the Indian use of peyote had to reappraise their image as opponents of Indian religious freedom, and with it the basis of their opposition.

By 1918 the Bureau of Indian Affairs had attempted to resolve the question of Pueblo lands by assigning a special attorney to handle the legal complications that had resulted from the *Sandoval* decision. When it appeared as if the bureau was not prosecuting the resolution of these land titles with sufficient enthusiasm, reform groups began to demand action, and the Pueblo lands problem now became a major item around which many reform groups began to rally.

In 1921 Albert Fall, former senator from New Mexico, was made secretary of the interior. Fall was known to be hostile to Indian rights, and he had previously clashed with Indian Commissioner Cato Sells over the question of allotting Indian lands in the Southwest. Sells refused to support allotment on the desert reservations because he realized that without adequate water no kind of successful adaptation could be made by Indians living on small tracts of unproductive land. Fall felt that the large tracts of Indian land inhibited white progress in the region and had vowed he would get things moving once he was in control of the Interior Department.

On May 31, 1921, Senator Holm Bursum of New Mexico, at the request of Fall, introduced a measure to resolve the Pueblo lands question by confirming all non-Indian claims to lands held for more than ten years before 1912. Thus began the great struggle over the Pueblo lands, which was finally resolved during the New Deal. Fall also supported or had introduced other measures that would have stripped the Indians of their federal protection and rights. One proposal, H.R. 9852,[7] would have authorized the secretary of the interior to appraise tribal property and pay tribal members a pro rata share and terminate them from the tribal rolls. In effect Fall proposed to buy out the federal responsibilities to Indians using the tribes' own monies. Other proposals, dealing with oil and gas leasing and the allotment of the Mescalero Apache reservation in southern New Mexico, were equally ruthless in their derogation of Indian rights.

This series of malevolent proposals issuing from the person of the secretary of the interior, whose duty was to defend and protect the Indians, created a tremendous stir in Indian affairs, and soon everyone from national Indian interest organizations to local women's clubs was writing the commissioner of Indian affairs and the secretary protesting the actions of the Interior Department. By 1922 the forces of reform were attacking the bureau on almost every front, leading with the issue of the Pueblo lands. The General Federation of Women's Clubs, under the inspired and determined leadership of Mrs. Stella Atwood, and the Indian Rights Association, under S. R. Brosius, began a general attack on the Bursum Bill. Mrs. Atwood, in what was surely one of the most insightful moves in Indian history, asked John Collier, a social science teacher at San Francisco State College, to assist in the fight against the Bursum Bill.

John Collier already had impressive credentials as a reformer and innovative social worker. He had worked in New York City and was a fringe member of Mabel Dodge's famous salon, where apparently he frequently bored the gathered assembly with very serious expositions on social organization and welfare theories. Collier had visited Taos Pueblo in New Mexico in December 1920 at the invitation of Mabel Dodge, and there he had a Damascus-like experience watching the Indians perform the Red Deer dance as part of their Christmas celebrations. As Collier reflected in his book *From Every Zenith,*

the discovery that came to me there, in that tiny group of a few hundred Indians, was of personality-forming institutions, even now unweakened, which had survived repeated and immense historical shocks, and which were going right on in the production of states of mind, attitudes of mind, earth-loyalties and human loyalties, amid a context of beauty which suffused all the life of the group. What I observed and experienced was a power of art—of the life-making art—greater in kind than anything I had known in my own world before.[8]

Collier was not the first non-Indian to appreciate the Indian tradition. He certainly became the first to understand, appreciate, articulate, and fight zealously for it.

The story of the reform movement thereafter is largely a story of John Collier's rise to prominence in the private organizational world that sought reform in federal Indian policy. He helped to organize the Pueblos to fight against the Bursum Bill and secure a much more favorable piece of legislation. From the Pueblo-lands fight Collier expanded his scope of activity, organized the American Indian Defense Association in May 1923, and remained its most important executive until its demise in the 1930s.[9]

The Bursum Bill greatly damaged the credibility and political influence of Warren Harding's Indian policy. Fall resigned in 1923, during the Teapot Dome scandal. President Harding appointed Hubert Work, his postmaster general, who set about immediately to repair the damage left in the wake of Fall's resignation. In May 1923 he appointed as a national advisory committee a blue-ribbon "Committee of One Hundred" concerned and influential citizens to keep him informed on Indian matters and make recommendations as to the administration of Indian affairs.

The Committee of One Hundred had the typical peculiar mixture of activists and celebrities. Included among the celebrities were Bernard M. Baruch, General John J. Pershing, William Jennings Bryan, William Allen White, Oswald Garrison Villard, Nicholas Murray Butler, and Roy Lyman Wilbur. Among the working activists in the Indian cause were Matthew K. Sniffen, of the Indian Rights Association, and John Collier, who had just organized his own Indian interest organization. Finally the committee included some prominent American Indian spokespeople, such as Henry Roe Cloud, Sherman Coolidge, Charles Eastman, Thomas Sloan, and Arthur C. Parker, a Tuscarora anthropologist who became chairman. Nine white anthropologists were included in the group, most prominently Frederick C. Hodge, Alfred L. Kroeber, and Clark Wissler. Work demonstrated by this selection that he was keenly aware of the role that the private citizen played in formulating and defending the government's Indian policy, and he hoped to still opposition by including everyone in his committee. Despite its peculiar alliance of interests, the committee made a valiant effort to speak to the things that had proved explosive in the previous decade or that seemed important for the future, especially to the new president, Coolidge, to whom they found themselves reporting in the fall of 1923.

With due caution, the committee recommended that the government support better-quality education for Indians, assist young Indians with federal scholarships for college and vocational training, seek the admission of Indians to public schools, and secure more adequate health and sanitation programs on the reservations. It also endorsed a new study of peyote by the National Research Council and supported opening the court of claims to Indian tribes, urged the resolution of the question of the status of executive-order reservations, and expressed an interest in concluding the Pueblo-lands questions.

Work took the recommendations of the Committee of One Hundred seriously, and the Coolidge administration did move quickly on many, if not all, of the committee's suggestions. In June it secured the passage of the Indian Citizenship Act and the Pueblo Lands Board Act on June 7, 1924.[10] A seldom noticed but equally important act authorized the payment of tuition for Indian children attending public schools.[11]

We can best understand the scope and direction of the reform movement in the twenties if we survey the incredible array of large and frequently profound studies of the conditions of Indians that that period produced. Since the days of Senator Dawes, who had almost single-handedly secured passage of the General Allotment Act which was eventually named after him, federal Indian policy had been made sporadically on the basis of personal belief and philosophy among administrative and legislative members. The belief in private property, deeply held by the reformers of Lake Mohonk, was sufficient to carry the day and get allotment affirmed without much evidence of the effect it would have or was having on the Indians themselves. The reform movement of the twenties, on the other hand, began to concentrate on the actual conditions under which Indians then lived and sought some major effort by the federal government to improve the situation.

The first major report in this respect was *The Red Man in the United States,* written by G. E. E. Lindquist for the Inter-church Movement in 1919. This study exposed the conditions of poverty on the reservations, documented the existence of tuberculosis and trachoma on the reservations, and pointed out that over twenty thousand Indian children were without schooling because there were no facilities for them. The impact of Lindquist's report on federal policy was minimal because it was written in the old-style missionary language and spoke optimistically about those Indians who walked the "Jesus Road." When the Committee of One Hundred visited the White House to submit its report, it was given to President Coolidge by a brash young Cherokee girl named Ruth Muskrat, who would later play a critical role in Indian affairs.

Even before the authorization of the Committee of One Hundred, however, the Bureau of Indian Affairs itself began to act. In March 1922 Commissioner Charles Burke wrote to the American Red Cross asking them to undertake a study on Indian health needs. The report by Florence Patterson, a registered nurse with considerable experience in public health nursing and hospital administration, was entitled "A Study of the Need for Public Health Nursing on Indian Reservations"; it was submitted to the bureau in the summer of 1923 but was kept relatively secret until December 1928, when Secretary Work reluctantly submitted it to the Senate Indian Committee. In testimony before the committee Ms. Patterson showed that poor health was widespread throughout the reservations and in the government boarding schools and that little was being done to correct conditions.[12]

The major impetus for studies came, however, midway through the Coolidge term, in 1926, when the Bureau of Indian Affairs rather crudely introduced a measure to formalize the reservation courts of Indian offenses by giving them jurisdiction over certain enumerated offenses and civil matters under rules and regulations prescribed by the secretary of the interior.[13] Most controversial of the proposals contained in this bill was the plan to prohibit customary Indian marriages and divorces and replace them with authority vested in the superintendents to issue marriage licenses to Indians. The bill stirred up a hornet's nest of Indian protests. Tribes that had never given testimony on federal legislation appeared and recited a litany of abuse steadfastly opposing the proposal. C. Hart Merriam, of the Smithsonian, and John Collier led the list of witnesses hostile to the bill. The bureau's lame excuses for its operation of courts of Indian offenses could not stem the tide of criticism. The hearings lasted from February until May, and the transcript filled over two hundred pages, mostly of vituperative protests. About all the hearings demonstrated was the inadequacy of the bureau's management of Indian affairs.[14]

The humiliation of the hearings had an immediate impact. A few weeks after the hearings Secretary Work wrote to the Brookings Institution and asked them to undertake some studies on the Indian situation. Two major studies resulted, and together they cover the complete administrative causes of Indian discontent. Laurence F. Schmeckebier produced in 1927 his monumental book, *The Office of Indian Affairs,* a history and a careful analysis of the work of the bureau. The following year *The Problem of Indian Administration* by Lewis B. Meriam (no relation to C. Hart Merriam) and associates was released. Although Schmeckebier's monograph is superior to Meriam's in its scope of comprehension of the manner in which Indian affairs evolved, the Meriam Report, as it is popularly known, received considerably more attention because, unlike Schmeckebier's historical account, it offered policy recommendations. The Meriam Report also came out in a national election year and became embroiled in the political considerations of the national campaign.

The Meriam Report made no apologies in stating what it found to be the conditions of Indians in the United States. "The poverty of the Indians and their lack of adjustment to the dominant economic and social systems produce the vicious circle ordinarily found among any people under such circumstances," the report began. "Because of interrelationships, causes cannot be differentiated from effects."[15] The report blasted the allotment policy and the halfhearted manner in which the government pursued the goal of assimilating Indians through the use of private property:

> When the government adopted the policy of individual ownership of the land on the reservations, the expectation was that the Indians would become farmers. Part of the plan was to instruct and aid them in agriculture, but this vital part was not pressed with vigor and intelligence. *It almost seems as if the government assumed that some magic in individual ownership of property would in itself prove an educational civilizing factor, but unfortunately this policy has for the most part operated in the opposite direction.*[16]

"The fundamental requirement," the report stressed,

> is that the task of the Indian Service be recognized as primarily educational, in the broadest sense of that word, and that it be made an efficient educational agency, devoting its main energies to the social and economic advancement of the Indians, so that they may be absorbed into the prevailing civilization or be fitted to live in the presence of that civilization at least in accordance with a minimum standard of health and decency.[17]

Although almost every commentator on Indian matters credits the Meriam Report with providing the motivation and framework for the subsequent reforms initiated by the New Deal, there is not much evidence to support such an idea conceptually or in execution. Indeed, the major emphasis in that report was the upgrading of the Bureau of Indian Affairs; the tone and direction of the recommendations continued to assume that Indians had to be led benignly, if not driven, to certain preconceived goals, which were assimilation or a mutually imposed isolation within small Indian enclaves.

In June 1928 an equally important report was issued. A year before, on March 15, Secretary Work authorized Porter Preston, an engineer with the Bureau of Reclamation, and C. A. Engle, the supervising engineer of the Bureau of Indian Affairs, to study Indian irrigation problems. The study took a year and was over five hundred pages long, complete with a history of the various Indian irrigation projects, charts on their feasibility, and recommendations regarding further irrigation projects. One of the major problems with Indian irrigation projects was the provision that construction and maintenance charges were laid against the Indian lands, making it impossible to manage them properly and repay the reimbursable debts accrued in construction of the projects.

The *Report of Advisors on Irrigation on Indian Reservations*—or the Preston-Engle Report, as it was popularly known—caused little stir until 1930, when Commissioner Charles Rhoads was called to testify before the Senate Indian Committee. The committee soon reached the subject of reimbursable debts, and John Collier, representing the American Indian Defense Association, presented testimony critical of the Bureau in which he cited liberally from the Preston-Engle Report to show that irrigation by the Bureau of Indian Affairs was a dismal failure. The Preston-Engle report recommended tightening the provisions under which Indians could use their lands, whereas Collier demonstrated that in almost every reservation the number of acres irrigated and used had declined radically and that much of the cost of construction had been charged to the Indians, even though white farmers had been the major beneficiaries.[18]

Another study authorized by the bureau was one dealing with reservation law-and-order problems. The topic had been simmering since the hearings on the courts of Indian offenses, and the bureau wisely asked the Brookings Institution to undertake another study on this subject. Authorized in December 1929, the Brookings Institution report, *Law and Order on Indian Reservations of the Northwest,* was submitted to the Senate Committee on Indian Affairs in June 1932. Directed by Professor Ray Brown of the University of Wisconsin School of Law, this report stressed anecdotal information that placed the bureau in a dreadful light. The report gave support to the upgrading of the courts of Indian offenses but made it imperative that "the persons selected as judges should be lawyers with social training and interests, who would be regarded as equipped for the duties of juvenile court judge in a progressive white community, or social workers with juvenile court or probation experience and the necessary training in law."[19] The report recommended a substantial adjustment in the manner in which the government perceived Indian offenses on the reservations:

> Important among the causes of Indian offenses are lack of interests, boredom, poverty, and family and community degeneration. Courts and laws can, of course, punish but they are not, unsupplemented, the agencies to remove causes in the great bulk of Indian cases.[20]

So, the report concluded, "the system adopted by the Federal Government should fit into its entire program for advancing the social and economic condition of the Indians."

The final report authorized by the Bureau of Indian Affairs was one involving the use of agricultural lands on Indian reservations. *An Economic Survey of the Range Resources and Grazing Activities on Indian Reservations,* by Lee Muck, P. E. Melis, and G. M. Nye, was authorized on April 26, 1930, and transmitted to the Senate Indian Committee in late January 1932. Although the report was very technical, its basic thrust was the suggestion of a new management plan for grazing and agricultural lands that emphasized conservation practices that would limit carrying capacity to a sound sustained-yield form of use. Unlike other reports, which chastized the bureau for its past practices, this report looked forward to the institution of new management practices consonant with other plans to enhance the economic status of the tribes.[21]

As the thirties began, the Bureau of Indian Affairs and the Senate Indian Committee had more information on the conditions of Indians than any previous administration or Congress. Part of the thrust to produce these reports came from the natural propensity of the bureau to protect itself by defining the nature of the problems Indians faced. Though the bureau was reluctant to submit its reports until the Senate Indian Committee demanded them, it is surprising how little white-washing there was of the conditions of Indians. A good deal of this honesty was no doubt caused by such Indian advocates as John Collier, who frequently skewered the bureau in congressional hearings and forced administrative officials to admit mistakes and inadequacies.

While these reports were being prepared, Congress was not idle— and in 1928 the Senate launched its own investigation. Following a resolution passed on February 1,[22] a subcommittee of the Senate Indian Committee—composed of Lynn Frazier of North Dakota, Robert La Follette, Jr., of Wisconsin, W. B. Pine of Oklahoma, Burton K. Wheeler of Montana, and Elmer Thomas of Oklahoma—toured Indian country, generally at the suggestion of John Collier, to specific places where bureau wrongdoing would be most evident and conducted hearings on various aspects of Indian administration. These hearings were invaluable in educating the senators on the real poverty of the Indians and the abuses that the Indian Bureau visited upon them. More than anything else these field trips demonstrated that if the tribes were given some form of political recognition, they would be able to withstand the most blatant abuses of the bureaucrats and protect themselves from the worst situations. It was, in effect, the first sign of congressional interest in the idea of self-government (or at least government of the reservations) since the 1916 failure of the Johnson Bill, which had been the last attempt to establish the right of Indians to elect agents in their reservations.

The experience was an eye opener for the senators. Invariably at a field hearing at one of the reservations, a member of the subcommittee would inquire about the kind of local representative organization the Indians used. Most senators were astounded that the Indians had little in the way of formal organizations to express their wishes, and on some occasions they would recommend that the Indians immediately gather together and form a council to represent themselves. The following exchange between Senator Burton Wheeler, Senator Frazier, and Mr. Johnson, a Yuma from Arizona, captures the confusion and frustration of these conversations:

SENATOR FRAZIER: Are you a member of the business council here—the business committee?

MR. JOHNSON: No.

SENATOR FRAZIER: Well, you have some office among your people, have you not?

MR. JOHNSON: Well, we had a council, but it is not recognized by others of the Indians.

SENATOR FRAZIER: It is not recognized by the Indians?

MR. JOHNSON: Some Indians do not recognize us.

SENATOR WHEELER: How do you elect your council?

MR. JOHNSON: We had an election here. I believe it was in 1920.

SENATOR WHEELER: That is a long time ago.

MR. JOHNSON: I am not certain. The election went through and was witnessed by Inspector Linnen.

SENATOR FRAZIER: Why do you not have another election? Why do you not get your Indians together at a meeting like this and elect a business council and then let the majority rule?

MR. JOHNSON: We tried it. There are so many factions every time.

SENATOR WHEELER: You ought to be able at a meeting like this to get together and elect a business council. The majority should elect. Then there could not be any complaint.

MR. JOHNSON: That would be all right if they could agree.

SENATOR WHEELER: A majority of them should agree. Why do they not get together? They ought to get them together, call them together every year and elect them for a year.

MR. JOHNSON: We tried that, but it is always a failure.

SENATOR WHEELER: You have not tried it since 1920?

MR. JOHNSON: We have tried it after 1920.

SENATOR WHEELER: Could you not elect anybody?

MR. JOHNSON: No, sir.

SENATOR WHEELER: Why not?

MR. JOHNSON: It is on account of the disagreement.

SENATOR WHEELER: But there is a majority of Indians and they could elect somebody. If there was a majority voted for some man, he would be elected.

MR. JOHNSON: That might be, but I doubt it.[23]

Throughout the hearings, in spite of their best efforts, the senators could not understand why Indians did not act like whites and organize a committee forthwith to conduct their own business. Mr. Johnson, politely turned aside the senator's questions with vague responses, knowing that spontaneous political organization according to the white man's ways would be futile because the traditional element in the tribe would not recognize it. It is important to note that the senators were concerned that the Indians had no official organization to represent themselves to the government; they were not concerned with allowing the Indians to govern themselves.

Even before the Senate Indian Committee began its investigation of Indian conditions, one tribe, the Klamaths of Oregon, had come to Senator Charles McNary in 1927 and asked him to help them draw up a bill that would make their reservation a federal corporation and that would eliminate the Bureau of Indian Affairs from their reservation affairs. The Klamaths owned a large tract of virgin timber in the area around Crater Lake, Oregon, and they believed, with good reason, that the bureau was not getting an adequate price when it sold their timber. The Klamaths felt that with a little assistance from experts of their own choosing, they could do better for themselves.

McNary introduced one proposal[24] in 1928 and two other versions the following year,[25] but they received little attention. The Indian committee did not regard the Klamath proposal as relevant to its investigation of Indian country. The third and most complicated version spelled out in detail a management scheme favored by Wade Crawford, an aggressive Klamath leader, and his followers. When Crawford's political opponents within the tribe learned of his efforts to transform the reservation into a federal corporation, they came to Washington and attempted to get legislation that would have liquidated the reservation and distributed the proceeds among the enrolled tribal members. Naturally the people in Congress were baffled at the sudden appearance of two groups of Indians each claiming to represent the true feelings of the tribe. Both proposals seemed radical in the context in which the Congress understood Indians. People could not believe that Indians wanted to liquidate their lands or that they wanted to manage the lands themselves—and had devised a plan to do so.

The Crawford proposal was complicated but had many innovations and was singularly important in distinguishing the idea of peoplehood from self-government. It would have established the Klamath reservation as the "Klamath Indian Corporation," a federally charted municipal corporation upon the petition of two thirds of the adult enrolled members of the tribe. All property of the tribe, real and personal, including claims outstanding in the court of claims on which the tribe hoped to recover, were to be turned over to the corporation. All outstanding liabilities of the tribe, including existing contracts and obligations made by the bureau on behalf of the tribe, were also to be assumed by the new corporation so that the bureau could not use them as an excuse to involve itself in tribal affairs after the corporation had been established.[26]

All enrolled tribal members would receive shares of stock in the new corporation. They could not sell or transfer their shares except to the corporation. Allottees could cede their allotments to the corporation and receive additional shares of stock according to the value of the land. There was, however, no provision made for children who would be born after the corporation had been established. Presumably they would simply inherit their parents' stock and become tribal members in that way. The membership provisions, considering the Indian refusal

to make wills, only forecast a very serious heirship problem a generation later, but the idea that the members of the tribe would be transformed into corporate stockholders did have a certain fascination and
innovation.

The corporation was to have a board of directors elected by the
shareholders according to the number of shares they possessed. During
the first years of its existence, the corporation would also have a board
of supervisors, three in number, with at least one member appointed by
the president of the United States. Considerable confusion existed whether
the board of supervisors or the board of directors would control the
day-to-day operations of the corporation. This point was never well
explained by the Klamaths, and at one point they suggested that a
federal district court judge have continuing supervision over the activities of the board of directors—an unworkable arrangement that only
indicated the Klamaths' mistrust of the executive branch of the federal
government.

The Klamaths proposed a fifty-year trust period, during which the
new Indian corporation could learn to conduct its own business. The
land would remain free from state property taxes and any form of state
control. After the expiration of the trust period, and diplomatically
phrased "at the will and discretion of Congress," the tribal corporation
would finally assume all responsibilities of other private and public
corporations. Presumably the cultural adjustment problems would work
themselves out as the people learned to conduct their own affairs. No
provisions existed for the tribe or corporation assuming civil or criminal
jurisdiction, and hence the bill was primarily a business management
plan rather than a movement toward some form of political independence. Though many of the provisions were ill conceived and overly
idealistic, at least the Indians had articulated a clear direction, established
a goal, and suggested a means of reaching some final resolution of their
relationship with the federal government.

Among the people giving testimony on S. 4165 in 1930 was John
Collier, then director and organizer of the American Indian Defense
Association and within three years to be commissioner of Indian affairs.
At first Collier praised the policy that the bill exemplified as "the most
important new step in Indian affairs since the general allotment act."[27]
He then went directly to the substance of the bill, noting that:

the conception is that the guardianship of the United
States shall be kept intact with all of its plenary power; that for the time being,
at least, all of the immunity enjoyed by the Indians from taxation shall be
preserved; that there shall be created a local instrumentality of the Govern-

ment, which is here called a board of supervision; and that board of supervision, which is distinct from the board of directors chosen by the tribe, shall be charged with the duty of assisting the tribe in setting up its business operations.[28]

Collier then raised the question of how the children born after the corporation was established would participate in the affairs of the corporation. Here Crawford could not explain the bill, stating one time that the Indians would vote democratically by tribal membership, one person one vote, at other times seeming to imply that they would vote according to stock ownership, the children inheriting from their parents.

Both the senators and Collier were skeptical that the Klamaths were ready to govern themselves, and with good reason. The Klamath proposal did not establish self-government as much as it advocated a way of allowing Indians some voice in how their natural resources were to be exploited. "Now," Collier told Senator Kendrick,

> if we imagine the Menominees, and again the Chippewas of Minnesota, and again the Navajos—and the situations are very diverse—and we have a dozen incorporated tribes working out under various conditions, it becomes evident that the United States can not, in advance, by hearings in committees, decide on the exact method that is going to be appropriate in those cases; that there is going to be needed some Federal agency which will oversee and keep track of all these developments; compare one of them with another of them, compare this year's results with last year's results, and report to Congress periodically.[29]

The continuing need for supervision over the decisions Indians might make with respect to the disposition of their property presented Congress with a dilemma. It might have to create another agency simply to supervise the various corporate experiments it authorized tribes to make. What, then, would be the role of the Bureau of Indian Affairs?

The basic problem, of course, was that discussions centered on allowing Indians to control their property to the exclusion of any mention of the political rights they might want to exercise. Although there was a continuing problem of cultural adjustment, even Collier saw it as one of qualifying future tribal members to vote in corporate elections, not as the larger question of providing some vehicle for cultural expression and some protection of the Indians' right to be culturally different. When we compare the Klamath proposal with the earlier General Allotment Act, we find no fundamental difference in outlook. Under allotment the government assumed that a vesting of the tribal land estate in the individual members in farming tracts would produce social and economic independence for Indians. This proposal simply updated the philosophy of economic assimilation by making it a corporate enterprise instead of an agricultural venture.

In the first phase of Indian reforms at the turn of the century, Congress and the public had usually dwelt on the sentimental-historical aspect of Indians; the initial motivation for reform came as a result of the desire to make amends to the Indians of the past for wrongs visited upon them. The burgeoning reform movement of the late twenties and early thirties proved at first no exception to this rule. In spite of the hundreds of pages of testimony and special reports that outlined the dreadful state of Indian affairs and the impending collapse of the Indian economy through government mismanagement, Congress in 1930 still spent its time honoring Indians of the past. Even the Klamath proposal in 1932 gained little more than a perfunctory hearing, which added virtually nothing to the discussion two years earlier.

A glance at the legislation of 1930 will eloquently demonstrate that until Congress dealt with past misdeeds, it could not bring itself to face the future of Indians. Among the laws passed in 1930 were the following:

- 46 Stat. 147—Providing for the recording of the Indian sign language through the instrumentality of Major General Hugh L. Scott, retired.

- 46 Stat. 168—Providing compensation to the Crow Indians for Custer Battlefield National Cemetery.

- 46 Stat. 169—Authorizing the Secretary of the Interior to erect a marker or tablet on the site of the battle between Nez Perce Indians under Chief Joseph and the command of Nelson A. Miles.

- 46 Stat. 258—Authorizing the Secretary of the Interior to erect a monument as a memorial to the deceased Indian chiefs and ex-servicemen of the Cheyenne River Sioux Tribe of Indians.

- 46 Stat. 431—Authorizing the erection of a marker upon the site of New Echota, capital of the Cherokee Indians prior to their removal west of the Mississippi River, to commemorate its location, and events connected with its history.

• 46 Stat. 1045—Authorizing the Secretary of the Interior to acquire land and erect a monument at the site near Crookston, in Polk County, Minnesota, to commemorate the signing of a treaty on October 2, 1863, between the United States and the Chippewa Indians. [This legislation was actually passed January 31, 1931.]

So the first reforms of the Congress were a series of monuments that commemorated some of the worst abuses of the past that the government had inflicted upon the Indians. Once satisfied that they had paid sufficient tribute to the past, Congress then began to consider more critical legislation.

The only noteworthy effort of Congress in 1932, one of the worst years of the Depression, was the passage of the Leavitt Act of July 1, 1932.[30] The statute gave the secretary of the interior permission to adjust or eliminate the reimbursable charges on Indian lands within reservation irrigation projects. The Meriam Report had recommended this cancelation, and the Senate survey had shown that many of the charges laid against the Indian lands in fact benefited non-Indians. Since the government had promised, when the lands were allotted, that it would deliver them free and clear of any encumbrance at the end of the trust period, it seemed natural to insist that levying reimbursable charges against these irrigated allotments would be contrary to the general land policy of the United States. The passage of the Leavitt Act eliminated one of the most burdensome problems of the previous two decades, one that made land consolidation almost impossible.

The presidential election year virtually eliminated any further consideration of Indian legislation. All the elements were in place for a complete revitalization of the Indian Bureau and needed only a steady and determined person able to bring together a synthesis of ideas and actions, to make the radical changes in federal Indian policy that were required. The Leavitt Act demonstrated that Congress would reverse itself, given a compelling argument against existing conditions. But the act did not go far enough in helping to resolve the Indian irrigation deficiencies, indicating that Congress could not, by itself, make the innovative changes the Indians needed.

The Meriam Report, the various bureau in-house reports, and the studies done by agencies external to the Interior Department had also suggested various adjustments in the Indian programs, but their major recommendation, when all was said and done, involved the appropriation of more funds and the increase of efficiency in delivering existing government services to the Indians. The Meriam Report sought to convince the bureau employees that their mission was primarily educa-

tional and not administrative in the traditional sense. Bringing this recommendation to fruition would have been the most taxing of efforts
because it required a complete change of orientation by people who had
spent their lives convinced that Indians were incapable of succeeding.
The report *Law and Order on Indian Reservations of the Northwest* had
suggested that no reforms would be lasting or significant unless they
were tied to a larger revision of federal Indian policy. The conclusions
of this report could not be overlooked and in a sense prepared both the
Congress and the Bureau of Indian Affairs for the eventuality of massive
and profound institutional change. It was now up to the new president,
Franklin D. Roosevelt, to take the bold step toward making that change—
and he did it through the appointments first of Howard Ickes as secretary of the interior and then of John Collier as his Indian commissioner.
The reform movement of the twenties had well prepared the groundwork for the fertile years of the New Deal.

The Vision
of the Red Atlantis

The effect of reform in the field of Indian affairs, with the solitary exception of the Indian Reorganization Act, has had two major thrusts: change in the rate of delivery of federal services and change in the efficiency in administration. The assumption of Congress, and generally of the executive branch, is that some kind of well-conceived federal infrastructure already exists on Indian reservations; the task is to make it more responsive to Indian needs or, in the conservative alternative, to dismantle it and allow social and economic Darwinism to take its course. Lawrence Kelly noted that "the genius of John Collier . . . was that he saw the bankruptcy of federal Indian policy more clearly than anyone else in his generation."[1] But Kelly is only partially correct. Everyone knew that federal Indian policy was bankrupt, but no one had any idea what could be substituted in its place. Almost all of the suggestions for reform prior to John Collier, and all of the suggestions since Collier, have accepted the federal institutions as a given element in the equation and sought to adjust other factors. Collier alone attempted to transform institutions themselves.

When we look back at the decade of controversy surrounding John Collier, we discover a fundamental fact of reform proposals that perhaps only Collier was able to recognize: Any reform inevitably affects countless areas of life peripheral to the central issue under discussion. Even John Stephens's seemingly simple proposal to allow Indians to appoint their own agents had as much to do with the adjustment of Indian lands, the recognized competency of Indians, and the distribution of tribal funds as it did securing protection for the Indians against arbitrary actions of their agents. The studies of grazing, law and order, the courts of Indian offenses, health, and education all pointed out the interconnected nature of Indian problems. It was apparent, then, as Collier took charge of the Bureau of Indian Affairs, that reform had to touch almost every aspect of Indian life deliberately if it were to accomplish anything lasting or significant.

The record of Collier's American Indian Defense Association (AIDA) gives clear clues to the nature and direction Collier sought for the recognition of Indian interests, as it would actually take form in the Indian Reservation Act and after. Kenneth Philp points out, in his excellent study of Collier's crusade for reform, that with the beginning of the Hoover administration a brief honeymoon period existed between the Bureau of Indian Affairs and the private Indian interest groups of which AIDA was the most aggressive and prominent. "When Commissioner of Indian Affairs Charles Rhoads sent four letters to Lynn Frazier, chairman of the Senate Indian Investigating Subcommittee,"[2] they were sent under Rhoads's signature, but were all written by John Collier. Filed the same day, they represented Collier's ideas for reforming the Indian Bureau.

The first letter raised the question of the irrigation construction and maintenance charges the government had placed against Indian allotments. By 1929 they totaled a staggering twenty-five million dollars and were regarded as an insuperable burden on the use of the land. The letter asked whether—given the promise of the General Allotment Act that the United States would convey the allotments to the Indians, or their heirs, at the end of the trust period free of any debt or encumbrance—there was not a constitutional question involved in the practice of burdening the Indian lands with these charges.[3] If the General Allotment Act could be read literally, then the liens were not constitutional. Collier's second point concerned the practice of selling allotments on the death of the original allottee. "The consequences are mathematically certain," he noted, that "the allotted Indians of the second generation largely become landless. By the time the third generation has arrived, substantially all of the allotted Indian land will have passed into white ownership."[4] The government, then, was facing a disaster of the first magnitude in a few years unless it radically revised its Indian land policy. Passage of the Leavitt Act in 1932 resolved the problem of reimbursable irrigation charges; it would be up to Collier to resolve the question of the forced sales of allotments.

The second letter dealt with what Collier called the "indivisible tribal estates," estimated at a value of perhaps a billion dollars. He pointed out that present practices placed most of the responsibility for management on the government and noted that "unless existing law be changed it may well be that the Government 100 years from now will find itself still charged with the responsibility and still maintaining the paternalistic administration." Collier's solution was the organization of tribal councils but not as an administrative matter, since "such action of the administrative kind would be revocable by any succeeding administration." He then cited positively the Klamath incorporation bill introduced by Senator McNary, remarking that he did not suggest that

the problems raised in this letter can be wholly met through the method of tribal incorporation, but it would seem that a complete study should be given to the subject of passing over to the Indians themselves a collective responsibility for their tribal business and ultimately of terminating the present absolute responsibility of the Government for the management of these multitudinous properties.[5]

Collier was strongly inclined to pursue the creation of a corporate structure for the reservations that would transfer the decision-making powers regarding the management of property to the Indians and away from the Bureau of Indian Affairs.

The third letter covered the subject of Indian claims against the government. Pointing out that many valid claims were not being prosecuted because of the tedious requirement that the Interior Department comment on them before they were submitted to Congress in the form of proposals for enabling legislation opening the court of claims to the tribes, Collier laid the groundwork for the later discussions of what kinds of claims the government should recognize. He advocated an Indian Claims Commission, independent of the Interior Department, whose members would be named by the president subject to confirmation by the Senate.

This claims commission might be given the power to reach final settlements—essentially judicial power—in specified classes of cases where the Indian claims rested on a legal right assertable as such. *But the commission should hear all causes, those that are human and moral as well as those that are legal and equitable; and its findings, submitted to Congress, could be the basis of settlement of a gratuitous kind which Congress might authorize* [emphasis added].[6]

The letter added that "There can be no liquidation of the Government's guardianship over Indians until this inheritance of treaties and alleged broken treaties and governmental laches of the past is absorbed."[7] Collier thus anticipated both the scope of the Indian Claims Commission and the major motivation of Congress in securing its passage in 1946.

The final letter returned to the reimbursable features of the irrigation problem and suggested that the bureau's irrigation projects be transferred to the Bureau of Reclamation. This suggestion differed from the content of the first letter in its effort to have the bureau's responsibilities transferred to the Bureau of Reclamation, primarily in order to place Indian water development in the hands of more expert people. Presumably, under the new agency, those projects that would never be satisfactorily operated would be closed out with a savings in funds for both the Indians and the federal government.

Collier, according to Philp, grew disenchanted with the bureau in the spring of 1930 and finally sent a bitter letter to Secretary Work denouncing the bureau's failure to initiate the needed reforms.[8] The reason for Collier's alienation was that his agenda was not the only program suggested for renewal of Indian fortunes. The Meriam Report received and continued to receive much recognition, and its agenda was more widely discussed than the specific items that Collier wanted changed. Part of the support the Meriam study received was based upon its enthusiastic emphasis on family and educational concerns, which seemed more in tune with the mood of the day and which, of course, were easier (or less problematic) to accommodate in legislation. Although chastising the federal government, the Meriam Report nevertheless seemed to be indicting past attitudes more than present propensities. "The Indian Service has not appreciated the fundamental importance of family life and community activities in the social and economic development of a people," the report noted, adding that "the tendency has been rather toward weakening Indian family life and community activities than toward strengthening them."[9]

One place where Collier and the Meriam study agreed, however, was the importance of providing an alternative to assimilation. "The position taken," the Meriam study related, "is that the work with and for the Indians must give consideration to the desires of individual Indians. He who wishes to merge into the social and economic life of the prevailing civilization of this country should be given all practicable aid and advice in making the necessary adjustments. He who wants to remain an Indian and live according to his old culture should be aided in doing so."[10] Collier could not quarrel with this conclusion, but he felt great uneasiness at the idea that simply changing the orientation of some bureau programs would correct the longstanding abuses in such tangible fields as land, water, and natural resources.

The Meriam study did not actually advocate, as Collier did, the "restoration of Indian societies and culture"; it only sought a "removal of restrictions on their activities."[11] Always a methodical thinker, Collier then felt compelled to outline his distinct set of guiding principles and goals. Of particular importance were the following:

- Indian societies "must and can be discovered in their continuing existence, or regenerated, . . . and made use of."

- Indian societies must be given status, responsibility, and power.

- Land held and used by Indians is fundamental to their lifesaving program.

- Each and all freedoms must be extended to Indians. This envisions the enforcement of cultural and religious liberty.

- The grant of freedoms must be more than a remission of enslavements. The government must give Indians the freedom to organize and extend credit as well as provide technical assistance of both a business and civic nature.

- Tribes must be extended the experience of responsible democracy.[12]

These six principles differed substantially in their orientation from anything the other supporters of reform had conceived. They showed that the government's job was to enable Indians to recapture their own genius, whereas even the Meriam Report had not believed that there was anything of value in the old ways, nor did it believe that the principles of Indian tribal life could be successfully revived and transposed into procedures that could energize and provide substance for modern corporate existence.

In the winter of 1932, convinced that the social and political needs of Indians had to be debated publicly, Collier helped to draw up a proposal to give some form of self-government to the reservations. Senator Lynn Frazier introduced the draft bill S. 3668 on February 16 that authorized the creation of tribal councils. Representative Edgar Howard, chairman of the House Indian Committee, introduced a companion bill, H.R. 11080, on April 4, but the need to get the Leavitt Act passed took priority, and consequently no hearings were held on the tribal councils proposal.

Interestingly, we find within the framework of the tribal councils bill not only the major underpinnings of Collier's concept of social institutions but also some of the very elements of self-government the Senate Committee would eventually adopt as their alternative to Collier's grand self-government proposal. Closely examined, the Tribal Councils Bill offers all the essential ingredients of self-government that would be debated during the first years of the Roosevelt administration, including a formula that Collier hoped would alleviate one of his greatest fears—that the adoption of the corporate structure would disenfranchise future generations of Indians.

The bill provided that when 25 percent of the adult members of any Indian tribe residing on a reservation petitioned the commissioner of Indian affairs, he was authorized to call an election to choose a committee to draft a constitution and bylaws for the tribe. Within sixty days after the committee was elected, it was to notify the tribe and call a general meeting to discuss the organic documents that it was authorized to create. The constitution was to provide for the number of council members, for their annual election, and for a referendum on any policy on petition of at least 15 percent of the tribal members.

The tribal councils created under the new constitutions were empowered to represent the tribe before Congress or the executive department and its agencies, and the expenses of the councils were to be paid out of funds the tribe had on deposit in the federal treasury. No tribal lands or interest in lands could be sold or leased, nor could permits or contracts be made regarding them without the permission of the tribal councils. The councils were authorized to employ legal counsel subject to review by the attorney general but not, significantly, by the Department of the Interior. Section 5 required the secretary of the interior to submit to each tribal council all estimates for expenditures of funds credited to the tribe's account in the federal treasury. Section 8 allowed the Pueblos to retain their traditional customs and established tribal governments and vested powers of government in these traditional institutions. The concluding sections enabled the secretary of the interior to dismiss any employee who interfered with the exercise of tribal political rights in any respect and made it a misdemeanor to do so, subject to a fine of five hundred dollars and imprisonment of not more than six months.

The genius of the plan was its simplicity, though it made it vulnerable to attacks by those who did not or could not understand human social processes. But the basic reason the Tribal Councils Bill failed to gather any support was that Collier was outside the institutions of government, not inside directing the kinds of policy changes that this proposal envisioned. When Franklin D. Roosevelt swept into power, Collier as well as other reformers saw their opportunity to secure a new Indian policy and certainly a new Indian commissioner who would be more responsive to their ideas.

Political maneuvering is difficult to follow when it is happening, and even the best politicians will not reveal, later in their lives, how things really came to be. So it is with Collier. He maintained in his book *From Every Zenith* that Harold Ickes was his first choice as Indian commissioner. Kenneth Philp suggests in his study that Collier, Margold, and Lewis B. Meriam had made an agreement that each put forward his own name and withdraw should the president decide in favor of one of them. We will undoubtedly discover even more twists and turns to this particular story as more historians pore over the records of that era. What is certain, however, is that the powers and interests in Indian affairs each had its own candidate and took strong positions in regard to its favorite choice. In particular, the Indian Rights Association, which continued to have great influence in Indian matters, favored the retention of the incumbent commissioner, Charles Rhoads, one of their members, and Senator Joseph T. Robinson, the Democratic majority leader, favored Edgar B. Meritt, who had been the assistant commissioner during the Harding and Coolidge administrations.

Collier reported that the choice for commissioner boiled down to himself or Meritt and that Ickes publicly announced Collier as his choice and then refused to submit more nominations until the Senate had confirmed him as Indian commissioner. Roosevelt then asked Robinson to withdraw his support for Meritt, and Collier was unanimously confirmed by the Senate. Collier's first move as commissioner was to hold a long conference with the bureau personnel in Washington, describing his hope to form policies that, he said later, "expressed a philosophy intended to reach beyond the United States Indians to all Indians and to all colonial peoples, and generally to the government-citizen relationship. In administration, they related essentially to the equation between government viewed as a necessity, and the Indians viewed as groups thinking and striving in their own being."[13]

Beginning on April 20, 1933, when he was approved as commissioner, Collier immediately began to put his own personal imprint on the Bureau of Indian Affairs. He selected William Zimmerman, who was an old family friend, as assistant commissioner. Nathan Margold became solicitor of the Interior Department, and Charles Fahey and

Felix S. Cohen were appointed as his assistants. All three were attorneys who had been active in the work of the American Indian Defense Association and had worked with the Pueblos during the struggle to protect their lands. Since Ickes had long been active in Indian causes (his wife spoke Navajo and had written a popular book on southwestern Indians), this group looked more like a cabal than a happy circumstance of appointments.

Collier immediately announced that Indians would be able to exercise their right to religious freedom and could engage in their traditional ceremonies without fear of harassment from the bureau. To emphasize this new policy, he forbade forced attendance of Indians at Christian religious services in federal boarding schools, canceled debts against tribal treasuries that had been incurred without tribal approval, and successfully pressured President Roosevelt to abolish the Board of Indian Commissioners, which had been dragging its feet on reforms.[14] Collier avoided antagonizing the Indian Rights Association on this front by simply having Roosevelt refuse to seek appropriations for the board on the excuse that expenditures had to be reduced. In all probability Collier did not want a board looking over his shoulder, as he had once done with Burke and Rhoads during his heyday as an activist.

The first year of his tenure brought a few legislative successes. He secured passage of the Pueblo Relief Act of 1933, which prohibited the secretary of the interior from spending funds on the Pueblos of New Mexico without first obtaining authorization from the Pueblos themselves.[15] Included in this legislation was the fulfillment of a personal promise Collier had made a decade before. It authorized the secretary of agriculture to contract with the Taos Pueblo for the exclusive use of the sacred Blue Lake area for their religious ceremonies. Collier also strongly supported the repeal of several repressive "espionage" acts passed a century before, which restricted the activities of Indians.[16]

Much of 1933 was devoted to connecting the existing programs of the Bureau of Indian Affairs with the new agencies that the New Deal was then creating. Very shortly after he assumed the post as commissioner, Collier established the Emergency Conservation Work program, using the Civilian Conservation Corps (CCC) funds made available to him through interagency cooperation. This program gave an immediate infusion of money into the reservations, which so desperately needed a source of income during that stage of the Depression. Following up this success with another cooperative venture with the Soil Conservation Service, Collier tested his ideas of Indian communal planning with small activities in which Indians were given a role in determining how conservation programs were to be operated on their reservations. His experiences in this regard only strengthened his resolve to vest reservations with full governing powers.

In August 1933 Collier launched the biweekly magazine *Indians at Work*. It was financed by the CCC and bureau funds and basically served as a propaganda organ to publicize Indian efforts to help themselves. With his own newsletter chronicling his successes, Collier was able to secure additional funds from other federal relief agencies in the next several years, immeasurably assisting the bureau in providing new programs for the reservations. It is not difficult to see Collier's clever strategy. If a variety of federal agencies that did not ordinarily serve Indians were already involved with the reservation programs, it would be much easier to secure landmark legislation, since more of the federal establishment would have a stake in the outcome. In this respect Collier had an opportunity to do more for Indians quickly than had any previous Indian commissioner, and he made the most of his chance.

By fall Collier was ready to present his major legislation, but he could not decide whether it should be written as a series of bills or as one large and comprehensive package. He credited Ward Shepard with the suggestion that he incorporate all his proposed reforms into one major package. Collier conceived of the new legislation as replacing almost everything that had gone before. While correct theoretically and conceptually, it was hardly realistic administratively, since the old laws would remain on the books unless they were specifically repealed, and Collier lacked the political influence to repeal the major part of federal Indian law. Nevertheless, it seemed important at that time to emphasize the scope of his proposal and to characterize it as all-encompassing in order to convince people that it truly represented a new departure in federal Indian policy.

In early January 1934 Collier called together a conference of the major personalities and organizations that had been active in Indian affairs during the past decade. The meeting was held at the Cosmos Club in Washington, D.C., and was regarded by everyone in Washington as the beginning of a major effort to reform the federal Indian programs and policies. Prominent in attendance were representatives of the American Indian Defense Association, the National Association of Indian Affairs, the Indian Rights Association, the American Civil Liberties Union, the National Council of American Indians, and the General Federation of Women's Clubs, which had been Collier's closest political ally in past struggles.[17] Neither the issues raised nor the positions taken were new. Much of the discussion centered around the recommendations of the Meriam Report, which had now assumed the status of canon law in reform ideas. Among the more notable topics that received a good deal of support at the conference were

- Repeal of the old policy of allotment

- Consolidation of Indian heirship lands and other trust lands for agricultural purposes

- Promotion of tribal ownership of productive lands for grazing and forestry

- Securing land for landless Indians

- Developing a system of credit for Indian economic development

- Returning the Five Civilized Tribes of Oklahoma to federal control

- Settling claims arising from broken treaties[18]

With the exception of Indian claims, which always seemed to exist outside the regular channels of reform, most of these points were later included in Collier's proposal package.

Collier determined to move forward quickly, using the momentum and good will from the Cosmos Club conference. He sent out a memo on January 20 entitled "Indian Self-Government" to superintendents, tribal councils, and individual Indians, indicating that he planned to reorganize the Indian Service. Collier implored all organizations to consider alternative measures to the allotment program and to consider plans for enlarging the scope of tribal self-government. Unfortunately, Collier received an uneven and largely negative response. Assimilated Indians were opposed to any change, a number of superintendents feared they might lose their jobs, and several tribes evidenced a reluctance to return to the old Indian traditions.[19] Collier, not realizing that he was endangering his program with such rapid moves, continued, and on February 12, 1934—appropriately, Lincoln's birthday—the Indian Reorganization Act was introduced in Congress as H.R. 7902 and S. 2755 by Congressman Howard of Nebraska and Senator Wheeler of Montana, respectively.

Hearings were called almost immediately, and on February 19, two days before he was to appear before the House Indian Subcommittee, Collier sent out a memorandum to all the superintendents, tribal councils, and selected individual Indians, announcing the convening of

Indian congresses at selected cities across the country. The Collier blitz had begun. Rather foolishly, the new commissioner had made himself and his ideas vulnerable to Congress, the bureau, and the Indians all within a week's time, and he would later regret the speed with which he attempted to push through his radical revision of federal Indian affairs.

The Collier Bill

Compared with any other legislation that the Indian committees in Congress had ever considered, the Collier proposal was overwhelming. Forty-eight pages long, the bill was divided into four titles, dealing with self-government, special education for Indians, Indian lands, and a Court of Indian Affairs, respectively. Each title included policy statements introducing the concepts at issue and outlining the distinct authority in new powers to be granted. Each title was itself more comprehensive than any previous legislative proposal, including the General Allotment Act, and spelled out in copious detail how the new relationship between the Indians and the government was to be conceived and administered. Since the material in each title is so extensive, prudence demands that each title be examined separately before any comments on the scope of the whole proposal be made. There is no question, however, that when Collier remarked that the bill was designed to replace almost all of existing federal Indian law, he had not understated his case.

Title I: Indian Self-Government

Unlike previous Indian legislation, which provided authority to the executive branch without clarifying the intent of Congress, this title clearly defined for the federal government what it was doing. "That it is hereby declared to be the policy of Congress to grant to those Indians living under Federal tutelage and control the freedom to organize for the purposes of local self-government and economic enterprise, to the end that civil liberty, political responsibility, and economic independence shall be achieved among the Indian peoples of the United States," read the first sentence of this title. The section then went on to describe the policy that would gradually relinquish the functions of government then exercised by the federal government over the reservations to the Indians, who were to be organized for municipal and other purposes as their ability to perform those functions was demonstrated.[1]

Section 2 spelled out the conditions under which the secretary of the interior would certify the corporate nature of tribal government. If one fourth of the adult Indians residing on any reservation petitioned the secretary for a charter, he was then to investigate the conditions on the reservation and define for Indians the conditions under which they could adopt an organic document for self-government. The charter, when submitted to the tribe, would have to be approved by an affirmative vote with at least three fifths of the Indians resident within the territory to be governed voting in a popular election. The secretary would then submit his findings and a record of his action to the Congress. The secretary could purchase land upon which landless Indians could settle and determine a charter for these people, to take effect at a later date. Presumably the requirement of submission to Congress would preclude the arbitrary actions of the Interior Department that had plagued earlier efforts to organize reservation councils.

The charters of each Indian community were spelled out with a precision that the constitutional fathers would have admired. Territorial limits and membership were to be included in the charters but, more important, the charter had to prescribe a "form of government adapted to the needs, traditions, and experience of such community."[2] Collier did not visualize a single formula for tribal charters. He rather believed that the traditions of each group of Indians could be expressed within the organic documents, thus allowing the Pueblos and other Indian communities with an already strong governing tradition to articulate the particular principles upon which their governments would rest. In formulating a charter, Collier saw old values and customs transformed, not replaced or transmuted.

Each charter was to provide a guarantee of civil liberties that reflected the traditional American beliefs of freedom of conscience, worship, speech, press, assembly, and association. Members were also to be free to sever their relationship with the community and to receive some compensation for their share of the tribal assets. This particular withdrawal provision was already a part of the federal law[3] but had not been rigorously exploited by tribal members. Although it might in the future provide a means whereby the economic power of the tribes would be depleted if any large number of people decided to withdraw their membership, it was nevertheless made a part of this section, since it could be maintained that organization under the bill was wholly voluntary on the part of individual Indians and that the proposal offered them an alternative to living in a communal setting.

Not only did the charter specify the powers of self-government that each community would assume, it was designed to extend those powers as the community demonstrated its ability to govern itself. Whether Collier eventually conceived of the reservations as having municipal powers to the extent of receiving back from the federal government jurisdiction over the major felony crimes, which had been assumed after the *Crow Dog* case, was not clear; it could be implied by the optimistic but also denied by the bureau. Continuing supervision over the financial affairs of the reservations by the bureau, to the extent necessary to prevent the dissipation of capital assets, was required. Here we have a check against the Indian propensity to distribute on occasion tribal capital in the form of per-capita payments. But here again the charters were supposed to describe the manner in which financial supervision would also eventually be terminated.

One defect in the self-government title was the apparent indiscriminate use of percentages when determining what powers the reservation community was to possess. For example, only three fifths of the people needed to ratify the charter in section 2, but suddenly section 4 required three-fourths approval to receive the powers the charter enumerated. Presumably approval of the governing document would not be nearly as controversial as accepting specific powers of government, and hence Collier wished to ensure that Indians understood reception of specific powers and the responsibilities they entailed with a good deal more precision and seriousness than simply receiving the charter to organize.

The form of organization was described as a federal municipal corporation. This status, as yet undefined, placed Collier's idea halfway between the Klamath proposal of the late twenties and the old traditional forms of government, which maintained the federal relationship by receiving municipal powers from their recognition and charter rather than from an inherent sovereignty, which previous cases[4] indicated might still exist in Indian tribes. In addition to other regular municipal charitable functions, the tribal municipalities were to "cultivate and encourage arts, crafts, and culture,"[5] which placed them in the uncomfortable position of having to represent traditional culture while performing contemporary, and basically non-Indian, functions of government. Collier assumed that no conflict of interest existed in this respect, but he most certainly should have visualized this as a problem area, considering the tensions between traditional and assimilated or progressive Indians, which then existed in most of the tribes.

Tribal courts were specifically provided for in the charter, and though their powers were spelled out, the manner in which they were to be established was not made clear in this title. The new tribal corporation was empowered to condemn and take title to any lands or properties, in its own name, when it was necessary to accomplish any of the purposes of the charter. This provision was dangerous and can be cited as an example of Collier's profound but rather naive belief that Indians would work together once they had been given self-government. Here we can see that Collier only anticipated benign acts by the tribal government in using this power of condemnation. The corporation could acquire property, make contracts, and perform other traditional corporate functions in the management of properties and funds. It could also, however, compel the transfer of any employee of the federal Indian Service for inefficiency or other cause and could exclude from the community and its territory nonmembers who, it believed, endangered the community's health, security, and welfare. This particular power was subject to the approval of the secretary of the interior, but it is important to note that the tribal municipal corporation could act as a political body in insisting upon this kind of exclusion. In that respect this title gave the Indians considerably more status in selecting federal employees and administering the reservations than they would have acquired if Congressman Stephens's proposal for elections had been revived.

Section 4 contained a provision that was certain to antagonize the traditional Indians, and Collier's inability to perceive this area of conflict is strange, considering his admiration of the traditional forms of government of the Pueblos. "An Indian community chartered under this Act shall be recognized as successor to any existing political powers heretofore exercised over the members of such community by any tribal, or other native political organizations comprised within the said community, not withheld by such tribal or other native political organization" was the critical phrase. Once the charter had been drawn up and the people had voted to accept it, of course, the traditional or native political organization would have effectively been bypassed and could not withhold any political powers it might formerly have exercised. Thus, although Collier professed great admiration for traditional Indian social genius, his proposal was phrased in such a way as to deliver to the mixed-blood and more acculturated Indians the controls of the tribal government.

The real power contained in this title, apart from the formal recognition of the tribal government as a federal municipal corporation, was in section 6, where the secretary of the interior was directed to prepare annual estimates of expenditures for the administration of the reservation and submit these to the authorized representative of the Indian community. The representative was then to submit his comments, which were to be transmitted by the secretary to the Bureau of the Budget and to Congress. Though this provision did not give veto power to the tribal government, it severely cut into the arbitrary exercise of the secretary's power and, in the hands of a skillful tribal council, could have been a devastating weapon in the perpetual struggle with federal bureaucrats. Within section 6 were also requirements that the secretary submit copies of any bill for the expenditure of funds and the flat declaration that no reimbursable debts could be charged against the tribe unless its duly constituted authorities had previously approved the expenditure.

The commissioner of Indian affairs was authorized, upon passage of the bill into law, to arrange and classify the functions and services administered for Indians by the United States and to make them severable one from the other so that Indians could choose which services and functions they would like to assume as the new program got under way. Depending upon the manner in which these services and functions were broken down, a tribal government might choose to perform only minor functions or assume responsibility for small services to specific segments of the reservation community, or it might, if the bureau felt it capable, undertake much larger projects and responsibilities. No indication was given concerning precisely how these functions and services were to be classified, and presumably Collier had in mind a gradation of functions, which could be relegated to communities depending upon their sophistication and willingness to undertake projects. Basically this general authorization was unworkable, if only from the perspective of monitoring the activities of over three hundred reservations, and it was inevitable that some sense of conformity would have emerged with the actual operation of this provision.

There is no question that Collier was attempting to do too much in this title of the bill. He simultaneously sought to recognize tribal corporations as federal municipal corporations, vest them with certain powers of self-government, and provide them with a set of tools to fight against arbitrary actions of the Bureau of Indian Affairs. While comprehensive, it allowed little leeway for growth in the experience of government. Such powers as budgetary review, transfer of federal employees, and condemnation were potent things to give to the best-conducted municipalities, and to provide them with tribal charters was asking considerably more from the Indians than they were prepared to give. Nevertheless, self-government virtually leaped from every page of the title, and the phraseology of the respective sections left no doubt that Collier saw his task as one of accomplishing as much as possible while it was in Congress's good humor to grant self-government.

Basically the title conceived of self-government as a balance-of-powers situation, in which, as Indians gained more experience, the federal government would surrender its powers of supervision and began to fade away. One minor point hidden in the final sections of the title enabled a tribal government to appoint anyone to the vacancies that then existed in the bureau on their reservations, subject to the individual qualifying under existing federal rules for employment. Again we have here an echo of the old Stephens proposal, and it is not clear whether the tribal government could exercise this power whenever a vacancy existed. In theory within a few years there would not be much difference between the tribal government and the bureau organizational structure on the reservation, and presumably the stocking of reservation posts with people compatible with the tribe would hasten the day when the tribe could assume responsibility for all functions and services on the reservation.

Title II: Special Education for Indians

The second title of the Collier Bill dealt with the problems inherent in Indian education. This title constituted the shortest and least controversial portion of the bill. Though there were a number of congressional statutes dealing with Indian education, the concern in this title was limited to the training and development of young Indians so that they could qualify for positions in the technical trades and professions, as well as in government service. The bill expressly directed the commissioner of Indian affairs to provide training programs for young people of at least one-fourth Indian blood so that they could become employed in a wide variety of positions in the Indian Office. These jobs would include posts in education, public health work, law enforcement, forest management, bookkeeping, and social services. The training for these positions could be conducted in Indian boarding schools, colleges, or professional schools, such as those for law and medicine. The bill called for an appropriation of not more than $50,000 (later increased to $250,000) annually to finance this training. One half of the amount was to be expended in the form of low-interest loans. The commissioner was further authorized to award outright scholarships to qualified students, and a sum not to exceed $15,000 was suggested to support these educational benefits.

Section 2 of the title contained potentially explosive provisions: "It is hereby declared to be the purpose and policy of Congress to promote the study of Indian civilization and preserve and develop the special cultural contributions and achievements of such civilization, including Indian arts, crafts, skills, and traditions."[6] In attempting to establish his own vision of Indian culture as a distinct civilization, Collier was going far beyond any previous recommendation. The Meriam Report had only suggested that if an Indian wished to live in the old ways, he was to be allowed to do so with minimal discomfort and indignity. Collier, on the other hand, was seeking to elevate the traditions of Indians to full civilized status, which radically undercut all previous statements regarding Indian culture made by other commissioners and by most of the interest groups and churches. In view of his strong support for the free practice of tribal religions, it is not surprising that Collier included this policy statement in his educational title. There was no question, however, that it was going to wave a red flag in front of the missionary establishment and antagonize those Indians who had already accommodated themselves to the white man's ways.

This section also directed the commissioner to take certain steps to ensure that Indian culture was respected and taught whenever the opportunity presented itself. The commissioner was directed to prepare curricula for Indian schools adapted to the needs and capacities of the Indian students and to employ individuals familiar with Indian culture and the contemporary social and economic problems of Indian administration. No funds were suggested for this ambitious program, and the individual programs were to be supported from regular educational appropriations.

Title III: Indian Lands

Indian lands had become a critical issue since the Burke Act[7] enabled the secretary of the interior to accelerate the rate at which Indian lands went out of trust. Every annual report of the commissioner of Indian affairs during the twenties contained a section on land sales, and the bureau customarily regarded one of its jobs as that of transferring Indian lands to white ownership. Collier's proposal aimed to reverse this practice completely and restore, insofar as it was possible, the land estate of the tribes. Because the Indian land situation was then so complicated, this title of the bill was highly technical, contained many explosive and revolutionary departures from established practice, and proved to be as controversial among Indians as it was with Congress.

The first command of the Indian land reform title was the termination of any further allotments for tribes who organized under its provisions. The prohibition reversed the policies of a half century completely and absolutely. To assure that Indians then holding allotted lands would be protected, the title stipulated that existing periods of trust on allotted and unallotted tribal lands would be extended until otherwise directed by Congress.[8] This relieved the president from making his annual declaration of the lands over which he was extending the trust period, as he was authorized to do under the act of June 21, 1906.[9] Prior to this time, Indians crossed their fingers every December, hoping that no bureaucratic mistakes would be made and that their lands would be included in the list of lands kept under trust by the government. For all practical purposes, this provision meant that an indefinite if not perpetual trust was extended over Indian lands, since any removal by Congress would almost certainly be met with strong political pressure. Furthermore, the forced "fee patenting" practice, which permitted the secretary of the interior to declare Indians "competent," was withdrawn by section 4.

As an additional protection, and in an effort to provide a measure of redress and source of new tribal lands, section 3 of the title authorized the secretary to withdraw the remaining surplus reservation lands that had been opened for sale or disposal. Under existing practices, the secretary could sell or dispose of all excess land that remained after allotment to individual Indians. Though some tribes had already lost all their surplus lands, other reservations had only recently been allotted, and their surplus lands had not been settled by white homesteaders. These lands were now to be returned to tribal control. The government, in most instances, was not losing money on these lands by returning them to the tribes. Many of the agreements to allot had provided that the tribes would be paid for their surplus lands as the settlers paid their fees into the federal treasury. So in theory these lands still belonged to the tribes.

Restoration of the surplus lands really signaled a complete reversal of federal land policy. Tribal property could no longer find its way into white ownership except through the (highly unlikely) voluntary sale by tribal governments. Tribal governments were to be given the power to control, preserve, and *expand* their land holdings with the assistance and cooperation of the secretary of the interior. Section 5 put teeth into this policy by prohibiting the sale, devise, gift, or transfer of any allotted lands *except to the Indian tribe or community*. Section 7 made it more explicit by authorizing the secretary to acquire additional lands for existing reservations and for landless Indians as well.

The secretary was given authority to establish new reservations for landless Indians on property obtained under the provisions of section 16, which authorized land purchases for Indians by the Interior Department. Theoretically, the secretary could have covered the West with both new Indian reservations and new Indian tribes—only public opinion and the availability of funds for land purchase preventing such a course of action. The secretary was also given the power to acquire property in the checkerboarded areas of the reservations. Over the years reservations had become very fragmented when allotments were sold to non-Indians and they lost their trust status. Until the land could be consolidated, Indians would not be able to put together economic units that would produce any significant income for themselves. Congress was asked to provide not more than two million dollars annually to implement this land acquisition and consolidation program.

Within the reservation areas, Indian communities were empowered to acquire or purchase a tribal member's interest in reservation lands.[10] This authority complemented the secretary's authority and gave the tribal governments the authority and incentive to pursue a constructive land consolidation policy. In addition, section 8 contained an extremely controversial provision. This section permitted the secretary, when he deemed it necessary for the purpose of land consolidation, to transfer to the tribe any individual Indian's interest in grazing, farming, or timber lands. The tribal member would be issued a nontransferrable certificate in exchange for title to his property, giving the Indian a proportionate share in tribal property. These tribal certificates could descend to an Indian's heirs but not to the nonmembers of the community. Though the title to the property would be lodged in the tribe, the right of the individual Indian to continuous use of the property was to be preserved. This "right of use" was also inheritable. These ideas differed in few respects from the idea proposed by the Klamaths for consolidating their allotted lands and certainly must have come from Collier's involvement with the Klamath Incorporation Bill.

This effort by the Collier Bill to provide the secretary with this extraordinary power of mandatory land acquisition became a thorn in Collier's side throughout the legislative hearings on the bill. The concept was simply too radical a change to be accepted quietly by either the Indians or the Congress. This power, however, was but the first of two highly volatile issues contained in the Indian-lands title. The second of these issues dealt with the very rigid restrictions placed upon allotted lands that were to descend to the heirs of a tribal member. Title to all restricted and allotted lands, under this title, passed not to the individual heirs but to the tribe upon the death of a tribal member.[11] The heirs would receive a certificate of interest in tribal lands equal to the proportionate share that he or she would otherwise have received under the will of the deceased. No will attempting to dispose of the allotment other than in this manner would be approved by the secretary. In addition to the certificates, the heirs could also be extended additional benefits, such as the right to the continued use of the property. In effect, Collier was attempting to change the Indian land use patterns from inheritable allotments to lifetime assignments by the use of a forfeiture provision.

The power vested in the secretary to acquire reservation land for consolidation purposes and the provision that stipulated that title to allotted land holdings of an Indian reverted to tribal ownership upon the Indian's death were both *mandatory* provisions; anything less, Collier believed, would defeat his overriding goal of keeping land in Indian hands. By making these provisions mandatory, however, the choice of land use by individual Indians was abruptly withdrawn, and this confiscation made the land consolidation more a departmental project than an Indian goal. The team of experts drafting the bill undoubtedly anticipated the real opposition to these provisions. They may not have envisioned, however, the magnitude of the emotions that these provisions evoked in those people who saw this part of the land title as a real threat to the personal freedom of individual Indian landholders.

The final features of the Indian-lands title put the finishing touches on the consolidation and conservation philosophy of the proposal. The secretary was given the authority to classify and adjust tribal lands into economic units for farming, grazing, and forestry purposes.[12] Furthermore, he could issue rules and regulations to preserve and protect reservation lands from overharvesting and overgrazing by stockmen.[13] This conservation authority could, however, be delegated to the tribe, and in his memoirs Collier commented on how he eventually had convinced several tribes to go along with this idea, most notably the Acomas, Lagunas, and Navajos.[14]

There is little doubt that the Indian-lands title of the bill was comprehensive, complicated, and provocative. Its importance to the overall concept of significant Indian reform, however, cannot be underestimated. Land has always constituted the heartbeat of Indian life, and unless significant changes that recognized its primacy were made in this area, little progress could be made in changing the conditions under which Indians lived. Collier's problem, however, was in his effort to reverse both the policy of allotment and its effects in one title of his legislation. Though he could prevent future loss of Indian land, he could not erase the effects of half a century of allotment and forced land sales without trampling on the rights of individual Indians, many of whom had made their peace with the idea of private property and wanted to keep what little remained to them personally.

Title IV: Court of Indian Affairs

The final title of the Collier Bill concerned the administration of Indian justice and its relationship with the other judicial institutions of the nation. As noted earlier, those people charged with drafting a comprehensive document on Indian reform were well aware of the deficiencies in the existing system of law. The hearings on the bureau's proposal to make the courts of Indian offenses a regular part of the federal judicial system had demonstrated that the enforcement of law on the reservations was a very fragile and volatile subject.

To remedy some of these problems, the Collier Bill called for a dual system of Indian courts. The first level was to be organized under the self-government title of the proposed act. Tribal communities could establish and staff their own local courts or tribunals to handle the legal problems that arose at the community level. At the same time, a national Court of Indian Affairs would be staffed with seven judges appointed by the president and subject to confirmation by the Senate. The court would always be in session and would be held in a number of different circuits.[15] Each judge would be responsible for a particular region. One judge, for instance, might cover the Sioux Indian reservations in North and South Dakota. Another might assume responsibility over the reservations in Arizona and New Mexico. A judge would stay on each reservation for several weeks, hearing cases that were covered under the act.

The jurisdiction of this special Court of Indian Affairs was spelled out in section 3 of the title. It would assume responsibility for hearing all major criminal cases, which at that time fell within the purview of the federal district courts under the Major Crimes Act. In addition, it would entertain cases in the following instances:

- Cases where an Indian tribe or community was a party

- Cases involving questions of commerce where one litigant was an Indian and the other a non-Indian

- Civil and criminal cases involving a tribal ordinance where the party was not a member of the Indian community

- Questions involving the validity of a federal law or regulation pertaining to an Indian tribe

- Issues involving Indian allotments where the rights of an Indian were involved

- Issues involving the determination of heirs and the settlement of estates, land partitions, guardianships, and so on

The establishment of a Court of Indian Affairs was quite a significant departure from the existing system of law, both as it had been practiced in federal courts and as it had evolved on the reservations. Since it was difficult for many Indians to get to the federal district courts because of their geographical isolation, judges of the Court of Indian Affairs were authorized to go to the reservations. The newly created Indian court was to assume much of the responsibility previously exercised by the federal district courts. And though a suggestion such as this one was bound to provoke controversy in Congress, the problems inherent in the existing system of federal Indian law suggested that a material change was badly needed.

A number of provisions in the Court of Indian Affairs title would have changed the traditional concept of Indian justice rather significantly. For example, all the rights accorded to an accused in a federal criminal court proceeding were to be extended to an Indian accused.[16] The right to trial by jury and other procedural guarantees expressed in the United States Constitution were to be observed.[17] The rules of evidence as used in federal criminal court proceedings were to apply in the new Indian courts.[18] In essence, the Court of Indian Affairs was in many respects to duplicate the system of justice that prevailed in the Anglo-American courts. White judicial norms and traditions were to be imposed upon the Indian system, which had been informal on the reservations and reflected neither Indian nor non-Indian jurisprudential concepts. The inclusion of these Anglo-American requirements may have been a reflection of the fact that at this stage of the political game, there was virtually no Indian thinking considered in drafting this title of the bill. Forcing such practices on the administration of Indian justice was hardly consonant with Collier's avowed purpose of returning power to Indian communities so that they could decide what was best for themselves.

Despite the difficulties that might arise from the imposition of non-Indian procedural and substantive norms on Indian proceedings, the Collier Bill did go a long way in attempting to bring an improved system of justice to the Indian legal arena. The new court would be given authority to establish its own rules, and these rules were to conform as nearly as was practicable with those of the federal district courts.[19] It could remove a case falling within its jurisdiction from a state or tribal court[20] and could hear appeals from local tribal courts.[21] Furthermore, the secretary was authorized to appoint ten special attorneys to provide legal advice and representation, both to tribes and to individual Indians, before the Court of Indian Affairs. Like the Indian-lands title, this part of the Collier Bill would generate a great deal of controversy during the legislative hearings.

Although the description of the bill specifically mentioned economic enterprise, there was curiously little direct discussion of the subject of economic development in the proposal. Collier originally believed that once a reservation had formally adopted a charter, it would assume control of both political and economic life and begin to revive its fortunes. There was, consequently, no distinction between the political and the economic functions of an Indian community outlined in the bill. After the bill had been introduced in Congress, however, Collier found it necessary to move his ideas a good deal closer to the Klamath economic proposal. Inserted later was the authorization for an Indian tribe, once it had adopted its constitution and bylaws defining the powers and limitations of self-government, to petition the secretary of the interior to issue it a charter of incorporation. This charter would permit the tribe to establish a corporation that could engage in business, acquire property, obtain loans, and do all things necessary to the conduct of a business agency. Once incorporated, the tribe could apply for loans from a proposed revolving credit fund. The revised bill called for Congress to appropriate five million dollars (later increased to ten million), which could be loaned to the Indian corporations and business enterprises to foster economic development. Collier hoped that a good many of the loans would be used to repurchase allotted lands that had left Indian hands in the interim half-century. The loans were to be repaid to the revolving credit fund so that they could be reloaned to other Indian organizations. In theory, the fund would continue to grow and provide the necessary capital for continued economic growth.

In evaluating Collier's proposal, we must view it in the context of his immediate political situation. There seems to be little doubt that he used the Cosmos Club conference to generate support for reforms that were described in general terms of policy direction, even while he was developing very precise and complicated proposals implementing them. Collier included a number of ideas that were peripheral to the groups attending the Cosmos conference but central to his own ideas of social engineering. Unfortunately, he tried to act as if *all* these ideas had come from the group he had assembled. The titles of his bill only remotely related to the issues identified and defined in the January meeting. Some of the land proposals went far beyond the condemnations of allotment that had been voiced by the Indian interest organizations. They bordered on fanaticism, with an authoritarian ring that suggested that Collier did not believe he would ever get another chance to reverse the loss of Indian lands. Collier's provisions for the revival of Indian cultural practices seem naive today; in 1934 they were exceedingly radical because few people saw any value whatsoever in reviving Indian culture, let alone giving it an aura of academic and educational respectability.

The Collier proposal was clearly a fully developed version of the Indian Tribal Councils Bill of 1932. Its problem was that it was too well developed; it pronounced in the most aggressive and determined language a philosophy of culture and self-government that most members of Congress could not possibly support. Each title could well have been a major legislative proposal of any administration. Its impact was overwhelming, and no one could fathom the degree of change it would entail. Only Collier's sociological concerns saved him from the outpouring of abuse that might have been his lot had people really understood what he was doing. His eloquence about culture mixed with specific proposals for letting Indians have a voice in their own affairs masked the fundamental political philosophy that lay under his words and concepts. The sad fact was that had Indians really understood the implications of Collier's thinking—the restoration of some kind of political sovereignty, with few exceptions—they might have been more violently against him themselves. Too many of them had adjusted to the idea of individual allotments and did not want to constitute a formal government which might eventually impinge on their use of their own lands.

The House Hearings

Although the Supreme Court has characterized congressional decisions regarding Indians as an exercise of the plenary power and has suggested that Congress deliberates in all its wisdom when considering Indian legislation, American history suggests otherwise. The two legislative houses have been at odds with each other on almost every major piece of Indian legislation they have considered. Compromises have eventually been reached on important bills, but on the whole it is not unusual to find the House of Representatives thwarting a senatorial initiative or the Senate blocking a proposal submitted to them from the lower house. Some commentators have suggested that this natural competitive spirit comes from the constitutional allocation of treaty making to the Senate and the origination of revenue bills in the House of Representatives.

In the period prior to the New Deal, the Senate had taken the lead in Indian matters. The Subcommittee on Indian Affairs had investigated the conditions of Indians in the United States and used this platform to demand concessions from the Bureau of Indian Affairs on a number of matters important to it. The House had attempted to deal with Indian matters, but its only significant hearings, dealing with the disastrous Interior proposal to make the tribal courts a part of the federal judiciary, had not been successful. The congressmen had been surrounded by angry delegations of Indians who believed that they were being abused by Congress. Enraged at the accusations made against them, most of the representatives were content to let the Senate take charge of Indian policy.

The House Committee on Indian Affairs, however, was mostly responsible for the conditions of Indians. It had insisted on placing crippling amendments on Indian legislation since the 1890s and tended to involve itself in the land problems of the Indians that never became resolved. Beginning with Representative Charles Burke's efforts to devise a formula for allowing Indians to achieve citizenship through the sale of their allotments, the House Committee on Indian Affairs had supported most of the detrimental land legislation of the previous two decades. Collier was not eager to come before this committee, since he had, on occasion, proposed alternative ways of resolving Indian problems that had made committee members look inept and foolish.

In the Senate Collier felt more at home. He had been allowed to participate in most of the hearings of the late twenties and on occasion had assisted senators in drafting legislative proposals that, if they did not pass, at least drew the approval and admiration of the private Indian interest groups and some of the tribes. It was Collier's practice to provide senators with information they could use to embarrass the administration, and he was considered a valuable ally in the perennial war between the legislative and the executive branch over domestic policies.

One must understand a bit about congressional protocol in order to understand Collier's dilemma as the hearings on his legislation opened. Traditionally the two Indian committees of Congress were not popular assignments. Careers could not be built on minor legislation that affected a small racial minority, and many members of Congress studiously avoided being assigned to these committees. As a consequence, they were generally filled with people from the western states, particularly those people whose supporters had business with the Bureau of Indian Affairs. There was unquestionably a conflict of interest in these committees, and it meant that often a major piece of legislation would be shelved because of a minor and trivial complaint on another matter voiced by one of the members.

The chairman tended to dominate committee meetings. He had almost absolute power with respect to legislation because few members cared to devote the time necessary to formulate new policy or programs. Whatever wisdom Congress had was not being exercised on behalf of Indians. Few members bothered to attend hearings and did so only when the matter affected people in their states. It was into this rigid political arena that John Collier had to venture, forgetting that he was no longer a private citizen who could act with impunity. Thus it was somewhat a *tour de force* that Collier was able to get Congressman Edgar Howard of Nebraska to sponsor his bill in the House of Representatives and Senator Burton K. Wheeler both to sponsor his legislation and to serve as chairman of the Senate Committee on Indian Affairs. With the chairmen of both Indian committees at least initially on his side, Collier overcame one of the major institutional barriers that thwarted the passage of legislation—support from the standing committee chairmen, though his support eroded as the hearings progressed. In retrospect, we can be certain that Wheeler, at least, eventually felt impelled to put his own imprint on the proposal in order to escape identification with the zealous Collier.

The legislative context in which the Collier Bill had to operate during the year 1934 was neither conducive nor detrimental to its chance of passage. While the Roosevelt administration was struggling in its formative years, it did not hesitate to address itself aggressively to the economic problems of the day. Clearly the issues attendant to Indian self-government were not among the more salient ones that occupied the attention of either the administration or Congress. This, however, may have been to John Collier's advantage, for it prevented the conservative assimilationists in the legislature from mounting a determined effort to stop the movement toward Indian self-government. This permitted Collier to enter the congressional arena in such a fashion that he could move forward without significant or at least organized opposition.

While the opposition to Collier in the House may not have been well organized, there still existed a strong nucleus of committee members who opposed the concept of Indian self-government. Prominent among this group were Representatives Theodore Werner of South Carolina, Isabella Greenway of Arizona, Thomas O'Malley of Wisconsin, and Oscar De Priest of Illinois, a formidable block of adversaries whose subtle criticisms and questions kept Collier and his staff of Interior experts in a constant state of tension. A number of these representatives opposed the bill simply because they believed it would delay the time needed to assimilate Indians into the mainstream of white society. Others, such as Isabella Greenway, came from states (like Arizona) where the reservations possessed a great deal of mineral wealth. Representative Greenway had always been a staunch supporter of the mining interests and the forthcoming hearings would afford her an opportunity to live up to her reputation. A number of other congressmen who opposed the Collier measure even went so far as to boycott the hearings at times. All of this was complicated by the fact that the bill was so long and complex that it posed problems of understanding. Congressman Will Rogers of Oklahoma confessed that few members of the House really comprehended the measure, and he was at a loss to see how the Indians could possibly understand it.[1] Opposition to the bill became so vocal in late April that Secretary Harold Ickes sent a memo to Indian Service employees warning them not to engage in activity designed to defeat the bill.[2]

Hearings on the Collier Bill, designated H. R. 7902, began on February 22. At the start of the hearings, Collier announced that a number of Indian congresses were to be held around the country so that Indians would not only receive information about the bill but would have an opportunity to contribute ideas for changing it as well. Ten of the congresses were to be scheduled throughout the months of March and April. Feedback from the Indian community would then be transmitted to the committee members to assist them in their deliberations.

Collier, the first witness to appear before the committee, began a detailed explanation of his omnibus proposal. The commissioner meticulously examined the problems that allotment posed to Indians, the disastrous loss of their lands, and the erosion of self-government, with its resultant bureaucratic stranglehold exercised by the BIA over Indian affairs. Throughout much of this discussion, Collier concentrated on the difficulties inherent in the existing governmental policy of assimilation—with much resistance from the many committee members who favored integrating Indians into white society. The commissioner tried to explain that the ultimate goal of assimilation was not to be completely abandoned;[3] his argument seemed ambiguous by design. In his politic manner, he reasoned that the proposed legislation would, on the one hand, prepare those who wanted to enter into white society, while at the same time, assist those who wanted to continue their traditional way of life on the reservation.

As adept as Collier was at verbal fencing, he was never able to convince the proassimilation congressmen that his bill would not segregate Indians into isolated communities in Indian country. This issue reappeared with frequency throughout the hearings. At one point it was raised in the guise of the alleged Indian failure to accept the responsibilities of citizenship. Might not the Collier Bill, reasoned Isabella Greenway, place Indians in a situation in which they would be less likely to undertake their civic responsibilities?[4] Collier responded by noting that existing policy dissuaded Indians from fully accepting their citizenship obligations. In allotted areas, Collier noted, Indian lands were largely controlled either by whites or by the Indian Bureau. Indians could not even enter into contracts without bureau approval. They had little if any control over their public services, and the whole network of bureaucratic restraints over their lives left Indians with little incentive to assume a more vigorous role in exercising civic responsibilities. Under the proposed bill, a great deal of the power now exercised by the Indian Bureau would be returned to the tribal communities so that they could assume a more active role.

Congressman Theodore Werner joined the argument, noting that Indians enjoyed "all of the rights of citizenship, but would not participate in any of the direct burdens under the proposed legislation."[5] Collier denied this contention, indicating that the only civic burden the Indians would not assume under his bill would be that of state taxation. When Werner turned to the potential isolation of the Indians' tribal communities, Collier drew a parallel between Indian communities and the colonies the Mormons had developed in the western regions of the country. The Mormons were American citizens but had established a productive system of cooperative living. Their colony did not segregate them socially or economically, and neither, Collier argued, would the development of Indian communities result in isolation.[6] The complexity of this assimilation/citizenship/guardianship issue is crystallized in the following exchange between Collier, Werner, Greenway, and Theodore Christianson of Minnesota:

MR. WERNER.   The Mormon is a citizen.

MR. COLLIER.   The Indian is a citizen.

MR. WERNER.   Certainly he is, but he has no control over his affairs.

MR. COLLIER.   He will get some control under this bill.

MR. WERNER.   This will still hold him within the power of a bureaucracy.

MR. COLLIER.   The guardianship of the Indian is definitely ended by this plan.

MR. WERNER.   A man cannot maintain the right of citizenship and still be subject to guardianship. He remains a ward nevertheless.

MR. COLLIER.   The guardianship will not be what it is now, something that takes away from him his initiative, his self-respect, his power, his liberty and self-support, but this will be something in which he will be urged to accept liberty and acquire the habit of self-support.

★　★　★

MR. COLLIER.　　The guardianship in this is simply not guardianship at all.

MRS. GREENWAY.　But is there the established policy among those who are working with and for the Indians all the time to build into an absorption into citizenship in the United States future generations of Indians?

MR. COLLIER.　　I would answer that by saying it is entirely a matter of personal equation what different people think about that. I will go on from what I said, that this would be the means if the policy were to terminate the guardianship—this would be the conservative and humane way of doing it.

MR. CHRISTIANSON.　Could we clarify this question by distinguishing between two classes of guardianship which the law recognizes, guardianship of the person and guardianship of the estate? Is not the guardianship the Government is exercising here more in the nature of the estate of the Indian than the person?

MR. COLLIER.　　It becomes that under this bill.

MR. CHRISTIANSON.　I think if we bear that distinction in mind, it might help us. Ordinarily when a guardianship is established over his estate, that guardianship terminates whenever the incompetent becomes competent to manage his own affairs, and is resumed if he becomes incompetent again, but I presume that the policy of the Government in this instance is to assist the Indian until he develops full competency and then terminate the guardianship.

　　The vigorous debate on assimilation ultimately focused on a clear and fundamental conflict. The rekindling of an effective governmental mechanism was directly at odds with the existing policy of assimilation. In an effort to avoid this controversial issue, Collier concentrated much of his testimony on the problem of removing the bureaucratic stranglehold of the Indian Bureau from Indian communities. "It is the chief object of the bill to terminate such bureaucratic authority by transferring the administration of the Indian Service to the Indian Communities themselves."[7] Collier went on to note that the bill "contemplates that the Office of Indian Affairs will ultimately exist as a purely advisory and special service body, offering the same type of service to Indians of the Nation that the Department of Agriculture offers to American farmers."[8] In essence, Collier adopted a strategy that would place the Indian Bureau in the position of a "whipping boy." Since the BIA was held in so little repute on the Hill, it was difficult for the committee members to take exception to this type of argument. Collier was at least temporarily able to deflect attention away from the delicate issue of how the development of effective tribal governments might erode the existing policy favored by the proassimilation congressmen.

The tactic left him, however, in a paradox. On the one hand, he stressed the enormous authority—"inordinate in its width"[9]—which the Indian Bureau possessed over Indian affairs. It had the power to remove restrictions on allotted land, approve wills, determine heirship, control the selection of attorneys, establish the procedures of litigation, terminate employment, hire those who were qualified to work in the Indian Service, supervise contractual relations made by Indian wards, arrest and prosecute the criminally accused, and set up a court of Indian offenses to try those that violated the law. But after criticizing these vast powers, Collier had to defend the provisions in his bill that continued to reserve enormous authority in the hands of the secretary. The phrase "at the discretion of the Secretary" loomed large in the commissioner's proposal, particularly in section 4 of the self-government title, which required the secretary's approval over many of the functions to be performed by the newly created or revised tribal governments. Fortunately, the members of the Committee on Indian Affairs raised few questions concerning this reservation of power; it posed a greater problem when Indian groups testified before the committee.

After stressing the need to cut the cord that tied Indian communities closely to the BIA, Collier then had to make clear that the federal government would continue to provide funds to tribal governments in the same manner that it had in the past.[10] The guardianship responsibility of the government to the Indian was to remain intact, Collier noted, but the federal government would not be financially liable for the debts and acts incurred by the chartered community. If a tribe entered into a contract with a white corporation and ultimately defaulted on that contract, it would be the Indian community and not the government that would be financially responsible.

This "liability issue" provoked a good deal of concern among several committee members. According to existing law, a businessman who entered into a contract with an Indian community had only limited recourse if that contract was violated by the tribe. The law provided the federal government with immunity from suit; hence, the aggrieved businessman could not proceed against the federal government as guardian for the Indian tribe. The Collier Bill did not change this policy. Congressman Dennis Chavez of New Mexico argued that the Indian communities themselves should be responsible whenever they breached a commercial contract.[11] The problem with this solution was that there were certain debt limits that had to be written into each tribal charter, beyond which the tribe could not be responsible.[12] To complicate the matter even further, the concept of sovereign immunity protected tribes from having their property levied upon for execution to satisfy a debt. The only possible recourse available to an aggrieved party would be to seek a "relief bill" from Congress, a special act compensating the party for his loss as a result of the tribal breach of contract. This whole issue not only confused the committee but disturbed it as well. Some members were afraid that this would effectively discourage white businesses from trading with the Indians. The matter was finally brought to a close when it was suggested that Collier submit a revised version of this section of the bill, incorporating the committee's thoughts.[13] The committee, of course, assumed that Collier would be able to discern with some clarity the mixture of diverse ideas suggested by the committee members.

As the third day of the committee hearings approached, Collier was ready to submit part of his economic development plan for tribal governments. This new section authorized Congress to create a revolving credit fund in the amount of five million dollars annually for loans to Indian communities.[14] The total credit extended to Indians under the present system worked out to be about 55 cents per year per capita to cover farming, education, grazing, and local operations. Collier noted that one of the reasons Indians were at the mercy of white traders was that they lacked sources of credit, and at times had to submit to a virtual state of peonage. The committee was moved to double the figure.[15]

Though the issue of tribal self-government was troublesome for the committee, most of the controversy during the House hearings revolved around the Indian-lands title. The Committee showed grave concern over the amount of power given to tribal governments in their area. Under the proposed bill tribes were permitted to obtain allotted land from tribal members in exchange for shares in the tribal corporation, which would be issued to the individual Indians. Since these exchanges were to be voluntary, they generated but minimal opposition. In addition, however, tribal governments were given the power of eminent domain over reservation property. The justification for bestowing this grant of power on the tribes was tied to the experiences that the Pueblo Land Board had encountered in its attempts to get non-Indian landowners to accept reasonable compensation for their holdings.[16] Inability to condemn lands delayed and impeded considerably the transfer of white property back into the hands of the Pueblo Indians.

Closely related to the condemnation issue were problems confronting those Indians who simply did not want to participate in the Indian community. What would happen to the lands they owned that were located within the reservation boundaries? Collier noted that these lands could be sold to the tribe. But where would the money come from to purchase this land? It would have to come, according to Collier, from such community sources as grazing revenue or timber cutting. The suspicion was never laid to rest that this need for funds might require mortgaging the joint property of the Indian community, thereby frustrating the economic enterprise before it even got started.[17]

Of all the burdens carried by Collier in presenting his bill to the committee, perhaps the heaviest dealt with those provisions that threatened the vested property rights of Indians. Continuously throughout the proceedings, the Indian commissioner stressed the fact that the vested rights of tribal members must be protected, but without absolute dominion. At times these rights would have to be adjusted.[18] Clearly Congress, through its guardianship and supervisory powers over Indian affairs, had made adjustments in the past. In emphasizing the contingent nature of vested Indian rights, Collier was preparing to grant the secretary several dramatic powers that could fundamentally affect vested Indian rights to their landholdings.

The first of these controversial provisions provided the secretary with the power to sell or transfer to a tribal government any farming, grazing, and forest lands owned by a community member when, in the secretary's view, it was necessary for purposes of land consolidation.[19] The secretary did not have to obtain the consent of the individual Indian. Hence, certain tribal members could be stripped of the title to their reservation land and paid off immediately in cash or by installments if it was impossible for the tribe to make up a lump-sum payment. The primary goal was to consolidate the lands into economically productive units. A representative of the Interior Department attempted to placate the fears of committee members on this issue. He noted that one of the reasons for making these transfers compulsory was that at times a party might want to hold out and simply not sell. If this property was an integral part of the consolidation program, the program of combining land into productive units could be defeated.[20] If an Indian preferred not to sell his property, the bill provided for mutual exchanges by which the tribe could receive title to the property and the individual member in turn would receive a certificate for a proportionate share in the tribal community property plus enjoy continued use of the land. The fact that the provision gave *mandatory* power to the secretary to divest an Indian of his reservation land if necessary for consolidation purposes provoked a sharp debate between Collier and members of the committee.

Section 11 stipulated that all restricted lands passed to the tribal community upon the death of a tribal member. The land could *not* descend to the Indian heirs. The tribal government would receive title to the property and the heirs would receive a certificate of interest in the tribal lands of similar monetary value. No will attempting to dispose of such lands in other than this manner would be approved by the secretary. The heirs, of course, could continue to use and work the land. Like the earlier consolidation provision, this section was of a mandatory nature.

This controversial heirship section was designed to overcome the immense difficulties encountered under the allotment system. Landholdings were fragmentized in such a manner as to render them useless. In many instances, each heir possessed such an infinitesimally small share of the property that his or her interest was economically worthless. Consequently, the Bureau of Indian Affairs had become in many respects a real estate agency, leasing these parcels out to non-Indians. At the time of the hearings on the Collier Bill, seven million acres of the best allotted land, having passed into the hands of heirs, were awaiting lease or sale to whites.[21]

Though recognizing the problem of fragmented landholdings, many committee members nevertheless rebelled against a measure that would automatically deprive Indian heirs of their lands. Congressman Werner was emphatic in his argument that Congress could pass no law that would deny any Indian his vested rights.[22] Collier responded by noting that the heirs would receive an equitable share in the tribal property; their interest would in no way be diminished. Fortunately for Collier, this sensitive discussion became confused with another issue and ended, but only temporarily. In the Senate hearings, the controversy would prove more explosive.

On occasion, concern was expressed over the subsurface rights to the land. Isabella Greenway of Arizona was interested in knowing what would happen to those Indians who owned land with oil and mineral wealth. Could these lands under the Collier Bill be sold or transferred by the tribal government into the oil business?[23] No, oil and mineral rights were expressly excluded from the bill. This prompted an argument over timber rights, which were *not* excluded. Was the bill designed only to satisfy one region of the country? Here Collier indicated that the administration of mineral rights had never been a real problem. The issue with reference to timber, however, was different. Timber had to be "slaughtered," and when it was cut down, it interfered significantly with the underlying governmental policy of conservation.[24]

One final point regarding the Indian-lands title concerned the committee. The New York Indians specifically requested that this title of the bill not apply to them. Indeed, they felt that their condition was so different from other Indians that the only part of the bill they wished to have applied to them was the section pertaining to education.[25]

Title II, which dealt with Indian education, was given a warm reception by the committee members. They listened attentively as Collier unveiled the educational provisions and linked them to the desperate problem of Indian unemployment. Most of the commissioner's testimony dealt with the lack of Indian personnel in the BIA. In spite of the millions of dollars spent on Indian education, there were more Indians employed in the Indian Service in 1900 than there were in 1934.[26] One of the major obstacles was that otherwise qualified Indians simply could not pass the Civil Service examination, which was a prerequisite for employment with the federal government. The Civil Service exam in practice always resulted in the employment of a "degree man." But a degree from college, which disqualified Indians every time, did not necessarily qualify a person to deal with Indian affairs. Since the Civil Service kept upgrading the exam requirements, Indians kept losing ground.

The educational training contemplated by the Collier Bill would enable Indians to secure positions in governmental service in forestry, teaching, nursing, administration, and other jobs required in the conduct of Indian affairs. Courses of a practical nature would be introduced, and students would be extended scholarships and loans from a congressional appropriation of not more than fifty thousand dollars annually. A Filipino forestry program was cited by Collier as an example of what could be accomplished under such a policy. After fifteen years of training, native Filipinos were able to take over and run their own forestry program without American assistance or interference.[27]

When asked by Congressman Peavey if an executive order instructing the Civil Service to employ more Indians would not suffice, Collier voted that he had already sought civil service reform on two occasions in the past but felt it was not the answer.[28] The real need was to create a list of eligible Indian candidates for governmental positions.

★   ★   ★

The Court of Indian Affairs title of the Collier Bill was mentioned sporadically throughout the hearings before the House committee, but it was ultimately decided to postpone considering this issue until the committee could hold a joint session with the House Judiciary Committee. When they convened on May 4, Collier and Charles Fahey, an assistant solicitor in Interior, were the only witnesses to appear. By the time the meeting was held, however, Collier had apparently already come to the conclusion that it would not be possible to get the Court of Indian Affairs through Congress. There was opposition to this title in both houses, but it was particularly strong in the Senate. At the beginning of the session Collier immediately signaled that the court provision of the bill was expendable. Indeed, he specifically noted that it could be eliminated without materially affecting the other provisions in the proposal.[29]

Having pretty much surrendered his position at the beginning, Collier nevertheless proceeded to discuss the need for judicial reform in Indian country. He mentioned that the bill envisioned a two-tier system of courts. One would be a local tribal court handling minor reservation issues; the other would be a national Court of Indian Affairs to serve as an appellate body for the local tribal courts and to handle major Indian problems. The jurisdictional problems in Indian country were in such a state of legal chaos that it was imperative to bring some type of order to the Indian legal arena. Charles Fahey then assumed the role of advocate and proceeded to examine the legal and political reasons why a Court of Indian Affairs should be created. He explored the jurisdictional maze that had resulted from the impractical operations of three-court systems—federal, state, and tribal—attempting to deal with legal problems on the reservations. There were simply too many areas of neglect where no legal institution was assuming responsibility.[30] To complicate matters, tribal customs and laws had been breaking down in Indian communities over the years because of the policy of assimilation that the federal government had been pursuing. The provisions in the Collier Bill calling for a two-tier Indian court system were designed to remedy this decaying situation.

Several congressmen were considerably reluctant to accept such an abrupt reorganization in the existing judicial system. Congressman McKeown of the Judiciary Committee conducted a vigorous if friendly cross-examination of Fahey. There seemed to be little disagreement that real problems confronted Indian nations in their attempt to gain access to an effective and responsive legal system. The fact that Indian communities were widely dispersed and geographically remote from the existing courts of justice could not be denied. Indeed, the members of the two committees appeared cognizant of the fact that Indians lacked understanding of the highly technical aspects and procedures inherent in the Anglo-American system of law. Even with all this evidence, though, there remained a deep-seated reluctance to tinker with the existing legal mechanism. In the long run, it all proved academic. Everyone, including Collier, quietly assumed that the Court of Indian Affairs would become the sacrificial lamb to be surrendered in order to preserve the remaining provisions of the bill.

While the members of the Committee on Indian Affairs engaged Collier in a firm exchange of ideas during the hearings, their dialogue was gentle compared with the confrontations that were provoked by interest groups and tribes that opposed the bill. One of the more vocal opponents of the bill was the Indian Rights Association, an organization that embraced the existing policy of assimilation. While supporting the education title of the bill, the Indian Rights Association took vigorous exception to the bill's other provisions. Jonathan Steere, speaking for this group, argued that old structures and traditions were dying away. The real need was to educate Indians in a manner that would speed up the assimilation process.[31]

Vern Thompson, appearing on behalf of the Quapaw tribe, focused his attention on the fact that the bill was inappropriate for small tribes such as the Quapaw. They had leased their lands, which contained valuable mineral rights, to white companies, and they did not want to be cut off from their share of the "bounty."[32] Equally important was the fear that under the Collier Bill Indians would be deprived of their right to devise property to their heirs by will. The Quapaws, therefore, had passed a resolution requesting that they be excluded from coverage.[33] The Yakima tribe also opposed the bill, fearful that they would lose their private ownership of property. As small as their holdings were and as little profit as the land brought in, the tribe was still against the concept of communal ownership.[34]

The concern with reservation land almost completely preoccupied the Indian opponents to the Collier bill. Robert Yellowtail, a Crow Indian, presented his tribe's case.[35] The Crow reservation had become badly checkerboarded because of allotment, and the most valuable parcels had passed into white hands. Many of the whites had indicated that they would not sell their land back to the Indians, or, if forced to sell, would ask an unreasonably high price for their property. How could the Crows possibly deal with a situation such as this? Collier admitted that this posed a difficult problem. Condemnation was limited to what the state law would permit, which might not be sufficient. Yellowtail also noted that almost all reservations were split into factions; it would be difficult to unite these factions behind the bill, and the committee members should be forewarned about this prospect.[36]

Although the Indian factionalism problem was important, testimony before the committee revealed other difficulties. James Saluskin, a Yakima, noted that great confusion and misunderstanding existed among the Indians.

Since this Wheeler-Howard bill has been interpreted to me, I never can get heads nor tails to the thing. I just imagine that it does not amount to anything to me. It seems as though if this bill were passed it would be no protection really for my children and that is the reason I want to protect myself and give my reasons for not wanting this bill passed.

In regard to this community play, I do not think that I am capable as a tribe of Indians to operate under the new system. I feel this way, that if we were to adopt this self-government, the people who are running self-government would be expecting some kind of a compensation, and we have no funds to pay them.[37]

Fear and confusion over the bill abounded. A good deal of the apprehension centered on the landless Indians who had sold their lands. Saluskin told the committee that the tribal members did not want to be ruled by those who had already gotten rid of their land. "I will put my land in and what has he got to put in against my land."[38] Saluskin proceeded to argue that he did not want the government to come in and take his land in order to give it to landless Indians who sold their property at an earlier date. Concluding, he indicated that the tribal members objected to the "proposed bill specially for the reason that we find it might result in placing in the hands of irresponsible Indians too much authority and power."[39]

This concern about the role of landless Indians was also expressed by Ute Arapaho of the Cheyenne-Arapaho tribe.[40] Would not the Collier Bill prevent landowners from holding on to their land and handing it down to their children? He also noted a strong feeling among tribal members against the idea of communal ownership of land. Ute Arapaho ended his remarks by commenting that he was in the dark about all this. Congressman Werner, not about to let this opportunity to criticize the bill slip by, responded by saying, "He is not any more in the dark than are the members of this committee."[41]

Not all of the critics of the Collier Bill opposed it because of its far-reaching scope. Some felt that the decentralizing measure did not go far enough. Thomas Sloan, an attorney for the Omaha Indians, indicated that too much discretion had been left in the hands of the secretary of the interior. The living conditions of the Omaha, Winnebago, Santee Sioux, Yankton Sioux, and Rosebud Sioux tribes were deplorable. Much of this poverty could be traced to the neglect of the secretary in failing to exercise his "discretion" to assist these tribes.[42] The real power exercised over the reservations, according to Sloan, resided in the superintendents, who were not sympathetic to the local community interests. So whereas the general notion of decentralizing power and placing more power in the hands of tribal governments was laudable, reserving so much power in the hands of the secretary would offset the ability of local Indian communities to govern themselves.

At times the committee hearings were used as a vehicle through which to continue local tribal disputes. Paul Willis, of the mission Indians of southern California, urged the congressional policy makers to adopt a strong provision enabling tribes to remove hostile superintendents, a concern echoed by Adam Castillo.[43] Upon conclusion of this testimony, Collier proceeded to explain to the committee that a terrible political battle was being waged among the mission Indians. According to Collier, the Mission Indians Federation, the political faction represented by Willis and Castillo, had tried to establish themselves as an authoritarian government and had virtually gone to war with the Indian Bureau. Paul Willis had wanted to become the new superintendent and hence had brought this local political conflict into the hearing in hopes of promoting his cause.[44] Furthermore, the federation, which according to Collier was really under the influence of the white community, had no official standing. It was not a tribal council. Collier also suggested that Willis had an additional ulterior motive in that he was attempting to get the government to purchase a ranch for $150,000. The government had refused, believing it to be worth only about $90,000.[45] Other such conflicts of interest occasionally found their way into the hearings.

The politics following from the House hearings were not limited to intratribal disputes. One of the early witnesses to appear before the committee was Charles A. Mitke, a consulting mining engineer from Phoenix. Under the Collier Bill, Mitke argued, local Indian communities could condemn and take title to existing mining properties. This authority would be in direct conflict with the plans of the governor of Arizona, the state legislature, the state Land Commission, and ten of the leading chambers of commerce in the state.[46] Mitke, of course, was not there representing the Papago tribe but rather the mine operators who had interests in the properties of the Papago reservation, and underlying this whole problem was a complex politicolegal battle involving the mineral rights on the reservation. This conflict, according to Collier, had no bearing on the bill and constituted an entirely separate issue that Interior was attempting to resolve—which did not keep it from occupying a good deal of time during the Senate hearings.

The House Committee on Indian Affairs received a number of other written objections from various tribes and interest groups opposing the bill. One complaint of interest came in the form of a letter from George Whirlwind Soldier, who accused Collier of recruiting Indians to campaign for the bill:

> The Government officials seem to be trying to force this Collier program upon the Indians. Collier has taken Roe Cloud away from his duties as superintendent at Haskell and is making a campaigner of him, the same as the politicians do before election. This appears to me to be entirely out of place to take a Federal employee and, in fact, several Federal employees, and make campaigners out of them instead of sending this bill to different tribes and letting them select some attorney to explain anything to them which they do not understand.[47]

Roe Cloud in fact did appear at several of the Indian congresses that were held, but only in the capacity of a moderator. A widely known and respected Indian figure, it was entirely proper for Roe Cloud to assume such a role. There is little doubt, however, that in his job as moderator, Roe Cloud was forceful in his strong support for the Collier proposal.

Not all the tribal testimony in the House hearings was critical of the Collier Bill. Indeed, the vast majority of the more than forty pages in the hearing records of communications were strongly supportive of the measure. Undoubtedly, the Indian Office had done a good job in promoting its cause. In addition, Collier could point with some pride to the votes taken by various tribal councils following the Indian congresses that were held during the months of March and April in 1934. A summary of the various referendums indicated that fifty-five tribes, composed of 141,881 Indians, voted to support the measure. Only twelve tribes, with a total of 15,106 Indians, voted to the contrary.[48]

It was not clear, however, whether these votes truly reflected an actual Indian head count. Whenever a tribal council voted, Collier simply assumed that the groups spoke for the entire tribe and counted the individual votes accordingly. "In other words, where a tribe was for the bill, it was counted as entirely for it, and where it was against the bill it was counted entirely against."[49] This method of computation raised a few eyebrows in the House. Congressman Roy Ayers of Montana was also quick to point out that some of the tribal councils voting to support the bill, such as the Blackfeet, were favorable only if certain amendments to the bill were accepted, and not necessarily as it was initially introduced.[50]

A number of tribal representatives provided Collier with more concrete encouragement by the testimony that they presented to the House committee. Ralph Fredenberg, a Menominee, told the committee how his tribe had gone to Congress several years before, seeking special legislation that would enable it to organize at the local level. Congress had refused to accommodate them. Since that time, the Menominees had attempted to close their reservation to whites for a two- or three-year period in order to restock the streams, which the whites had overfished. The tribe had been subjected to enormous pressure to prevent this conservation action.[51] Had the Indian community been possessed of a strong local government with the kinds of powers envisioned in the Collier Bill, Fredenberg argued, the Menominees would have been in a much better position to withstand the white pressure. The tribe was now being pressured by the white community to permit the development of a water power site on the reservation. The Menominees felt helpless to cope with problems such as these, according to Fredenberg.

Joseph W. Brown, of the Blackfeet tribe, advised the committee that initially the Blackfeet tribal council had been opposed to the omnibus Indian measure. After attending one of the regional Indian congresses and hearing Collier's explanation of the bill, however, the tribe later voted unanimously to support it.[52] The Blackfeet did suggest several amendments, which met with the commissioner's approval. Brown indicated that if the Collier Bill were passed, the Indians would be protected from losing more of their lands. More important, the tribe needed to obtain credit for economic development, and the revolving credit fund would meet this need. When an Indian went to a bank to obtain a loan, Brown stated, the bank always refused to extend credit because title to Indian property was in trust and inevitably suggested that the Indian go to the Indian agency for a loan. But the Indian agency never had any money to loan. Without the revolving credit fund, the future of economic development for Indians appeared bleak.

During the course of Brown's testimony, Congressman Werner discovered that the government had provided Brown with funds so that he could come to Washington to testify. Werner then noted that James Saluskin, a Yakima Indian who opposed the bill, was not reimbursed.[53] Werner wondered aloud whether or not the hearing had been rigged in favor of the bill, since the measure's supporters seemed to get reimbursed whereas the opponents did not. The congressman then asked Brown how he felt about the bill's taking away an Indian's right to bequeath his property to his heirs. Brown noted that this could be rectified by one of the several amendments the Blackfeet had suggested.[54] Both Congressman Werner and Congressman O'Malley then proceeded to engage Brown in a vigorous interrogation concerning the Court of Indian Affairs. Brown noted that the Indians believed the court to be a good idea but thought that they could probably get along without it.[55] The admission, interestingly, was identical to the position that Collier had begun to take. The court seemed to be expendable.

Earl Wooldridge, the superintendent of the Rocky Boy Indian Reservation, was in Washington on business and was asked by Collier to testify before the committee. Wooldridge was a strong supporter of the bill. Congressmen Werner, still concerned with dealing the Indian court proposal a death blow, asked Wooldridge about some earlier testimony regarding a criminal incident that had occurred on the Rocky Boy Reservation. An Indian who had stolen a horse worth fifty dollars had been arrested and jailed. A white court set the Indian's bail at fifteen hundred dollars, so the accused sat in jail for a long period of time. When Walter Woehlke earlier testified regarding this incident, he indicated that if a Court of Indian Affairs had been in existence, the matter would have been settled within three or four days and the Indian would have been out of jail. Werner then asked Wooldridge if this was the type of justice that would come from the new court—letting the guilty off in some back-office arrangement.[56] Wooldridge discreetly responded that the problem that needed to be rectified was that Indians were largely ignored by the Anglo-American courts. It was simply too hard to get cases heard, and white judges seldom understood or responded to Indian legal needs. Werner replied that he was only trying to indicate that a lot of deceptive statements were being made by the bill's proponents, which were providing the Indians with false hopes. Wooldridge indicated that he did not believe this to be the case. "But I do know," Wooldridge concluded, "that so far as our Indians go, they feel that this is one of the times that something is really trying to be done for Indians."[57] The day's hearing was brought to an end with Congressman

O'Malley extremely exercised over the fact that Wooldridge, a civil servant who was not supposed to get involved in politics, had come before the committee to support the bill.

Congressional hearings are not just formal rituals enabling Congressmen to demonstrate their rhetorical talents. They can and do have a meaningful impact upon the content and form of legislative proposals, which certainly was the case with the Collier bill. Actually, the initial changes in the measure probably flowed as much from the regional Indian congresses held in March and April as from the hearings. Testimony before the House committee began on February 22 and extended through May 9. Collier was able to measure both Indian and congressional opposition to the bill during this period. Where Congress and the Indians agreed, this seemed to be a politic point to make adjustments. A number of amendments to the bill were consequently offered by Collier, several of which were quite important.

The first significant change that Collier suggested involved the authority of the secretary of the interior to transfer land to the community even if contrary to the wishes of the Indian landowner.[58] The compulsory authority of this section was dropped, and the provision was made voluntary.[59] This change pleased a number of Indian groups and some members of the House committee, both of whom opposed the mandatory provision. On the issue of heirship, title to all restricted land was to pass, under the original bill, to the Indian tribe upon the death of an allotted Indian and not to the heirs.[60] Under the suggested new language, farm land or allotted farm land would continue to be inheritable as long as it did not have to be subdivided to the extent that it could not be used.[61]

Several of the amendments proposed by Collier dealt directly with the power of the secretary. Of particular importance was an amendment designed to limit the secretary's discretionary power with respect to the rental, leasing, or alienation of land. This amendment, which was a new addition to the bill, required the secretary to obtain tribal consent before taking such action.

An entirely new title was added to the bill during this interim amendment period. Title V stipulated that the act would not apply to any reservation where the majority of adult resident Indians voted *against* its application.[62] Congressman Rogers took exception to this wording, indicating that the act should require a majority of Indians voting in favor of the measure, not a majority voting against its application. This ratification procedure raised a number of sticky questions. Should women be permitted to vote in those tribes where by custom they were excluded? Should the vote be by a majority of all enrolled Indians or only those who chose to exercise their franchise? As with many other issues before this congressional committee, the exchange quickly moved to other subjects before resolving such pressing questions.

One amendment, designed to satisfy the concern of a particular committee member, concerned the unique situation of the Alaskan Indians. Initially it appeared that the Alaskan Indians would be excluded from the scope of the Collier Bill entirely because there were no reservations in the Alaskan territory. Congressman Anthony Dimond of Alaska was upset by this omission, for he wanted the Alaskan Indians to be able to take advantage of the educational provisions of the bill.[63] Unfortunately, the Alaskan Indians did not then fall under the supervision of the Indian Office, and including them in this bill would have created some very real problems. Collier advised Dimond that he would attempt to redraft the bill to provide Alaskan Indians with some of the bill's benefits. In keeping with his promise, Collier submitted an amendment that enabled Alaskan Indians to take advantage of both the self-government and the education titles of the proposal.[64]

More than thirty amendments were prepared and submitted for the committee's consideration, many of specific concern to a particular group or groups. There was, for example, a special provision protecting the "Sioux benefits"; another measure dealt with land appropriations for the Navajo.[65] Increases were made in the amount of funds that Congress could appropriate for educational loans and scholarships from $50,000 and $15,000 to $200,000 and $50,000, respectively.[66] The new version of the bill included a provision that prohibited transfer of individual title to minerals, including oil and gas, to the tribe.[67] Collier tried hard to accommodate concerned congressmen and tribes by these amendments, hoping thereby to minimize the opposition to his legislative package.

By the last day of the hearings before the House committee, Collier felt he had taken the necessary steps to make the omnibus bill acceptable to the divergent forces of opposition. Success, however, was still quite distant. Isabella Greenway remarked that she simply could not support the bill in its present form because a great deal of unexpected opposition had developed in the weeks just prior to the end of the House hearings.[68] But Collier was prepared to compromise further in order to meet this last-minute challenge. He responded to Mrs. Greenway by noting that title IV of the bill, dealing with the Court of Indian Affairs, was expendable and could be eliminated from the package.[69] Furthermore, he was willing to jettison the section that permitted Indians to force the removal of federal employees from the reservation. Though he hated to lose this provision, he acknowledged that it might become too political.[70]

Seeing that Collier was on the defensive, Mrs. Greenway then inquired as to whether it was not possible to strike a compromise so as to deal only with the nagging problem of allotment. Congressman Werner immediately introduced a motion to this effect. The Werner proposal read as follows:

> . . . all existing trust periods of Indian allotments, held under restrictions against alienation, and any new allotments which may hereafter be made, shall be continued under such restrictions, until further action thereon by Congress. The authority of the Secretary of Interior to issue fee patents, or certificates of competency or otherwise remove restrictions on allotted lands now held by individual Indians is hereby repealed, Provided, that the Secretary of Interior may approve sales of allotted lands or inherited interests in allotments where Indians needing such care and attention, and there is no relief available.[71]

Werner noted that if Congress would pass this law, there would be no need for hasty action on the more controversial parts of the Collier Bill. He knew what he was doing: The Werner compromise, if passed, could effectively kill the whole proposal.

Congressman Oscar De Priest of Illinois joined the anti-Collier forces, arguing that the omnibus measure was being pushed too fast. He proposed that a committee of five congressmen be sent out to visit the reservations so that they could make their own assessment of Indian needs.[72] Fortunately for Collier, Chairman Edgar Howard came to the rescue. He suggested that Werner's substitute bill be incorporated along with other suggestions into the omnibus bill. Congressman Peavey then noted that the committee owed it to the chairman to give the Collier Bill its courteous consideration. He went on to suggest that the committee consider the matter in executive session.[73] Congressman Gilchrist of Iowa and Mrs. Greenway, deferring to the chairman, agreed to go along with Peavey's suggestion, and the last-minute attempt to abort the Collier Bill came to an abrupt end. More important, consideration of the proposal in executive session provided an opportunity for the two sides quietly to reach an acceptable compromise. Negotiations thus continued, not only between Collier and the members of the House Committee on Indian Affairs but with people from the Senate side of the Hill as well.

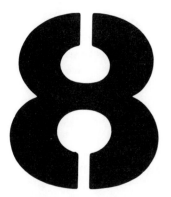

The Indian Congresses

On September 17, 1778, the United States entered into a treaty of alliance with the Delaware nation.[1] This treaty was significant not only because it was the first time that the federal government negotiated with the Indians, but because it established an important precedent. Indian nations were to be dealt with as sovereign entities on an equal footing with the United States. Agreements were to be reached bilaterally, with each side given an opportunity to suggest terms and provisions. Although bilateral agreements were the general rule in the latter part of the eighteenth century, they were certainly not a feature of the relationship between Indians and the federal government during the first three decades of the twentieth century.

The formal departure from this bilateral approach to Indian affairs probably occurred in 1871, when Congress unilaterally decided to cease making treaties with Indians, assuming instead the role that had previously been performed by the executive branch of government. For all intents and purposes, this change from treaties to statutes meant that Indians, conspicuous for their lack of political power, were now effectively precluded from playing any meaningful role in the development of federal Indian policy.

On February 22, 1934, John Collier announced to the House Committee on Indian Affairs that he intended to convene a number of regional Indian congresses. This device would provide tribal representatives with an opportunity to become acquainted with the Wheeler-Howard Bill and present their ideas regarding the measure. Collier's decision to take his proposal before the Indians broke with the established pattern of simply telling Indians after the fact how laws would apply to them. Congress in the past had apparently ruled out any kind of consultation with tribes prior to enacting laws that significantly affected their lives.

What provoked the Indian commissioner to take such a radical step? His motives may well have been—at least in part—altruistic; there is no doubt that Collier had true sympathy for the Indians and wanted sincerely to place more power in their hands. However, the Collier Bill had been drafted by non-Indians, with virtually no Indians participating in this initial phase. The ten conferences would afford the BIA an opportunity to clarify the bill's provisions and respond to Indian suggestions. At the same time, knowing he would meet a good deal of opposition both in Congress and among a number of tribes themselves, Collier felt that the regional congresses could become bastions of support for the proposal, giving him the opportunity in person to turn around objections to its provisions. There is nothing wrong with supplementing altruism with a good dose of practical politics. A master of self-confidence, Collier was convinced he could turn the Indian congresses to his advantage, and so he did.

Collier's public relations opportunities did not escape the attention of a number of the Indian commissioner's congressional opponents, who commented frequently to this effect during the legislative hearings. But this political combat over the bill should not diminish the importance attached to these Indian gatherings. For the first time in decades, the government was actually going out to the tribes to obtain their views on proposed Indian policies. While it was not a complete return to the bilateral approach of the federal government's relation to Indian nations, it was nevertheless a step in this direction. The congresses raised the hope that in the future prior consultation would replace administrative promulgation. Theodore Haas declared that these conferences initiated a new precedent. "They symbolized a new relation between the Indians and the Indian Office that the commissioner hoped would evolve. In lieu of administrative absolutism there would be developed between government officials and Indians a partnership in the determination of many policies."[2]

The Rapid City Congress

The first of the Indian congresses was held at Rapid City, South Dakota, on March 2, 1934. To this four-day conference came the Plains Indians, over two hundred representatives from forty tribes with a population of nearly sixty thousand.[3] The initial atmosphere was far from warm and receptive. As the Indian commissioner described it,

> The meeting, like many of the congresses, started amid a cloud of grimly silent fears. The lands of the landed Indians were to be confiscated, they feared, and given to the landless ones. The Indians were to be deprived of their citizenship and of the franchise. The Indians were to be interned, fenced in like buffaloes, compelled back into some (they were told) ancient and outmoded life. The Commissioner, it was said, had bribed a tribal leader, by offering him four sections of land, to support the Indian Reorganization Act.[4]

The task confronting the Indian comissioner was formidable indeed.

The format of the proceedings at the Rapid City congress set a precedent for the procedures that were used at all ten Indian conferences. Collier would begin with an extensive examination of some of the major problems confronting Indian country—allotment, inadequate land resources, inheritance burdens, insufficient self-government, and the need for judicial reform. Having set the proper climate of concern, the Indian commissioner would then embark upon a detailed explanation of the major provisions of his bill designed to deal with them. At each conference Collier was careful to use data and illustrations that related to the particular tribes in attendance. The delegates were then permitted to submit written questions to be answered by Collier and his accompanying staff of experts. The requirement of written questions provided Collier with a better opportunity to control the session and minimized the potential conflicts that might erupt with hostile factions among the delegates. If Collier could not respond to a question, one of the experts among the Interior entourage would rise to the occasion. In addition to the Indian commissioner, the representatives from Interior included Walter Woehlke, a field representative from the Indian Service; Ward Shepard, a specialist on land policies in the bureau; and Melvin Siegel and Felix Cohen, both of the Solicitor's Office in Interior.

Following the written question-and-answer period, representatives from each of the tribes were asked to speak. Sometimes the delegates would indicate their support or opposition to the bill, but more often than not they would speak without taking a position. In the latter instances, the delegates usually noted that they would take the information gathered at the conference back to their tribes or tribal councils for consideration. While the procedures at the end of each of the conferences varied somewhat, this format was usually followed.

In Collier's initial remarks to the Rapid City congress, he focused his attention not so much on the deficiencies of the Indian Bureau but on the inadequacy of the laws governing Indian affairs. "The United States is not making a mess of its Indian guardianship because its employees are wicked or stupid . . . but because the guardianship maintained by the United States is carried out under a body of laws which are wicked and stupid, and which make slaves even of the Government employees hired to enforce the laws."[5] By directing attention to the problems inherent in the laws, the Indian commissioner could more easily call for a change in the law—a change that could be achieved through the proposed Indian Reorganization Act. Collier then proceeded to talk about allotment and the enormous problems it had created for Indians all over the country. The Indian Office experts had come well prepared. They presented large maps of the reservations indicating where lands had been lost, which lands were held in trust, and where the reservations had been broken into a checkerboard pattern. Since the problem of checkerboard ownership of reservation land was particularly burdensome to the Plains Indians, Collier placed a great deal of stress on how his proposed measure would assist in resolving this situation.

A good deal of concern had been expressed by the Plains Indians about the power of the secretary to transfer title of the allotted lands to community ownership. Collier spent a considerable amount of time attemping to placate fears that Indian heirs could no longer expect to inherit title to allotted lands upon the death of the owner, but the emotional conern about this issue remained intense.

Collier's attempt to justify the transfer of land to tribal ownership simply fell on deaf ears. He explained in some detail the need to consolidate land to make it economically productive. Consolidation could only be achieved by providing the secretary with the power to transer fragmented property interests from individual to tribal ownership. The individual landowner would not lose anything, since he would receive a proportionate share of the tribal property in return. Furthermore, continued use of the land by the original owner or his heirs was permissible at times. Although vigorously presented, the Indian commissioner's argument seemed to go nowhere. It was at this point that Collier must have realized that mandatory property transfers were not going to be supported by the Indians. Their opposition to this provision was shared, of course, by a number of members of Congress. So Collier began to compromise by indicating at the Rapid City congress that some of the mandatory provisions might be made voluntary. Regardless, he pointed out, individual landowners would be able to retain all of the subsurface rights to minerals and oils even if land was transferred to community ownership.[6]

Not all the delegates were convinced by Collier's argument that the allotment system was at the heart of the Indian land problem. George White Bull, a Standing Rock Sioux, indicated that Indians had believed in the allotment program when it was initially presented and that they were now accustomed to the way it was being administered. He felt that the proposed legislation would jeopardize the rights of Indians to their personal allotments as well as many treaty rights that Indians had been enjoying.[7] Furthermore, White Bull argued that the Collier Bill was only supported by a number of landless Indians. These landless Indians were mixed-bloods who had already parted with their property. The bill would not be good for those full-blooded Indians who continued to live on their allotments. This mixed-blood/full-blood controversy appeared frequently throughout many of the Indian conferences.

In addition to this sensitive intratribal, factional issue, White Bull also questioned Collier about the effect of the proposed legislation on Indian claims against the United States government. Why did the proposal not contain a provision dealing with this important matter? Collier responded that the claims issue had to be considered as a separate measure. "This bill we have got before you is a big mouthful, and if we throw it into the Omnibus court of claims bill, then it will choke us to death. But to take them both on at the same time and as a part of one bill would be too heroic, it is too much, we couldn't get away with it."[8] Collier advised the delegates that Nathan Margold of the Interior Department had already drafted a separate claims bill that the Indian Office intended to introduce.

While a number of assimilation advocates stood firm in their criticism of the Collier proposal, another dissident group questioned the Indians' veto power over the expenditure of tribal money, fearful that the local governments might veto the use of funds to pay the tuition of children who attended the mission schools. This issue revived an earlier problem dealing with Catholic educational services in South Dakota. The church had received an 80-percent monopoly of the governmental funds for religious schools. When the law expired, Collier had suggested a policy in which the government would pay only for the physical maintenance of the Catholic schools and not for student tuition, the financial savings of which could be distributed to the physical care of Indian children attending mission schools (which would benefit Protestant institutions as well).[9] Collier laid aside this concern by indicating that the funds used here were not tribal funds and he was convinced that educational expenditures were not something that would fall under the control of the local governments.

One of the more delicate issues raised at the Rapid City congress dealt with the problem of Sioux benefits. These were payments guaranteed to members of the Sioux nation when they acquired their allotments, initially fixed by a congressional act in 1889 and later extended to future children by subsequent legislation.[10] Fire Thunder, from Pine Ridge, expressed the concern that if allotment was terminated and much of the land was returned to tribal ownership, they could no longer expect to enjoy these special benefits. Collier felt that this point was well taken, and indicated that he would submit an amendment to his bill expressly protecting and preserving the "Sioux benefits."[11]

As more and more delegates rose to comment on various portions of the bill, it became apparent that there was still a good deal of suspicion and opposition in the crowd. Oliver Prue, a Rosebud Sioux, put it like this: From "past experience in years gone by, we have come to learn to distrust all Government officials that come out here to negotiate with our people, and we really have been fooled so many times, time and again, that we just simply distrust every Government official that came out here, however true they may be."[12] The delegates vigorously applauded these comments.

Francis Red Tomahawk, a Standing Rock Sioux, admitted that the allotment system had had devastating effects upon his reservation, but the broad changes that the Collier Bill intended to bring about were too abrupt; they would do harm and injustice to the Indians.[13] Red Tomahawk felt that there was too much from the white man's culture in the bill and that Indians did not adapt well to that. Joe Irving, from the Crow Creek delegaton, stated that some Indians had said that John Collier was a Democrat; others said he was a Republican. But when he looked at the self-government part of the bill, he thought that Collier was just a plain socialist.[14] "In this bill, it gives the Commissioner of Indian Affairs power to take away from one Indian and give to another Indian, if he so desires. Now everybody knows this is not right. This is the United States, and according to this Bill if it were passed we could not exerecise our own rights and we might just as well live in Russia."[15]

Not all of the comments by the delegates were critical. The Blackfeet Indians, for instance, adopted John Collier into their tribe, a gesture that produced a good deal of applause among the delegates. They gave him the name Spotted Eagle. "The name represents the Indian Reservations, the way they are checkerboarded. We hope that these spots will be rubbed off so that every Indian Reservation will be all in one spot."[16] Sam La Pointe, a Rosebud Sioux, praised the educational provisions of the bill. He also suggested that they refer to Collier as the Iron Man because "I know he has worn out every interpreter we have got."[17]

Many of the delegates really did not say much of substance. Often they just thanked Collier for coming and talked briefly about their tribe. Typical of this posture was Felix White, a Winnebago:

> We were sent up here to be open-minded and we have tried our best to be, although some things are not clear. I am praying that tomorrow I will have a clear vision of all things. I want to express appreciation that the Commissioner brought this ball of light out here. We are probably the last on the list—last but not least. I believe Adam and Eve were Winnebago. We are thankful that we came up here. We have learned a lot and will learn some more."[18]

Not infrequently humor was interjected into the proceedings. On one occasion, Collier wanted to take a standing vote to see if the delegates would like to hold an annual Indian congress. Many people stood to be counted in favor of the suggestion. Only one person stood in opposition. Walter Woehlke noted that while the vast majority of delegates wanted to hold an annual meeting, the lone figure that stood in opposition had the courage of his convictions. The chairman of the Blackfeet delegation then jumped up and noted that "He can't help himself, his name is Standing Bear."[19]

As the Rapid City congress came to a close, it was clear that Collier had made significant progress. During the four-day congress, the Indian commissioner and his team of experts from Interior went a long way in overcoming the initial fears and hostility of the delegates. In addition to the formal hearings, Collier even held a special session with several tribes. The combination of energy, command of data, and political flexibility that Collier exhibited at the Rapid City congress paid off. By agreeing to a number of changes in the bill, including the provision protecting the "Sioux benefits," he moved the congress from opposition to support: Thirteen delegations in favor, with only four still opposed.[20]

The Southwest Congresses

Between March 12 and March 16, three Indian congresses were held in the southwestern region of the country. These included gatherings at Fort Defiance, Arizona; Santo Domingo, New Mexico; and Phoenix,

Arizona. Of these the most important clearly was the meeting at Fort Defiance, which was attended by representatives from the Navajo tribe, the largest Indian nation in the land.

For some time the Indian Bureau had battled with Navajo stockmen concerning their propensity to overgraze their herds. In 1933 Collier had called for a full-scale reduction of stock. The Navajos were informed that they would have to slaughter 400,000 head of sheep, goats, and horses.[21] Though the large stockmen were able to absorb this decrease by cutting their less productive stock, the small herdsmen were hurt badly by the new conservation policy, but the problem of overgrazing was real and had persisted for a long time. Collier flew to the Navajo reservation seventeen times between 1933 and 1938 to deal with it. He noted that "in my long life of social effort and struggle, I have not experienced among any other Indian group, or any group whatsoever, an anxiety-ridden and anguished hostility even approaching to that which the Navajos were undergoing."[22] The task thus presented to the Indian commissioner at Fort Defiance was one of some magnitude.

In addressing the Navajo gathering, Collier attempted to present himself and the Indian Bureau as friends of the Navajos. As long as he remained in office, they were to have no fear of either losing their lands or the variety of federal services extended to the tribe. But Collier warned the delegates that he would not be in office forever. Another administration might not be as receptive to Indian needs. The Collier Bill was designed "to guarantee through a solemn law of Congress the protections and the gains and the advantages that you have got and to make it impossible for a future administration to take them away from you."[23]

The Indian commissioner then proceeded to discuss the potential problems that could affect the Navajos in the future. While the allotment system had not touched the Navajo reservation to any large extent, their lands were ripe for exploitation by white entrepreneurs. He told the delegates about the Five Civilized Tribes in Oklahoma, which were allotted when the whites wanted their land, resulting in a loss of thirteen million acres and eventually producing 72,000 landless Indians.[24] Several years ago, Collier continued, the Quinault Indians of Washington thought that they would never have to fear this problem. Today, after allotment found its way to the Northwest, the Quinault Indians had become virtually landless.[25] Navajo lands were becoming more and more valuable. Oil deposits and the need for expanded grazing lands would inevitably result in white pressure to get hold of additional property on the reservation.

Collier's forceful presentation on the allotment issue did not satisfy all the delegates at the congress. Howard Gorman, who opposed the bill, engaged Collier in a heated debate, claiming that allotment was only a ruse that Collier had raised. Gorman was still incensed over Collier's stock-reduction policy. "He has taken our sheep, our goats, even our money, and it seems to me that the sooner Collier gets out the better it is."[26] Gorman finally concluded his assault by stating that Collier was looking at Navajos through communistic glasses.

In addition to the dissident stockmen, the Christian missionaries on the reservation opposed the Collier Bill. On the day that the Fort Defiance congress was held, the missionaries passed a resolution praising the policy of assimilation and condemning the attempt to resegregate the Indians. They suggested that Collier would "put the clock of Indian progress back at least fifty years."[27] The missionaries were supported in their opposition by the United Traders Association, a group of white businessmen who feared that the bill, together with the emergence of more Indian co-ops, would put them out of business.[28] On the whole, the gathering at Fort Defiance had been a difficult one for Collier. It is true that ultimately the Navajo tribal council voted to support the measure, but it was not clear whether this support accurately reflected the large-scale hostility and continuing resentment among many of the tribal members.

From the convention at Fort Defiance, Collier traveled to Santo Domingo, New Mexico, where he met with many old friends and associates on March 15. The Indian commissioner had played a prominent role in the defense of the Pueblo Indians in the defeat of the Bursum Bill, and Collier was received warmly. Since the Pueblos already possessed a traditional form of government, the All-Pueblo Council saw the Collier Bill as providing them with a number of advantages. Their support for the measure was thus firm, with but a few objections.

The last of the Southwest Indian congresses was held at Phoenix, Arizona, on March 16. Collier had to return to Washington and hence did not attend this meeting. A. C. Monohan, an assistant to Collier, and Walter Woehlke conducted the proceedings in the Indian commissioner's absence. The atmosphere at the Phoenix conference, not unlike the Rapid City meeting, was filled with an air of suspicion. The Papago Indians had been engaged in a long and bitter struggle with the Interior Department concerning a number of disputed land claims that were intimately connected with attempts by the mining interests in Arizona to gain access to some of the mineral wealth situated on the Papago reservation. Of late, the Department of the Interior had not been particularly sympathetic to the Papago position, and this performance had produced a reservoir of hostility.

Walter Woehlke began the major presentation before the Indian gathering by exploring the problems posed by the allotment system. But the Southwest Indians had not been faced with these difficulties to any great extent, and many of the delegates were more interested in the self-government provisions of the bill. The Papagos were not convinced that self-government would work on their reservation. Papago villages were well dispersed throughout this huge reservation and functioned pretty much as autonomous entities.[29] Ward Shepard of the Interior Department responded to this by noting that the bill did not set up any one form of self-government. Each tribe could decide for itself what kind of government it wished to establish—the Papagos could develop a local government that would fit their particular needs. Shepard also indicated that the bill would bring more power to the tribe by transferring a number of functions that were being exercised by the Indian Office to the local tribal community.[30] With regard to Indian employment opportunities, Shepard pointed out that there were proportionately fewer Indian employees in the Indian Service in 1934 than there had been twenty years earlier. The Collier Bill was designed to overcome this deficiency as well as to give tribal government the power to veto the proposed expenditure of tribal funds without the local government's consent.

During the question-and-answer period, a number of delegates wanted to know (as had others) why the secretary of the interior retained so much control over tribal lands? Melvin Siegel of the Solicitor's Office acknowledged that this might be a deficiency in the bill but noted that the measure could be modified to remedy this situation.[31] There was also concern over the fact that there was no provision in the bill protecting Indian water rights. Somewhat embarrassed, the representatives from Interior admitted that they had just not considered this subject, and the bill would of course be changed to correct this oversight.[32]

A great deal of misinformation still existed about the bill. The San Carlos Apaches were afraid that their cattle would be confiscated and placed under communal ownership.[33] These gatherings fortunately provided the Indian Office with an opportunity to correct many of these mistaken assumptions. But even more important, it demonstrated to the Indians that a meaningful effort was being made to consult with Indians prior to the enactment of a law touching their lives. John Rice, a San Carlos Apache, spoke of his gratitude regarding this development. "Long ago the government told us not to say anything, just put your head down, don't look around. Many years back they said that to us. Now I may have a voice in all things pertaining to my reservation and I think it is a good thing."[34] His comments were echoed by Harvey

Cawker, representing the Pima Indians. "It is up to you, brothers, if you want the possessions that you have fought for, if you want to keep them for the generations in the future of our own people. And if you do, it is up to you as I see it to accept this new plan. . . ."[35] Cawker went on to note that there were a few loopholes in the bill that needed to be filled, but this was not a basis for refusing to support the plan.

The hostility that many of the Indians held toward Washington emerged occasionally. Oliver Bellville, of the San Carlos Reservation, wanted the Interior representatives to know that the San Carlos Reservation belonged to the Indians. It always had and it always would. "These men sit up here, what do they know about our reservation? . . . I want to say to these gentlemen up here that I want them to make it known that the San Carlos reservation is mine and I want to keep it."[36] Walter Woehlke replied to Bellville that this was exactly what the Collier Bill was designed to do—to keep Indian land in the hands of Indians.

On the whole, the response at the Phoenix conference was supportive. But the bureau representatives never let up on their constant pressure to assure this support. One of the Indian delegates asked what would happen to the Indians if they failed to adopt the so-called New Deal law. Melvin Siegel did not mince words: "I don't know. The way they are going now they will probably be extinguished. There are many indications from the other parts of the country to this effect. In the future, they will lose all their lands and will gradually lose everything."[37] And Walter Woehlke implored the delegates to be wary of Congress. It was becoming increasingly difficult to get money out of the national legislature. "The time to act is now, not to wait and quibble over line 2, paragraph 3, and so on."[38]

The Oklahoma Congresses

Oklahoma was not friendly territory for John Collier. A large state with a large number of Indian tribes, it was the heartland of opposition to the Collier Bill, much of it emanating from Muskogee. One particularly vitriolic attack, which appeared in an article published in the New York *Herald Tribune,* was written by Ray Kirkland of Muskogee. It stated that if Indians voted for the Collier proposal, the government would start immediate "condemnation proceedings against properties on non-Indian residents in their areas."[39] It argued that once the soviet was started, the tribesmen would be shut off from the rest of the world. E. E. Lindquist, a former member of the Board of Indian Commissioners, was quoted as saying that "Collier's plan is socialism and communism in the rankest sense."[40] Lindquist later denied ever having made such a remark. The article went on to say that since Indians neither spoke nor read English, they were being told many lies by the white elites. They were informed that the bill would forbid Christian preachment and that their lands would be raided and seized.

The Kirkland article haunted John Collier throughout the hearings. He was constantly on the defensive, arguing that there was nothing communistic or socialistic about his bill. Collier also ran into opposition from Flora Warren Seymour, a former member of the Board of Indian Commissioners, which had been abolished by President Roosevelt at Collier's insistence. Seymour adopted the same type of "red baiting" tactics used by Kirkland. She suggested that the Collier Bill was "the most extreme gesture yet made by the administration in this country toward a Communist experiment."[41] All of this criticism forewarned Collier that the three Indian congresses to be held in Oklahoma would be no picnic.

The first Indian gathering in the "Sooner" state was held at Anadarko, Oklahoma, on March 20. Collier opened the conference by noting that it was not only important that he talk to them, but that the Indians talk to him as well, voicing their needs and desires. He advised the delegates that President Roosevelt was firmly behind the bill and that when the president wanted legislation, he got it. However, before formal action was to be taken on the measure, the president wanted to hear from the Indians, and that was the reason for this gathering.[42]

Collier began his explanation by focusing on Indian land problems. He told the delegates that the Indians of Mexico had been landless thirty years before but had recently increased their land holdings significantly. Why was it that the Indians of Mexico and Canada were increasing their landholdings, but Indians in the United States were unable to do the same? The answer, according to Collier, revolved around the evils of the allotment system. Under the Allotment Act, Indians were paid only $1.25 per acre for surplus land. This price, Collier said, amounted to outright confiscation. Of the twenty-three million acres of surplus land sold, twenty million were sold to whites. In one area where 5,846 Kiowas, Comanches, and Apaches resided, four out of every six Indians were landless.[43] The Indian commissioner did an exceedingly fine job of relating the general land problems to these local concerns.

During the evening session, Henry Roe Cloud, president of the Haskell Institute, assumed the role of moderator at the conference. Roe Cloud's presence lent a good deal of prestige to the bill's proponents, and even though in his role as moderator he was supposed to be neutral, it was abundantly clear that he was a great admirer not only of John Collier but of the bill as well.[44]

Before concluding his discussion of the Indian land provisions, Collier attempted to demonstrate how expensive it was to administer the real estate operations of the Indian Service. It cost, for instance, about eighty thousand dollars to run the Kiowa agency, sixty-five thousand dollars of which was used to deal with the problems attendant to allotment, leasing, and heirship problems.[45] These expenditures were simply eating up all the funds that the tribes were receiving from the federal government. It was folly to continue to waste several million dollars a year on the allotment system while there were fifteen thousand Indian children out of school because there wasn't enough money to support education.

Like the other conferences, the delegates were not uniform in their responses to Collier's presentation. Hoy-koy-bitty advised the delegates that the Comanches loved their land and that they wanted to hold on to their allotments. They opposed "community life and would just as soon stay without land and don't want to be segregated."[46] Kish Hawkins, to the contrary, stated that we "Cheyennes and Arapahoes have been sitting on the fence watching the procession go by."[47] They were ready to vote yes so that they could move ahead. Henry Chapman indicated that the Pawnees were opposed to the bill, for they felt that they were not capable of handling such a large undertaking.[48] Yet Thomas Alford, a Shawnee, told the gathering that though they did not fully understand all of the program, they were inclined to accept it.[49]

At the conclusion of the Anadarko meeting, several tribes submitted resolutions that had been passed prior to the conference. The Arapaho tribe of the Cheyenne and Arapaho reservation in Canton, Oklahoma, the Kiowa Council from Carnegie, and the Comanche Indians of Fort Sill all opposed the bill.[50] This opposition did not, however, reflect upon the success or failure of Collier's efforts at Anadarko, since these resolutions were passed prior to the meeting.

There is little doubt that the Indian Bureau representatives did an excellent job in prosecuting their case at this first meeting in Oklahoma. Indeed, the questions and answers shed a great deal of light on the substance of the bill. The large question remained: Was Collier persuasive enough? The Indian commissioner concluded this session with the following eloquent statement:

> If there ever will be a time when the Indians of the United States can get what they need, now is the time. Now is the time when

the government is doing big things in a generous way, making fundamental changes through the country. Three or four years from now conditions may have changed. There may not be the same spirit at work. There may not be the same men at Washington anymore, and the financial condition of the government may be such that we can't get appropriations for the purchase of land, for establishing credit. It may prove to be a case of now or never, and surely it is a time for every Indian to think seriously. Surely it is a time for every Indian to think of his children as well as of himself.[51]

From Anadarko, Collier and his entourage moved to Muskogee on March 22 for the second Oklahoma meeting. This gathering began with a festive opening, with each of the Five Civilized Tribes (Seminole, Creek, Choctaw, Chickasaw, and Cherokee) presenting greetings to the commissioner. As was his custom, Collier immediately began to focus upon the evils of allotment but particularized it to his specific audience. Using many of the same examples and statistics that he presented to the Anadarko conference, Collier attempted to show the delegates how the lands of the Five Civilized Tribes had been decimated over the years. Furthermore, the average per-capita income among Indians per year was only forty-seven dollars. No wonder, Collier reasoned, the vast majority of Indians were living on the remnants of land owned by relations. Whereas the national wealth had increased, the wealth of Indians was vanishing.[52]

Collier was emphatic in emphasizing that under the bill no land would be taken from landholding Indians and given to landless Indians. The sensitivity of the land issues, along with a strong pitch for the economic-development provisions of the bill, occupied most of Collier's attention during the session.

One of Collier's old nemeses, Joseph Bruner, attended the Muskogee meeting. Bruner, a dedicated assimilationist, headed up the National Indian Confederacy, which strongly opposed the bill. Bruner, however, was not given much of an opportunity to perform at the meeting. When the Keetoowah Society introduced a resolution praising Collier for coming to the session and calling for the conference to endorse his bill, Bruner raised a point of order arguing that the Keetoowah was only a clan and not a tribe and could not offer such a motion. The floor rejected this point, stating that the resolution had already been presented. Bruner then moved to adjourn but was ignored by the chair.[53] Earlier Bruner had asked a question concerning employment of Indians and whether they would be as capable as whites. Walter Woehlke responded for Collier, who had lost his voice by this time, brusquely noting that the question had been answered fully and exhaustively earlier.[54] Bruner, who played an important role of opposition during the congressional hearings, was isolated and summarily handled during the Muskogee congress, so that he had little effect upon the proceedings.

To conclude the Muskogee meeting, Collier went back to the refrain that it was imperative to act now. "In the history of countries and peoples, there comes a time when everything is possible. There are moments of destiny and if they pass by—are not used—it may be too late."[55]

Collier succeeded in convincing a number of delegates of the wisdom of supporting his bill. The Eastern Emigrant and Western Cherokees passed a resolution favoring the bill, and at a later date the Creek and Choctaws came forth with endorsements.[56] Joseph Hayes, a Chickasaw, provided quite a compliment to Collier in noting that his tribe supported the bill because John Collier "was one white man with a red man's heart."[57]

The final Oklahoma meeting, at Miami on March 24, followed pretty much the same pattern as the two other conferences in the state. The important feature from all of the Oklahoma conferences was that John Collier not only survived in what was considered hostile territory, but seemingly left Oklahoma with a reservoir of support. Considerable opposition continued to flourish among the proassimilationist Indians, but Collier must have been pleased with the Oklahoma achievements.

The West Coast Conferences

Two Indian congresses were held on the West Coast, one in Oregon and the other in California. The Oregon meeting was convened at the Chemawa Indian School in Chemawa, Oregon, on March 8 and 9. It was the second of the ten congresses, immediately following the convention held at Rapid City, South Dakota. The Chemawa gathering, however, was quite different from the Rapid City gathering in both form and style.

Collier was unable to attend the Chemawa conference because he had become physically exhausted at the Great Plains Indian meeting. The Sioux had referred to the Indian commissioner as the Iron Man because he had kept talking for fourteen hours and wore out four different interpreters. But the Iron Man apparently needed a little refurbishing before entering into battle again. William Zimmerman, Walter Woehlke, and Melvin Siegel shouldered most of the burden in presenting the Collier Bill to the Chemawa gathering.

The Oregon conference posed a special problem for the Indian Bureau officials. While all the Indian congresses were conducted with the use of native language interpreters, none presented the burden that hovered over Chemawa. Throughout the proceedings, delegates from the audience continually interrupted, wanting a more precise translation. Indeed, a person reading the minutes of the meeting might have thought that the Indian delegates were caustically toying with the representatives from Washington. The problem appeared to be more than just language confusion. The whole frame of reference of the Oregon and Washington Indians seemed different from that of Indians at the other congresses. They appeared to be less worldly and less aware of matters that were commonplace beyond the reservation boundaries. At one time, Ward Shepard of the Indian Office was talking about transferring lands to tribal ownership and noted that some of the critics of the bill had charged that this constituted communism. A voice from the audience called out and asked, "What is communism?"[58] Clearly it was hard to transpose the word *communism* into the Indian languages, but an equal difficulty seemed to be that there was a lack of understanding as to what the term meant.

Most of these Indians were not concerned with the problems of farming and grazing, as had been the case on other reservations; their livelihoods largely revolved around fishing, and there was nothing in the bill that expressly dealt with this kind of enterprise. Several delegates were concerned whether the bill would apply to them at all and/or would have to be amended specifically to include those Indians whose work related to fishing. The answer, of course, was that the bill did apply to the Oregon and Washington tribes. It would not have to be amended, and the Northwest Indians could take advantage of the bill's provisions just like other tribes throughout the nation.

When it came time for the delegates to speak, the convention seemed to be quite divided over the bill. The opponents were gracious in their criticism, but firm nevertheless. Chief Peter Moctum, a Coeur d'Alene, spoke eloquently about how the government had given his tribe nothing but broken treaties. "Have pity on me, on our Indians. The Government in my country has picked on our Indians. The white people have made me poor. Why do you not have pity and help me and give me justice? This is my suggestion to you."[59] Walter Woehlke attempted to respond to this by noting that this was what the government was trying to do in proposing the Collier Bill.

Two delegates from the Yakima tribe also voiced their opposition. A Yakima by the name of Seltica argued that the bill was "just like putting a big pack on a small horse. The content of that Bill is getting very heavy on my shoulders." While expressing the hope that his remarks would not hurt Commissioner Collier, Seltica stated that the

Yakimas had their treaty of 1855 and wanted to continue to live under that treaty.[60] Thomas Sam, another Yakima, supported Seltica's views. The Collier Bill, he noted, gave them self-government, but they were not able to take care of themselves yet. Woehlke attempted to show that the proposed Indian legislation would be of considerable benefit to the Yakima tribe. It would preserve their landholdings, extend the trust period on allotted parcels, and ensure future generations of Indians that they would have a secure reservation. "If the Yakima understood what this bill was all about . . . how it would help their children and grand-children they would change their minds."[61]

Much of the hesitancy on the part of the Northwest Indians stemmed from the deep distrust that they held toward the government. A southern Oregon delegate named Wasson noted that when the Dawes Act had been passed, it was supposed to be the greatest thing that ever happened to the Indians. "It was to remove them from their present environment and place them in the environment of the civilization of the world so that the children could learn the habits of the white man and learn to be self-supporting."[62] The Indians were left under this system and suffered because of it. What, then, Wasson asked, will happen in the future with regard to this new bill? "Will another commissioner come out from the seat of government and tell them this community system is a failure?"[63]

In contrast, other delegates urged the convention to take some positive steps to deal with the continuing problems plaguing Indian country. Christine Galler, a Colville, told the convention that Indians "have been led by the white people for 122 years since the white people came into this country. We have never been given the choice of our leaders. We have no voice in anything. . . . Let us try a new deal. It cannot be any worse than what it has been."[64] Nealty Olney, a Yakima, brought the Chemawa meeting to a close focusing on the same message that Collier had attempted to get over to the other conferences. Olney noted that Collier may be in office for only a few more years and that it was imperative that Indians take advantage of his office. "Don't delay too long and allow the white man, who is not posted in your needs and welfare as you are, to work out some plan which may rob you of your remaining properties. You must help [Collier] plan the destiny of your people while you have an opportunity to do so."[65]

The Chemawa congress turned out to be a mixed bag as far as the Indian Office was concerned. It proved to be the most difficult to conduct, given the more-than-usual language burdens. Though there did exist a fund of support, there appeared to be an equal amount of opposition to the bill. More than anything it seemed to crystallize the confusion that existed in the minds of many Indians with regard to the measure.

The second West Coast Indian congress was held at Riverside, California, on March 17 and 18, again without Collier. To this gathering came the mission Indians, tribes from the Nevada district, delegates from the Yuma, Arizona agency, and Indians from the southern section of the Sacramento Valley. A great deal of time at the Riverside meeting was spent on Indian land problems, particularly with regard to water rights, a pressing issue in this region of the country. Another major concern was the potential isolation of Indians. One delegate asked if a major objective of the measure was "to reverse the present policy of civilizing the Indians and forcing [them] to revert to old conditions?"[66] Melvin Siegel, speaking for the Indian Bureau, indicated that Indians could choose for themselves and could go in either direction. "If the Navajos wish to retain their ancient tradition, they may do so, but if the California Indian prefers to go with the white man, he will be given the opportunity to do so much greater than ever before. . . ."[67] Addressing the overall issue of segregation, Siegel attempted to temper the fears of several delegates:

Now the problem of segregation. There is no desire to put a closed wall around the Indian. We merely believe that the policy of forcing the Indian into the white community proceeded at much too fast a pace in the past. It was done much too rapidly. Indians were turned loose before they were able to compete in the white world. We recognize the problem of the Indian has changed since the white man came and there is no desire to bring about racial segregation through the new communities. . . . [Indians] should be allowed to stay on the reservation and only so long as they want to stay. We believe those Indians who want to stay there should be given an opportunity. This is all this policy means. It is not an attempt to segregate Indians.[68]

Much of the concern relating to segregation came from Indians who did not live on reservations.

Robert Miguel asked about the treaty rights that the Indians had negotiated with Mexico and later the United States. "We were on this continent first and you took the wild fruits, the water, and the lands we were living on. After the American Government got in this warm business, they promised us this and that and have fulfilled nothing on these promises. They forgot the rights our ancestors had, but now Indians get what is left and citizens get the best."[69] Miguel wanted to know what would happen to the claims they had against the federal government. Walter Woehlke assured the delegates at the meeting that the Indian Office was working on the issue. A separate bill would be introduced specifically designed to provide Indians with an avenue by which to pursue their claims against the government.

Hardly an Indian congress went by without one or two delegates condemning the Collier Bill because it was a plot to bestow a communist system upon Indian tribes. The Riverside conference was no exception.[70] When challenged, Melvin Siegel attempted to explain the quid pro quo of the Indian-lands section of the bill, noting that whereas title to property may be given over to the tribe, individual Indians would receive in return a proportionate interest in the community property. Mrs. Costa, who had voiced the concern here, was not about to be put off her position: "I am one hundred percent American. I tell you this bill preaches communism and socialism. We don't want none of it."[71]

The Riverside congress left many delegates undecided. They wanted to take the information back to their respective tribes. But the Indian Office representatives left with a good feeling about their accomplishments.

The Great Lakes Indian Congress and Back to Washington

The last gathering, with the Great Lakes Indians, was convened almost a month after the others, April 23 and 24 at Hayward, Wisconsin, with the Indians from Wisconsin, Minnesota, and Michigan. Collier remained in Washington preparing amendments to the bill before returning to testify before the Senate Committee on Indian Affairs, so William Zimmerman and Walter Woehlke handled the proceedings.

A number of the Great Lakes tribes were concerned about the lack of provisions relating to fishing and hunting rights in the bill. The Bad River band of Indians voiced the fear that the Collier proposal might strip Indians of these traditional rights. Indeed, so much time was spent alloying these fears at the first session that on the second day of the conference, Gabriel Saice of the White Earth Reservation announced that yesterday "there was too much talk of muskrats and fish to get anywhere."[72] He urged the convention to get down to the basic provisions of the bill so that the delegates could learn something. Woehlke thus proceeded to examine in detail the major titles of the bill, as he had done at past congresses.

The response of the delegates at this convention was very positive. Edward Wilson, from Grand Portage, Minnesota, indicated that this "bill as I look at it is a Godsend to the Indian—a blessing and salvation. . . . In his [Collier's] fight for the Indian he has been very useful—

very energetic—and always uppermost in his mind was the Indian."[73] Several representatives from the Mille Lac and Fond du Lac delegations rose to praise the bill. John Kingfisher, of Lac Court Oreilles, states that the young people of his tribe were ready for self-government and the old people were broadminded enough to accept the will of the majority.[74] George Seikirk, a Chippewa, however, signaled a note of caution. What the Indian wanted was not a new deal but a square deal.[75] Mitchell Red Cloud, a Winnebago, quickly moved the flow of comments back to a positive note, however, when he said that "Justice may be blind, but Mr. Roosevelt and Mr. Collier are excellent eye doctors."[76] The *pièce de résistance* that crowned the conclusion of the Great Lakes congress came from Reverend C. Aaron, of the Stockbridge delegation:

> My common sense tells me that John Collier is a member of the White Race, but my heart tells me John Collier is an Indian. Yes, indeed, John Collier is an Indian with a heart as big and broad as the day is long. This Indian is as capable as any class of people on earth—the only trouble is we haven't had the chance to prove it to the white man. We have been like a smudge. The blanket has been put over us and the smoke couldn't be seen, but through the provisions of the Wheeler-Howard bill we see a new day dawning.[77]

The Hayward Indian congress was an upbeat note upon which to conclude, providing the Indian Bureau officials with a great deal of much-needed enthusiasm when they returned to the battlefield of the United States Congress. True, the meetings were physically exhausting and filled with a goodly amount of criticism. But they prodded Collier to make changes in those areas in the bill where certain sensitive provisions simply could not be sold either to dissident tribes or to alienated congressmen. In addition, the regional Indian gatherings gave Collier more political ammunition to take before the two congressional committees on Indian Affairs. He reported that, in a preratification straw ballot, ninety-two tribes, with a total population of 180,163 Indians, voted on the measure.[78] Seventy-four tribes, representing a population of 158,279 Indians, voted to support the Collier Bill. Eighteen tribes, with an Indian population of 21,884, voted against the bill.

As we have noted, the accuracy of these figures is vague, particularly so because many of the votes were not cast by tribal members, but by a tribal council. However, regardless of the "vulnerable" nature of the vote taken, the regional Indian congresses had to be counted as a bonus to Collier and his efforts to achieve success in the legislative halls of Congress.

It is important to consider the Indian congresses in detail to see the issues to which Collier gave priority, and to hear the concerns of the Indians. Nowhere do we find any real discussion of self-government in the political sense. The arguments revolve primarily around the Collier plans for allotted lands. Many of the Indians who attended these congresses had adjusted to the allotment policy and did not wish to create tribal governments to represent them before the government. Indeed, they had devised their own criterion of tribal membership, which was simplicity itself: If you had kept your allotment while others sold theirs, you had kept the faith with the old people who had signed the treaties and later the allotment agreements, and therefore you were a recognized member of the tribe.

The congresses prepared the ground in a fundamental way for Collier's later efforts to address the question of tribal powers of self-government, because they demonstrated an Indian willingness to experiment but did not tie Collier to specific promises regarding how much authority the Indians would have in governing themselves. Collier could later develop the specifics of self-government and lead both the bureau and the Indians along paths that he alone determined. Had he been too precise in describing how the new tribal governments were to function, Indians might have opposed him more strongly after the Indian Reorganization Act had been passed, thereby precluding him from using the vast powers of administration on their behalf.

Nevertheless, it is a fact that apart from Collier's ideas on how the Indian Reorganization Act was to function, no one, Indians or congressmen, had any notion of what was in store for them. The multititled bill was exceedingly more complicated than the old Indian Tribal Councils Bill, and this complexity worked in Collier's favor. It would have been very simple to dissect the old bill and reveal the radical change in policy and program that Collier had envisioned. Trudging through the forty-odd pages of the new proposal, however, made it difficult to relate the various sections to one another and disguised from almost everyone the revolution that was taking place. Collier still had to face the Senate Indian Committee when he returned from the Indian congresses, and the turmoil he had stirred up in Indian country had made a profound impact on the senators on that committee who were waiting for his appearance in defense of his proposal. It seems likely that the congresses did demonstrate to Collier that even stronger measures had to be enacted to protect the basic idea of self-government from the Indians themselves. Hence we can suspect that as Collier prepared for his confrontation with the Senate Indian Committee, he was already formulating a new strategy for getting the legislation passed and was even then expanding his understanding of what self-government should be.

Political Conflict
in the Upper House

Former Senator Joseph S. Clark once described the operations of the Senate Establishment as "almost the antithesis of democracy. . . . It is what might be called a self-perpetuating oligarchy with mild, but only mild, overtones of plutocracy."[1] Within their congressional setting, United States senators are elected aristocrats possessing enormous power—particularly those senators who chair important committees. Burton K. Wheeler was just such a man. As head of the Senate Committee on Indian Affairs, he reigned supreme, not unlike the manner in which Henry VIII ruled England—absolutely.

The fact that Wheeler chaired the committee was at least an initial boon. Wheeler and Collier had been allies in the many assaults directed toward the Indian Service during the presidency of Herbert Hoover. Indeed, Wheeler, along with Edgar Howard, had agreed to co-sponsor the Collier Bill, hoping it would check the power (and abuses of it) by the BIA. If a close relationship ever existed between Wheeler and Collier, however, it disintegrated after Collier took over the Bureau, and Wheeler began to think of him as part of the established regime he disliked. By the time the omnibus Indian measure was formally introduced in the United States Senate, Wheeler, together with Elmer Thomas of Oklahoma and Henry Ashurst of Arizona, would form a troika set to savage the bill.

The Senate Committee on Indian Affairs held its first session on the Collier Bill, S. 2755, on February 27, 1934.[2] The bill, as initially introduced, was the same bill that had been submitted to the House of Representatives five days earlier, but it ran into immediate difficulty. Senator Ashurst interrupted the proceedings at the very start, wanting to know if the Collier proposal would have any effect on the Hunter-Martin claims in Arizona.[3] These claims, which were fraudulent in the eyes of Senator Ashurst, purportedly gave to the Papago Indians title to vast stretches of mineral-rich land in southern Arizona.

To protect the Papago livestock, former Secretary of the Interior Ray Lyman Wilbur had, in 1932, withdrawn from some of these lands the right of mineral entry, thus barring mining interests in Arizona from valuable mineral resources.[4] The conflict between the Papagos and the mining industry in Arizona had gone on for years, and neither the courts nor the Department of the Interior seemed to be able to bring the dispute to an end. Senator Ashurst was afraid that the Collier Bill might provide the secretary of the interior with the power to enlarge the boundaries of the Papago reservation, thereby restricting even further the availability of mineral extraction by the mining industry.[5]

Henry Ashurst was determined not to permit the hearings on the Collier Bill to proceed until he found out how Collier felt about the Papago conflict. Collier was in an awkward position. Although he had served as a self-appointed champion of Indian rights for years, the Department of the Interior had decided to oppose the Papago nation on this issue, siding with the Arizona mining interests. Although stressing that the Papagos obviously had to be accorded their day in court, Collier advised Ashurst that it was his belief that there was insufficient evidence to substantiate the Papago claims.[6] Though this position seemed to placate the senator from Arizona, this peripheral and largely irrelevant issue took up virtually the whole first day's session—not an auspicious beginning for the Collier Bill.

Nearly a month passed before Collier was able to return to the Senate committee to continue his presentation. During this interim period a great deal occurred. The regional Indian congresses produced information that made necessary adjustments and amendments to the bill to accommodate Indian desires and minimize opposition from certain tribes. The House Committee on Indian Affairs had also continued to meet, and several dissident House members had signalled that even more changes in the initial bill would have to be made if there was any hope of the bill passing the House. The bill Collier brought to the Senate Judiciary Committee on April 26 was a slightly modified one, including some thirty amendments. It was on this amended version of S. 2755 that the Senate committee discussion now focused.

As was his custom before the House, Collier began his presentation before the Senate Committee on Indian Affairs with a meticulous examination of the problems confronting the nation's Indians and the proposed solutions the Collier Bill offered. It was clear from the beginning that it was not going to be smooth sailing. Senator Wheeler declared that whoever had drafted the bill had "put in here a lot of propaganda and verbiage that have no place in a bill of this kind," referring to the broader policy statements in section 1 of the self-government title.[7] Collier claimed that the statements were simply a clarification of policy. The chairman then began to isolate the passages that concerned him. "The process of allotment and inheritance of allotment of restricted Indian lands has caused the subdivision of such lands into units which are not capable of effective domestic use."[8] That is not policy, Wheeler argued, it is propaganda. If Collier had any doubt about Wheeler's true disposition toward the bill, the vigor with which the chairman pursued this "propaganda" argument clarified the picture.

Wheeler's critical approach was shared by Senator Elmer Thomas of Oklahoma. At the beginning of the committee session on April 28, Thomas held up consideration of the substantive provisions of the bill while he interrogated Collier about an apparently critical statement about Congress that the commissioner had made at one of the regional Indian congresses held at Anadarko, Oklahoma:

> You know that at the present time President Roosevelt controls both houses of Congress. When President Roosevelt wants a piece of legislation, he gets it from Congress. The bill we are going to discuss today is an administration measure. It is a President Roosevelt measure. The majority of the Members of Congress do not pretend to understand the Indian question in detail at all. In other words, if the administration had wanted to put this bill through quietly and quickly, understand, they had the power and they have the power to do it. The administration, as I stated before, had adopted a new policy which is the policy of bringing all the Indians into consultation on the bill, even though it entails or may entail delay. That the administration is not trying to put something over on them, or stampede them, or steam roller them, because if that were the purpose of the administration these meetings would never have been called. The administration would simply have gone quietly ahead and put the bill through Congress. I am saying this in order to ease your minds and to get them open so we may think together on this problem.[9]

Thomas was incensed that Collier would have told Indians in his state that it made no difference what Congress thought about the proposed legislation. Though the Indian commissioner attempted to calm the waters by indicating that his remarks to the Anadarko congress were simply designed to assure the Indians that they would have some influence in formulating the bill, Senator Thomas was never fully placated by this explanation.

When the hearings were finally redirected back to an analysis of the substantive provisions of the Collier proposal, initial attention was again focused on the self-government sections. Senator Wheeler laid his cards right on the table: The bill's underlying thrust toward Indian self-government ran dead against the government's present policy of assimilation. Assimilation, according to Wheeler, was the best thing that had happened to the Indians. They should as "nearly as possible adopt the white man's ways and laws."[10] Wheeler went on to argue that promoting a program of self-government would isolate Indians from the white communities and have a terrible impact upon such tribes as the Blackfeet and the Indians living on the Fort Peck Reservation in Wheeler's own Montana. It would clearly be a step backward.[11]

Senator Thomas picked up the argument where Wheeler had left it. Thomas was particularly concerned about how a tribe was to finance itself if given increased responsibility. Once a tribe proved it was capable of undertaking some of the functions normally performed by the Indian Bureau, such as health services and education, where would it obtain the money to underwrite these tasks? Since Indians could not raise their own taxes, was this not impossible?[12] Collier responded that the money would come from the federal government, just as it did under existing practice. Only the administration of the programs would be assumed by the Indian communities. It would be not unlike the education program envisioned under the pending Johnson-O'Malley Act. Here the states provided the educational services to Indian communities but used federal funds. The Indian tribes, under the Collier proposal, would be like the states, an instrumentality of the federal government performing the services.[13]

Senator Wheeler did not agree and accused Collier of attempting to give hope to the Indians for something that Congress would never permit; the legislature simply would not appropriate money and turn it over to the Indians.[14] When Congress could be convinced that a tribe could administer these programs better than the Indian Bureau, Collier replied, then it would provide the funds. Wheeler refused to be moved and went on to say that if Indians were given the power to manage their own programs, they would be saturated with all kinds of corruption.

Congress would not appropriate money unless it was guaranteed that Interior would be supervising the programs.[15] Senator Thomas finally ended the discussion by indicating that he would not consider the bill seriously until these provisions were stated in a more businesslike fashion. In its present form, the bill would simply isolate Indians onto reservations "where you will have a gate, with an admission charge of so much to see the Indian zoo."[16] The existing policy of assimilation, the senators believed, was the only course of action to pursue.

Senator Wheeler's argument that power should be retained in the hands of the BIA posed an interesting paradox. On the one hand, Wheeler distrusted the Indian Service, believing it to be ill managed and authoritarian. Yet he could not quite convince himself that Indians had reached (or could ever reach) such a state of maturity that they would assume a greater responsibility over their own affairs. In presenting his bill before the Senate committee, Collier had concentrated heavy attacks on the Indian Service. He indicated that while the BIA was moving away from its old paternalism, a future commissioner might well return it to its former omnipotence vis-à-vis Indians. Indians thus had no stability; they were at the complete mercy of the bureau. If the Indians were going to "get on their own feet they have got to be allowed to have some power and not to be dependent on Washington for every decision affecting their lives."[17]

Elmer Thomas was determined not to let this discussion come to an end, doggedly pursuing the notion of the Indians' incompetence. The Collier Bill required different levels of ability. Some Indians would be competent for certain purposes and yet incompetent for others, resulting in administrative chaos. Collier tried to deemphasize the issue: There was absolutely no reason why we could not begin to give *local* powers to the Indians that were beyond the control of the bureau. Congress would still retain the authority to change or affect these matters if the need arose.[18]

He pointed to the Pueblos in the Southwest, who already functioned in this manner. Their municipal works, for instance, were controlled and run by the Indians. They had a magistrate court, ran their own schools, and controlled a host of other local activities. All these municipal powers were exercised, even though the Pueblos were wards of the federal government. Senator Wheeler responded by generalizing the point: Such a plan might work for Indians who lived in the Southwest, but in his state of Montana it would be a bad idea; self-government would provoke all kinds of conflict between Indians and white people.[19]

Senator Thomas, having started the argument using Indian incompetency as the crux of the issue, concluded the discussion on the same note. Collier had just finished providing the committee with an illustration of the value of self-government, using a colony of landless Choctaw Indians. They had been given about three thousand acres of tribal land and had been permitted to organize and develop co-ops. A credit union had even been created to assist the tribe. Thomas asked Collier to explain how "these Indians can do that when they are held to be incompetent for all purposes whatever? How can you legislate competency into an Indian or legislate it out of him?"[20] Collier, having been faced with the same problem before the House Committee on Indian Affairs, was prepared with an answer. Competency, he noted, was merely a legal fiction. "It is a status in law and not a condition of the mind and body."[21] If the Collier Bill stipulated that Indians were competent to organize a local government, as it did, that was all that was necessary. Congress would have declared its intent.

When it came time to consider the Indian-lands title, Ward Shepard, a specialist on land policy from the Department of the Interior, explained and defended this portion of the bill. Shepard had brought with him a number of charts and maps as an aid in his attempt to demonstrate the enormous problems that the policy of allotment had wrought upon the Indians. Wheeler told Shepard in a firm, indeed almost discourteous, manner that the committee did not want to waste its time looking at maps and hearing about problems. Shepard then began to discuss the connection between the Collier Bill and the problems of "checkerboard" reservations, complete with the difficulties confronting the Indian Service in the leasing of Indian lands. Again Wheeler rudely interrupted, stating that "we don't need any elaborate scheme of this kind to correct it. The fault is not with the present law so much as it is with the policy that has been adopted by the Indian Bureau in the past."[22] Why, demanded Wheeler, did Congress have to pass a new law anyway? Clearly the bill's cosponsor had come away from his initial enthusiasm.

Shepard provided Wheeler with this answer: It was imperative that Congress pass legislation to provide the Indians with some degree of stability and permanence. "The purpose of this bill is to prevent the Indians from . . . continuously in the future being made the victims of that particular kind, benevolent despotism which has lost them in the past 50 years 63,000,000 acres of land."[23] Furthermore, the stability provided by the Collier Bill was not limited to securing Indian land rights; it also provided them with some assurance that future administrations would not reverse the temporary policies of the Indian Bureau and commence a new period of exploitation. Bureaucratic regulations were transitory and changed easily from one Indian commissioner to the next. But a declaration of policy coming from Congress was relatively permanent and would provide Indians with a fund of security that they had not enjoyed in the past.

As in the case of the House committee, the inheritance problems attendant on Indian lands posed a good deal of difficulty for Senate committee members. Collier dealt with this issue at some length, offering his statistics about the problems of heirship and the administrative and financial load it hung on the Department of the Interior.[24] The cost of the heirship "real estate" operations was thought to account for about half of the Indian Service operations budget (excluding school funds).[25]

It was clear that a minor amendment would be of little help. The Collier Bill proposed a bold and dramatic, albeit controversial, solution—returning the lands to the tribal community, with corporate compensation for the heirs. This provision could protect the land from being sold or leased to whites and at the same time afford the tribe an opportunity to consolidate parcels into economically productive units. He battled with Senator Wheeler over making the system voluntary, which Collier knew would be self-defeating. The equity that Indian heirs possessed in their inherited lands was so small that it would be virtually impossible to obtain voluntary relinquishment.[26]

In order to justify the legality of the so-called "divestment heirship" provision, Collier turned to the federal guardianship power of the federal government. Congress was endowed with plenary power over Indian affairs, and though there might be some question as to the legality of transferring title from a living allottee, heirs were not vested with such legal rights. Collier cited *Lone Wolf* v. *Hitchcock* as his legal authority in support of the interpretation.[27] Apparently Wheeler was not convinced, and he periodically returned to this issue, at one point arguing that to divest Indians of their inheritable rights was not only legally wrong but morally wrong as well.[28]

In the final stages of this discussion Charles Fahey, the acting solicitor for Interior, Wheeler, and Senator Frederick Stiewer of Oregon engaged in a firm and frank exchange, each citing legal authority to justify their respective opinions. Fahey did not fare well in the initial exchange but concluded with a position of strength. He successfully argued that there was no vested right in inheritance until one inherits. Once an Indian inherited, then the right became vested, but until that time, due process of law could be satisfied by appropriate legislation. States, for instance, had the power to pass laws cutting off certain heirs unless specifically mentioned in wills. Congress had like power. In the Collier Bill, all that Congress was doing was modifying a *potential* inheritance. It was not a confiscation of property, since the heir received something of equivalent value in place of the title to the property—a certificate of interest in the tribal community property.[29]

The legal issues surrounding the divestment of Indians from private ownership of their allotted lands did not constitute as great a problem for Collier in the Senate as it did in the House. True, the Indian heir problem was thorny, but the other controversial provision dealing with the authority of the secretary to compel the transfer of land for consolidation purposes proved less difficult. The amended bill presented to the Senate committee had eliminated the mandatory nature of this section, at least with respect to farming lands. It still gave the secretary mandatory power with respect to timber and grazing land. The very fact that a modification had been made resulted in less visibility for this provision and hence less conflict. It mattered little, however, for the heirship issue provided enough conflict to occupy the attention of both the bill's advocates and its opponents.

One provision in the Collier Bill that did not provoke a great deal of controversy in the House, but that concerned several members of the Senate committee, dealt with the power of the secretary of the interior to purchase land for landless Indians. Senator Elmer Thomas of Oklahoma felt that local white communities would be adamantly opposed to this measure, since it would remove property from the state tax rolls. He betrayed his prejudices by adding that since the Indians were incompetent to begin with, it would be folly to lend them money to build "creameries and factories."[30]

Wheeler suggested that if anything was to be done, it would be limited to giving Indians a small piece of land so that they could engage in subsistence farming. There was no need for consolidation.[31] Senator William Thompson of Nebraska quickly noted that this sounded a lot like what the Indian Service had been doing for the Indians in Nebraska for a long time. The government gave the Indians land under the General Allotment Act, and it soon disappeared into white hands.[32] Was this not just a continuation of the old exploitative policy? Thompson continued to argue that the Indians in Nebraska were in a "pitiable" state because the government and the white community permitted other whites to steal the Indian blind.[33] While Thompson's remarks were demeaning and patronizing toward the Indian, they did afford Collier an opportunity to say that this situation was one of the principal problems that the Collier Bill was designed to remedy.

One might have thought that once the committee dropped discussion of Indian lands and took up the issue of Indian education, things

would have progressed more smoothly for Collier. After all, the education title was received rather warmly before the House committee. Not
a great deal of time was spent on Indian education, but Senator Wheeler
plunged into the issue with his inimitable hostile style. Wheeler was
primarily concerned with the problem of segregating Indian education
and isolating it on the reservations. He favored a policy of moving
Indian children into the white school system. The Collier Bill would
overturn the Indian educational programs in his home state of Montana,
which was now providing educational services for Indian children.[34]
Collier denied that a segregated system of education would evolve.
There were two basic purposes to this title: first, to permit Indian
communities the opportunity to assume a greater role in educating their
children; and second, to provide practical education for Indians to enable
them to qualify for government jobs. Collier did admit that there were
reservations, such as the Navajo, where segregated educational facilities
already existed, not because of a designed policy but simply due to the
geographic isolation of the Indian communities.[35]

While the senator from Montana served as the catalyst of opposition to most of the bill's provisions, he did come to its defense during
the testimony of Luther Steward, president of the National Federation
of Federal Employees. Steward wanted to bring the committee's attention to the fact that the Collier Bill would withdraw from the Civil
Service the entire personnel of the Indian Service and vest the appointment power in the hands of the secretary of the interior. There would
be absolutely no restrictions limiting the secretary's power in this area,
and no standards for appointment. Not even a test was required. Some
criteria were essential, he maintained, even if they weren't the same as
those that applied to Civil Service applicants in general.[36]

Wheeler responded to Steward by noting that the Indian Service
was different from other agencies in that Indians actually owned the
property that the government was supervising. In addition, he reasoned
that many Indians had the practical knowledge to function well in the
Forestry Service but did not have the academic background to qualify
for employment. This situation was precisely what the Collier Bill was
trying to remedy.[37] Senator Peter Norbeck of South Dakota interjected
that the Civil Service had simply done a bad job in that Indians were
almost entirely excluded. "The reservation is filled up with white people
who live off the Indians. . . . This may be going a little too far in the
other direction, but I am willing to go, inasmuch as I do not know
where else to step."[38] Collier finally concluded the discussion by illus-
trating how one tribe had begun a program where Indians were being

trained to do camp work. "We were able to pick Indians who were qualified [to do the work], and more than half of all the supervisory force [were] Indians. We could not have got those Indians in under any civil service examination designed for the general population."[39]

There was not a great deal of discussion on the Court of Indian Affairs before the Senate committee. There was no joint session with the Senate Judiciary Committee, no doubt because Senator Wheeler was firmly opposed to the court from the beginning, and by the time the issue came up for discussion, Collier seems to have decided that the court was expendable. Collier and Wheeler did occasionally confront each other on this issue, however. Early in the hearings the two tangled over the power of tribal courts to issue divorce decrees. Collier contended that the tribal courts possessed this power, and Wheeler argued firmly that they did not have such authority. The Indian commissioner indicated that the tribal courts were empowered to issue such decrees as a matter of custom, and many courts all over the country recognized these decrees. Wheeler responded that Indian courts were courts in name only; when they functioned, they did so only in minor areas of concern.[40]

An extended discussion of the proposed Court of Indian Affairs was held on May 3, at which time Alexander Holtzoff of the Department of Justice appeared before the Senate committee.[41] Holtzoff attempted to justify the creation of the national Indian court by noting that there were certain cases that the Anglo-American courts were either unwilling or unable to hear. These cases dealt with minor or specific types of crime, such as embezzlement or kidnapping. Wheeler responded by noting that Indians don't kidnap people; only white people kidnap, hence there was no need for any provision on kidnapping.[42]

When Holtzoff mentioned the crime of assault, the chairman of the Senate committee in a condescending and brusque fashion again refused to admit that any need existed. "But why should [assault] be included? After all, the Indians get into a fight and they do not hurt each other very badly unless they have dangerous weapons. . . . [T]here is not very much necessity for including common assault on an Indian reservation."[43] Much of the exchange during this session centered on the jurisdictional problems attendant to the court title. Would there be conflicts with the federal court and in what areas? Would whites be required to sue Indians before an Indian court? Wheeler finally noted that the whole provision was ridiculous and would never get through Congress.

At this remark Collier did one of his famous strategic backtracks. "Mr. Chairman, we have explained that we did not regard this section as an integral part of the bill, as indispensable at all."[44] The Court of Indian Affairs had apparently been given its "day in court" and lost.

When Collier returned to Washington following the regional Indian congresses, he was immediately faced with a major disappointment. M. K. Sniffen, editor of the Indian Rights Association's journal, *Indian Truth,* had published an article critical of the Collier Bill.[45] This defection was particularly disappointing to the Indian commissioner in that the Indian Rights Association had participated in the Cosmos Club meeting, where some key ideas of the bill had been formulated. In the May issue of *Indian Truth,* Sniffen again criticized the omnibus Indian proposal and urged that the self-government and Indian court titles be eliminated. Indeed, Sniffen felt that Congress should draw up a number of separate bills to deal with the various problems confronting Indian country.[46] Sniffen was joined in this criticism by G.E.E. Lindquist and Flora Warren Seymour, both former members of the Board of Indian Commissioners. Lindquist feared that the bill would revive tribalism and "wipe out most of the gains of the last fifty years."[47] Seymour raised the old specter of "communism," which had haunted Collier throughout his campaign to get the bill adopted.

The accusation that the Collier Bill embodied the worst of communist and socialist doctrine was used frequently as a vehicle to discredit both the Indian commissioner and his proposal. One of the leading critics to use this device was Joseph Bruner, president of the National Indian Confederacy. Bruner was a Creek Indian from Sapulpa, Oklahoma. A successful businessman, he dabbled in farming, real estate, and oil and gas. A strong advocate of assimilation, Bruner claimed that the Collier Bill would bring about a "Russian Communistic life in the United States."[48] Bruner accused Collier of favoring atheism as well as communism and suggested that Collier had been too much influenced by such people as Isadora Duncan, Bill Haywood, and Emma Goldman.

On April 30, 1934, Bruner wrote a letter to Senator Elmer Thomas, disputing the fact that Collier had Indian support in Oklahoma for his bill. He alleged that Collier had had a destructive effect upon Indian tribes and that the omnibus Indian measure would set Indian affairs back two hundred years.[49] Collier, according to Bruner, was neither sincere nor fair in his "assumed" friendship with Indians. The Collier Bill would not restore one acre of land lost under the allotment program. Furthermore, during his sixty-one years, Bruner had yet to witness one Indian standing in a "soup line," as the Indian commissioner had asserted. The measure was nothing more than a propaganda device orchestrated by Collier.[50]

Bruner's letter to Senator Thomas sparked a series of written exchanges between Collier and Bruner, each accusing the other of misleading and inaccurate statements circulated among members of the committee and higher officials in the BIA. This exchange became increasingly bitter, as in the following excerpt from one of Collier's letters blasting Bruner:

> [You are an] Indian, whose seeming passion is to impede the opportunity of his own people. One who gains attention at all only through being an Indian, and yet who gains the attention through presenting the anomaly of an Indian ferociously trying not to be one.
>
> But when an Indian is subconsciously driven not to be an Indian, almost unavoidably he falls into imitation of the less attractive traits of the white man.
>
> You are, unfortunately, made less interesting through your choice of the white-man qualities you will imitate. To be violent, to bluff, and to be recklessly inaccurate are not the traits which make white men attractive.[51]

Though Collier had maintained his poise through much of the legislative battle, even when he was verbally chastised by congressmen and Indians, he momentarily lost it in this ugly exchange with Bruner. He could accept the criticism and opposition of the American Indian Association, for instance, when it called for the bill's defeat "before it commits a fatal injustice against the American Indian in creating a definite perpetuation of this monstrous Indian Bureau system," but he could not control his feelings when he went to battle with Bruner.[52]

Several prominent Indians who had testified against the Collier Bill before the House Committee on Indian Affairs appeared in a similar role before the Senate committee. Joe Dann presented his argument that the Yakima tribe was simply not ready for self-government. They could not accept such a responsibility, for they would be unable to shoulder the burden. All the Indian landowners today were old men, Dann noted. The "smart" young leaders were given competency, along with fee patents, and still lost their land years ago. If this bill were to pass, Dann declared, "our best and ablest and smartest men, supposedly, would be the landless Indians. Therefore, the Yakima Indians feel that they do not want to be led by such a body of men."[53] The only portion of the bill that might be of benefit to the Yakimas, Dann noted, was the educational provision. But as far as the sections dealing with self-government, land, and the proposed Indian court were concerned, the tribe remained in firm opposition.

Though a number of interest groups and tribal representatives continued to express their concern over the Collier Bill, the Indian commissioner had his parade of witnesses primed and ready to testify as well. Oliver La Farge, a nationally noted anthropologist and president of the National Association of Indian Affairs, appeared before the committee in support of the bill. He spoke for a number of organizations, such as the General Federation of Women's Clubs, the American Indian Defense Association, and the American Civil Liberties Union.[54] Senator Wheeler immediately attempted to impeach the credibility of La Farge by arguing that organizations such as these would come in and give blanket endorsement to a bill without ever having read the individual provisions. La Farge responded by noting that he had studied the Collier Bill extensively and had attended numerous meetings and conferences at which the bill had been considered.

In La Farge's presentation before the committee, he stressed that it was important that Congress take action on the bill and take action now. Administrations change with too much frequency, La Farge noted, and with each change comes new revisions in Indian policy. Congress, therefore, through the Collier Bill, needed to provide permanent direction to Indian nations.[55] La Farge did suggest that a number of amendments would improve the bill, but most of these were amenable to the bill's sponsors.

Ralph Fredenberg, representing the Menominee tribe of Wisconsin, told of his tribe's experience in attempting to establish a logging plant on the reservation.[56] The plant had been developed, but it was not run by Indians. It was operated by the Indian Bureau, and the people hired by the bureau were mostly white. The tribe, according to Fredenberg, had been constantly exploited and was never permitted to do things on its own. Recently, however, a new foreman had been brought in and had begun to place Indians in department-head positions. Soon the tribe hoped to have the plant filled 100 percent with Indian employees. Senator Thomas interrupted Fredenberg here to indicate that the tribe did not need legislation to bring this about. Fredenberg responded by noting that under the old act, Indians were to be employed "as far as was practicable." But white people had been hired and the forest denuded. If the Menominees were given the power of self-government, they would be able to run their own timber industry and at the same time adopt measures to conserve the forest.[57] Fredenberg stated that his reservation was a long way from Washington, and it needed the power of self-government to do the things that had to be done in order to keep the tribal members prosperous.

Senator Thomas attempted to minimize the effectiveness of Fredenberg's testimony by commenting on how well qualified the Menominees were to function on their own. He was skeptical about other tribes. Why couldn't Congress simply pass a separate piece of legislation designed specifically for the Menominees without having to affect other, less able tribes? Collier then reminded Thomas that a few years ago the Menominees had come to Congress to get permission to set up a corporation on their reservation but that Congress had refused to pass such a law.[58] So ran the discouraging pattern whenever tribes came to Congress seeking authority to assume more responsibility.

If the record of Congress had been less than encouraging in assisting Indians in their various enterprises in the past, so had the Bureau of Indian Affairs. Thomas Sloan, an attorney and member of the Omaha tribe, described to the Senate committee the difficulties he had encountered in obtaining a simple land patent. Having developed a successful law practice, Sloan went to the Indian Office to purchase a fee patent for eighty acres of land. His request was denied by a three-member board of commissioners (all of whose income probably did not equal that of Sloan's at the time). The commission demanded a competency hearing, and by the time it was held, the land was sold off to someone else.[59] The attorney went on to say that while he was waiting for his hearing, a seventy-year-old Indian who was blind and neither spoke nor wrote English was given a fee patent by the Indian agent, a friend of whom in turn bought the land for a mere fourteen thousand dollars. The white purchaser actually gave the old Indian four thousand dollars plus a non-interest-bearing note. That four thousand dollars was all that the old Indian ever received for his property.[60]

Sloan's tale of exploitation and neglect had a telling effect upon several committee members, particularly Senators Lynn Frazier of North Dakota and William Thompson of Nebraska. Sloan went on to discuss at some length the real problems that allotted Indians faced. They were constantly exploited. When materials were given to assist them, they were shoddy and inferior. His sentiments were echoed by Elwood Harlan, also a member of the Omaha tribe. Harlan indicated that at one time, his tribe had access to 200,000 acres of land. This area had gradually decreased to about 25,000 acres, 4,000 of which were classified as surplus lands.[61] Sam La Pointe, a Rosebud Sioux, testified that at one time his tribe had owned practically six counties in South Dakota. At the time of the hearings their landholdings had shrunk to one county, much of which was itself checkerboarded and difficult to manage.[62] "Under the present system of Indian Bureau management, we have lost our initiative, that God-given gift. We have become a people dependent on somebody else to do something for us all the time."[63] La Pointe went on to note that it was the system that was at fault and that the Collier Bill could change this condition. As a passing salute to the Indian commissioner, La Pointe proclaimed that "Mr. Collier is the first Indian Commissioner who really had the welfare of the Indians down at the bottom of his heart. Sometimes I think he is an Indian himself."[64] A heartfelt sentiment, but unfortunately not a particularly popular one with Congress.

The legislative struggle in the Senate had been a real burden to Collier. The senators tended to probe much more deeply into the real workings of the bill, and he had also to defend himself against a number of unfair peripheral accusations. Whereas there was a nucleus of opposition to the bill in the House, Senator Wheeler as chairman, dominated his committee. A discouraged John Collier finally turned to the White House for support. He convinced Secretary of the Interior Harold Ickes and Secretary of Agriculture Henry Wallace to approach the president and urge him to give a high priority to the Collier Bill. Roosevelt responded on April 28 with letters to Edgar Howard in the House and Burton Wheeler in the Senate, strongly endorsing the Collier proposal.[65] He urged Congress to take immediate action, providing the break in the legislative logjam that had frustrated Collier for several months. Both Howard and Wheeler agreed to convene subcommittees to work out unresolved issues in the legislation. Collier and William Zimmerman of Interior proceeded to get together informally with the members of both committees to work out an acceptable compromise.[66]

On May 17, Senator Wheeler once again convened the Senate Committee on Indian Affairs to consider the compromised product that he and Collier had drafted. He noted that his initial idea had been simply to go over the original Collier Bill and amend those provisions he thought to be unwise. However, after due consideration, a decision was made to come up with virtually an entirely new bill, S. 3645.[67] The compromise had eliminated from consideration most of the important points of controversy, according to Wheeler. With a new bill in place, the Senate committee proceeded to examine the Collier-Wheeler compromise section by section.

A startling change had taken place. Collier was no longer the dominant force in command of the proposed legislation. Senator Wheeler had taken control. (The bill itself was eventually named the

Wheeler-Howard Act). Gone from the original version of the bill was the title dealing with the Court of Indian Affairs. Gone was the elaborate title on self-government, which would have endowed tribal governments with a large reservoir of home rule. In its place was substituted a much smaller provision providing Indian communities with some limited powers of self-government. Many of the mandatory provisions relating to land transfer and the problems of heirship were made voluntary. It appeared, for all intents and purposes, to be but a skeleton of the original bill that Collier had submitted to the committee for consideration.

With his personal imprint now on the compromise bill, Senator Wheeler began to direct it, actively through the committee hearings. Additions were made here and there, but only when they corresponded with Senator Wheeler's notion of how the bill should be constituted. At one point for instance, the issue was raised whether a tribe could be given the power to levy taxes on tribal members. Wheeler contended that the Congress probably did not have the power to permit tribal governments to levy such taxes. Collier responded by noting that tribes had done so in the past in Oklahoma. Wheeler simply indicated that Congress "may have done it . . . but I don't think they had any authority to do it. . . . We shall cut it out."[68] And it went.

On another occasion the committee debated whether to permit the tribe to contract with the secretary for the performance of certain services that under the present system were performed by the Indian Bureau. Senator Joseph C. O'Mahoney of Wyoming thought that since Congress had imposed these duties upon the Indian Office, it should perform them, not the tribe.[69] Collier felt that tribes could easily perform many of these services for themselves. Wheeler indicated that the Indian Bureau could let Indians assume greater responsibility now if it desired. O'Mahoney was not convinced. After a brief exchange Wheeler concluded the discussion by noting that "we shall just cut the whole provision out of the bill and concentrate on other sections." And so it was.

Occasionally a special-interest provision made its way into the compromised version of the bill. In order to accommodate the Sioux Indians, a section was included to protect the "Sioux benefits," which would cease if allotment was terminated.[70] Discussion proceeded in such a manner that differences, unless they were resolved as Senator Wheeler wanted them resolved, were left hanging. In an attempt to define what constituted an "Indian" living off the reservation, Collier suggested Indians have at least one-fourth Indian blood. Wheeler held out for one-half blood mixture. "If you use one-fourth, then all sorts of people are going to come in and claim that they should be put on the tribal rolls," Wheeler claimed. "What we are trying to do is get rid of the Indian problem rather than add to it."[71] The final bill incorporated the one-half Indian blood standard.

While finishing touches were being put on the compromise bill in the Senate, the House Committee on Indian Affairs was restructuring its version of the bill. On May 22 Congressman William Hastings of Oklahoma rose to criticize the bill as initially drafted by the Indian Office. Congressman Hubert Peavey interrupted Hastings to advise him that all the points he objected to had been stricken from the newly drafted compromise House bill. Peavey noted that the original bill "was so drastically amended that they took out everything but the title."[72] Peavey was certainly correct in his assessment of the situation. Without tracing the whole history of the hearings, there would have been no way to link the final version to the draft of the original proposal submitted by Collier.

But the compromise had been struck. Several amendments were added during the debate on the Senate floor. Senator Pat McCarren of Nevada succeeded in raising the percentage of voters required to ratify corporate charters from one fourth of the adult tribal members to one third. Senator Henry Ashurst was able to incorporate a provision for the Papago mineral dispute.[73] The Senate finally passed its version of the bill on June 12 by a voice vote. The House version was passed 258–88 on June 15.[74] While the two bills were not identical, the differences were slight, and they were worked out in a conference committee hearing on June 16. Two days later, on June 18, 1934, the Indian Reorganization Act was forwarded to President Roosevelt for his signature. The President signed the measure, and at long last the bill became a law.

The legislative journey had come to an end. It had been a singularly difficult struggle and in most respects represented a solid defeat for Collier. The final version bore little if any resemblance to what he had originally suggested. Gone were the great philosophical preambles that he had hoped would commit Congress to a clear support of the Indian right of self-government and cultural difference. There was in fact no clear statement of congressional purpose at all.

Collier saw in the bill a conglomerate of amendments that had no central theme. Allotment was prohibited for those tribes that chose to organize under the new statute. The sections actually dealing with self-government were vague and without much form or substance. Eager to compromise on the Court of Indian Affairs title, he had received nothing in exchange. Yet Collier was an astute and energetic man, and he determined to make the best of the opportunities that presented themselves. If he could figure out a way to keep moving forward with his ambitious program for Indian reform, even with the badly fragmented statute that Congress had given him, he would do it.

10

The Indian Reorganization Act of 1934 and the Collier Bill: A Comparison

June 18, 1934, must have been a bittersweet day in the life of John Collier. It was the culmination of months of hard work in which he devoted his full energy to the passage of a bill,[1] which was nearly unrecognizable when it finally became law. As an astute politician, Collier knew the art of political survival was compromise. But had the sinews of the Collier Bill been left out of the final product? A comparison of the original version of the Collier Bill with the provisions of the Indian Reorganization Act should provide an answer to this perplexing question. In addition, it should help to set the record straight for those people who mistakenly have viewed the act as if it had been passed in its original form.

The external contrasts between the original Collier Bill and the IRA are readily apparent. Collier's initial proposal was forty-eight pages in length, with four major titles, each divided in turn into a number of substantive sections. The Indian Reorganization Act as passed omitted the major titles and in slightly more than five pages simply organized the various provisions into nineteen succinct sections. According to Collier, the only provision of the initial bill that remained intact was the one that terminated the policy of allotment; actually several of the original provisions appeared in the final act. The most conspicuous omission from the IRA was the title dealing with the Court of Indian Affairs, which had disappeared entirely—hardly surprising, since throughout the congressional hearings Collier seemed ready to dispense with it. Although the three other major areas of concern—self-government, education, and Indian lands—were all reduced from comprehensive titles to individual sections, they at least found a limited home in the new Wheeler-Howard Act.

Self-Government

The Power to Establish Local Self-Government

One of the key ingredients in the original version of the Collier Bill dealt with self-government, with thirteen extensive sections designed to provide Indian communities with some basic powers of home rule. The Indian Reorganization Act reduced these to one principal provision that provided tribes with but a limited fund of power.[2] The IRA permitted Indian tribes to organize a local government to provide for the general welfare of the Indian community. The Collier Bill would have allowed groups or subdivisions of Indians on a reservation to organize as well, but the final version of the law limited this permission to tribal units only; each tribe could adopt a constitution and bylaws by which the community would be governed.

The first step in the process of drafting a constitution was the creation of a committee of representative tribal members. The committee could draft the constitution on its own or elicit assistance from the Department of the Interior. An election would then be held to determine if the community wished to ratify the constitution. A majority vote of the adult reservation members was necessary for adoption. Secretarial approval, of course, was also required. These procedures were similar to those expressed in the Collier Bill, except that the Collier Bill required ratification by a three-fifths vote of the community members. The IRA therefore was actually a bit more liberal than the Collier Bill in that it only required a majority vote for ratification. Under the Wheeler-Howard Act, a tribe also had the power to amend or revoke the constitution by following the same procedure as that required for ratification. Once the machinery for self-government was established, it could not be abolished by executive or administrative action. Only Congress was empowered to alter or interfere with its functions.

The Exercise of Tribal Power

The Indian Reorganization Act specified a number of powers that tribal governments could exercise without first seeking secretarial approval. They could, for instance, negotiate with federal, state, and local governments. They could exercise veto power over the sale, lease, or encumbrance of tribal property and assets. They were also accorded the right to be advised of appropriation estimates and federal projects that pertained to their reservation. Of equal importance was the grant providing tribes with the authority to exercise all of the *existing* powers that Indian governments possessed. In contrast to the IRA, the Collier Bill had been less generous in bestowing unrestricted authority to tribal governments. The original proposal had limited tribal governments to the exercise of existing community powers and the right to be advised of appropriation estimates. While the Collier Bill did provide local governments with a number of additional powers, they were all subject to the approval of the secretary of the interior. With relation to the unrestricted powers extended to tribal governments, therefore, the IRA actually went further than Collier originally intended.

A fundamental weakness in the authorization to exercise existing powers was that no one knew just what those powers were—and the act itself failed to enumerate them specifically. In October 1934, shortly after the act's passage, Nathan Margold, the solicitor of the interior, working with the sympathetic support of John Collier, attempted to address this cloudy area in an opinion designed to define the existing powers by name. This opinion is described at length in the next chapter, but its key elements were the recognition of the Indians' rights to adopt their own chosen form of government, to define the conditions for tribal membership, to regulate the disposition of tribal property, and to prescribe rules of inheritance on real and personal property. The impact that this opinion had upon the move toward Indian self-government was exceedingly significant.

One of the most important aspects of the Margold opinion, which we will again address later, is the assumption that these powers were inherent in the tribes' status as a domestic dependent nation—harking back to the old Marshall phrase—and were *not* merely delegated by overriding federal authorities. The opinion went far to clarify the bureau's position, though not necessarily to quiet controversy.

Tribal Powers Subject to Secretarial Approval

The phrase "subject to the discretion of the secretary" has always given

Indians cause for alarm. It inevitably meant that the power rested not with the local tribe, but in the hands of the Bureau of Indian Affairs and/or the secretary of the interior. While secretarial approval was required with reference to some of the major activities of a tribe, such as approval of the constitution, this reservation of power in the hands of the secretary was not prominent in the "homerule" provisions of the IRA. Indeed, the act referred to secretarial power only with respect to the employment of legal counsel and the fixing of fees.

The Collier Bill, in marked contrast, required that Indian communities seek secretarial approval in a multitude of endeavors, including the ability to organize a municipal government, elect officers, hire employees, define membership, fix salaries, regulate disposition of property, conserve resources, establish a court system, levy taxes, acquire and manage property, negotiate contracts with other governmental entities, and exercise other powers necessary to the fulfillment of local government responsibilities. When taken together, such functions constituted a firm foundation for exercising home rule.

If these powers could be delegated or withheld from tribal governments completely at the discretion of the secretary, what true authority was left for the tribe? Perhaps Collier had hoped that many of these functions might be written right into a tribal constitution and be approved by the secretary. Clearly, the Collier Bill did not suggest a wholesale transfer of power from the bureaucracy to the local authorities, an instant decentralization, as some commentators have suggested. It was a cautious transfer of powers that would be made only if the secretary deemed it advisable. The secretary, at his discretion, was also permitted to enter into agreements with tribes to have them perform local services heretofore exercised by the Indian Bureau, thus transferring certain BIA functions to tribes gradually as well. Furthermore, the secretary was authorized to convey the federal interest in property the government held in trust to the Indian communities.

None of these provisions found their way into the Indian Reorganization Act. The idea of decentralizing power, even gradually, and placing authority in the hands of the local Indian communities was anathema to the legislators. Collier's own ambiguity—his idealistic vision versus his bill's actual stipulations—probably did not help, but the final drafters were clearly not interested even in idealistic rhetoric. The home rule authority was denied.

Both the Collier Bill and the IRA called upon Congress to pass an annual appropriation to assist in the development of these community organizations. The Collier appropriation of $500,000 was cut in half.

The Establishment of Tribal Business Corporations

John Collier originally covered little in the area of fostering economic development, which had been one of the major trouble spots for Indian communities. The Indian Reorganization Act, in contrast, faced this perplexing issue head-on. Under the IRA, the secretary of the interior, upon receiving a petition from at least one third of the adult reservation Indians, could issue a charter of incorporation to the tribe.[3] The charter would become operative when ratified by a majority vote of the adult tribal members.

The chartered corporation permitted tribes to engage for the first time in a number of business enterprises. The corporation could obtain loans, acquire and manage property, issue certificates of interest in the corporate property, transfer land, and exercise other powers that were incidental to the conduct of corporate business. The corporation was limited, however, in that it could not mortgage or lease reservation land for a period that exceeded ten years. This limitation was to ensure that tribal land remained under Indian control. Once a charter was issued to a tribe, it could not be revoked except by an act of Congress.

For all intents and purposes this finally put an Indian tribe in the position where it could not only compete economically with its neighbors, but it could also control the internal operations of the corporation as well. The tribe could elect its own corporate officers, draft bylaws, pay dividends, and otherwise function independently of the Bureau of Indian Affairs. Indeed, the corporation could even sue and be sued. However, tribal trust property was immune from legal seizure or attachment. In refining these provisions Collier borrowed heavily from the proposal put forward by the Klamaths in 1930 and 1932, and it is singularly ironic that the Klamaths themselves rejected the Indian Reorganization Act and never organized a corporation under its provisions.

Revolving Credit Fund

Providing tribes with a corporate mechanism such that they could develop their resources economically was one thing. But a corporation could not survive without the benefit of operating funds and credit. To remedy this problem the Indian Reorganization Act authorized Congress to appropriate a sum of ten million dollars to establish a revolving credit fund for purposes of economic development[4]—twice the sum Collier himself initially suggested. The unavailability of credit had been a major factor in preventing Indian nations from developing themselves economically, so the increased authorization was a major boon.

The secretary of the interior was charged with developing regulations for lending funds to the tribes. The loan repayments would be deposited in the revolving fund so that the monies could be loaned out again to other tribes. There was one problem in obtaining access to the revolving credit funds: Funds were available *only* to the tribal corporations; they in turn could lend money to individual Indians. If a tribe did not elect to participate in the IRA and establish a tribal corporation, it would be barred from using the fund.

It can't be denied that the Indian Reorganization Act extended a good deal of power and responsibility to tribal governments. Even without the great fund of home-rule authority, the basic powers of organization, negotiation, property control, and other general existing functions previously exercised by tribal governments provided Indian communities with a firm foundation upon which to build. To these must be added the benefits of business incorporation, complete with access to a revolving credit fund. The situation was not ideal, but it was a pretty good bargain, nevertheless.

Education and Employment

The education provisions in the Collier Bill were neither extensive nor controversial. The original proposal charged the Indian commissioner with providing training for students of at least one-fourth Indian blood so as to prepare them for jobs in the Indian Service. To accomplish this task, an appropriation of not more than fifty thousand dollars was requested from Congress. Half this amount was to be expended for low-interest loans. In addition, the bill authorized Congress to appropriate fifteen thousand dollars for outright grants to Indian students.

The Indian Reorganization Act changed the Collier version of the bill rather significantly. The final act called for an appropriation in the amount of $250,000, but it was to be limited to governmental loans. There was no mention of outright grants. Furthermore, no more than $50,000 could be used for high school and college students. The basic thrust of the law was to foster vocational and trade school education.

Much of the debate on the Collier Bill during the congressional hearings focused on the fact that few Indians were qualified to work in the Indian Service, since the Civil Service examination prevented otherwise qualified Indian applicants from being hired. The new act directed the secretary of the interior to establish new standards of eligibility, without regard to the Civil Service requirements, for employment in the Bureau of Indian Affairs.[5] Furthermore, Indian applicants would receive preference for vacancies that occurred in the Indian Service.

Collier's controversial provision allowing tribal governments to nominate Indians for vacancies was omitted.

One other notable provision was excluded from the Wheeler-Howard Act. The Collier proposal stipulated that it was to be the policy of Congress to promote and preserve Indian arts, crafts, and culture, and the Indian commissioner would have been permitted to employ personnel and develop programs in the existing Indian educational facilities to achieve this goal. No separate funds, however, were to be expended for the program, which would be funded out of existing school budgets. Apparently Congress believed that the Indian commissioner could initiate this policy on his own, without the sanction of law, and omitted it from the IRA.

Though the final education and employment provisions of the Indian Reorganization Act were not very extensive, the changes they brought about were significant. The appropriation requested, though admittedly for loans only, was increased fivefold. Furthermore, the new provisions for preferential Indian employment opened a real—and realizable—path toward self-management, if not self-government.

Indian Lands

The Indian-lands provisions of the Collier Bill constituted the most controversial, and possibly the most important, part of the proposal. The original twenty-one sections were reduced to eight, and significant changes in the compromised measure diminished much of Collier's hopes for land reform. Still, a new policy direction was charted in the IRA that could not help but benefit Indian nations.

The most important provision of the Indian Reorganization Act was spelled out in the first section of the measure: The IRA brought to an end the old policy of allotment. Top priority was extended to terminating this devastating program, and a new policy was outlined to prevent Indian lands from being broken up in the future and sold to non-Indians. In addition, the trust period on allotted land was to be extended indefinitely, that is, until otherwise directed by Congress.[6] Under the existing system, allotted land was to be held in trust for a period of twenty-five years. At the expiration of that time, the land would be vested absolutely into the hands of the Indian landowner and become subject to state taxation. The Collier Bill, in addition to extending the trust period, had attempted to take the protection of Indian landowners even further. It would have terminated the secretary's power to force "competency" and fee patents upon Indians, a tool that had been used successfully to force Indian landowners into a position where their property could be lost to whites. The IRA said nothing about dismantling this system, however, and failed to incorporate these additional important protections in the final version of the bill.

Both the Collier Bill and the Indian Reorganization Act withdrew surplus Indian lands that had been opened for sale to nontribal purchasers.[7] The secretary was authorized to turn these surplus lands back to the tribe so that they would remain under Indian control. This restoration was of considerable importance, since the sale of surplus land to whites had been one of the major factors contributing to the wholesale reduction of Indian landholdings. This portion of the act, however, did not apply to lands designated for reclamation projects. In order to accommodate the interests of the Arizona mining industry and Senator Henry Ashurst of Arizona, the order withdrawing certain Papago Indian lands from mineral entry was revoked.[8] Damages were to be paid to the Papago nation for the loss of any improvements made, and a yearly rent (not to exceed five cents an acre) was to be given to the tribe for the loss of use or occupancy. In effect, the Papagos' claims were sacrificed as part of the price of getting the compromise measure through Congress.

The principal disputes concerning Indian lands in the Collier Bill largely revolved around when and how property could be taken away from individual landholders and transferred to the tribe. Collier would have authorized the secretary to *mandate* a transfer of farming, grazing, and timber land to tribal ownership whenever he felt it was necessary for purposes of consolidation. This authority was designed to bring together fragmented parcels that by themselves could not be productive, but once consolidated would be capable of economic development. Equally controversial was the mandatory transfer of allotted land to the tribe upon the death of the Indian landowner.

The Indian Reorganization Act changed these provisions significantly. Section 4 of the IRA stipulated that sale, devise, or transfer of Indian lands could be made only in the following three ways:

1. Restricted land could be transferred by an owner to a tribe or tribal corporation with the secretary's approval. This was to be a *voluntary* transfer only.
2. Restricted land could be exchanged for other lands of equal value, with the secretary's approval, as long as the exchanges did not interfere with consolidation. This again was to be a *voluntary* exchange only.

3.   Restricted land could be inherited by tribal members or nontribal heirs, whether Indian or non-Indian.

The mandatory procedures were jettisoned; all transfers were to be of a voluntary nature. Furthermore, there were to be no restrictions placed upon the rights of heirs. Upon the death of an Indian landowner, his title would descend to the heirs and not to the tribe. The IRA did stipulate, however, that wills disposing of restricted Indian land had to be approved by the secretary and that approval would be forthcoming only if the heirs were members of the deceased's tribe. Though the need to modify Collier's thoughts on the mandatory nature of land transfers became apparent during the congressional hearings, the Indian commissioner still suffered two major defeats here. His program to consolidate fragmented Indian parcels was dealt a deadly blow—any voluntary alternative would be impractical. While the IRA made some advances in attempting to keep land in the hands of Indians, they shied away from the problems confronting the Indian Bureau in its attempt to deal with thousands of heirs possessing a minute interest in a piece of inherited land. The bureau would have to continue functioning as a real estate agent in regard to such inheritance problems.

While the land transfer provisions of the Indian Reorganization Act must have been disappointing to Collier, several less important sections of his bill did find a home in the IRA. The secretary, for instance, was given the authority to proclaim new Indian reservations on land acquired under the act.[9] The secretary was also empowered to acquire land, water rights, and surface rights for tribes.[10] These acquisitions could be to add property to an existing reservation or to obtain land for the benefit of landless Indians. This provision was quite important for those reservations that had a "checkerboard" appearance due to white acquisitions of reservation land. It afforded a tribe an opportunity to purchase the white properties and consolidate tribal holdings. The act authorized an appropriation of not more than two million dollars annually to assist in this program. It is also interesting to note that the IRA, unlike the Collier Bill, specifically included the power to acquire water and surface rights. This issue had been raised at several of the Indian congresses, and the final version of the law acceded to these Indian demands.

For a long period of time Indian lands had suffered for want of local or national conservation policies. The Indian Reorganization Act, like the Collier Bill, attempted to take steps to remedy this problem. Under the IRA, the secretary of the interior was charged with the obligation of conserving Indian resources.[11] This responsibility included maintaining sufficient stands of timber, restricting grazing on ranges, and preventing soil erosion. The secretary was also given the power to issue rules and regulations to carry out the spirit of this newly articulated conservation policy. The last section of the IRA relating to Indian lands dealt with the issue of Indian property that was located in the public domain. This land, be it allotment or homestead, was not to be affected by the act unless the property fell within the boundaries of an Indian reservation.[12]

The land sections of the Indian Reorganization Act were a hodgepodge of good and bad. Collier's efforts to establish a basis for economic development through land consolidation and tribal control of property through changes in the heirship rules never reached fruition. These revisions were not just minor policy changes but major undertakings that Collier hoped to effect. He failed. But he still succeeded on a number of important fronts. The Indian Reorganization Act brought about a major change in federal policy by terminating allotment. Surplus land was to be returned to tribal control, trust periods of allotted land were extended indefinitely, money was authorized for land acquisition, new Indian reservations could be proclaimed, and the secretary of the interior was provided with an opportunity to develop a conservation program for reservation lands. Though short of what the Collier Bill had originally envisioned, these changes constituted impressive steps forward.

Miscellaneous Additions

The other modifications and changes that the Collier Bill experienced in becoming a law were plentiful; several important new additions were also appended to the final law. Most of them were a direct result of pressure brought by special-interest groups or dissenting tribes. We have already mentioned the fact that the Arizona mining interests were able to insert a provision in the bill revoking the administration order withdrawing certain Papago lands from mineral entry.[13] This section was hardly designed to please the Papago nation, but it did win the important support of Senator Henry Ashurst of Arizona, who in the absence of such a provision probably would have opposed the measure.

The Sioux Indians were also successful in inserting a provision in the Indian Reorganization Act designed to preserve a special interest. Section 14 permitted the secretary of the interior to continue the controversial "Sioux benefits," which had been bestowed upon them by an act of Congress in 1889, and which Collier had promised in Rapid City would be protected. Another demand that was raised at almost all Indian congresses also found its way into the final act. The law specifically noted that nothing in the act "shall be construed to impair or prejudice any claim or suit of any Indian tribe against the United States."[14] It further stipulated that benefits received under the IRA would not be deducted from any future judgment that an Indian tribe might secure against the government.

In order to accommodate a number of Indian nations that did not wish to participate in certain of the act's provisions, a special section was included to provide for these exclusions. Senator Elmer Thomas of Oklahoma wanted the Indians from his state excluded from six of the act's provisions:

Section 2: Extension of the trust period
Section 4: Restricting the transfer and alienation of land
Section 7: The proclamation of new Indian reservations
Section 16: Tribal organizations for self-government
Section 17: Tribal incorporation for economic purposes
Section 18: Tribal referendum

Section 4 of the act was not to apply to the Klamath Indians of Oregon at their own request. And finally, none of the provisions of the act were to apply outside the confines of the United States. The Indians of Alaska were therefore excluded except with reference to five provisions:

Section 9: Funds to assist in the development of self-government
Section 10: Revolving credit fund
Section 11: Indian education funds
Section 12: Indian preference in employment
Section 16: Tribal organization for self-government

During the congressional hearings, a dispute arose concerning the definition of what constituted an Indian. John Collier and Senator Burton Wheeler wrestled over this issue on several occasions. The Indian Reorganization Act finally resolved the issue in section 19. The term *Indian* was defined to include three classes of persons:

1. All persons of Indian descent who are members of a recognized tribe, whether or not residing on an Indian reservation and regardless of the degree of blood.
2. All persons who are descendants of any such members of recognized tribes residing within an Indian reservation on June 1, 1934, regardless of blood.

3.   Persons of one-half or more Indian blood, whether or not affiliated with a recognized tribe, and whether or not they have ever resided on an Indian reservation.

Collier, who had argued for the one-fourth rather than the one-half Indian-blood criterion, lost this battle to Senator Wheeler who preferred the one-half standard. Eskimos and other aboriginal people living in Alaska were to be considered Indians under the provisions of the act that pertained to Alaska.

The final section of the Indian Reorganization Act that merits our attention describes the manner in which Indian tribes were to indicate their acceptance or rejection of the act. Section 18 of the statute provided that the secretary of the interior, within one year from the date of passage of the act, was to call for a referendum election. The Indians were to be given thirty days notice, during which time they were expected to discuss the provisions of the act. Then they were to vote either to accept or to reject the act by secret ballot. The vote, however, was somewhat different from votes usually required in federal statutes. The IRA would become operative on a reservation unless a majority of the adult Indians, members of the tribe or reservation, voted to *exclude* themselves from the provisions of the act.

This particular provision had been the subject of bitter controversy between Collier and Senator Wheeler. Wheeler championed the notion that the law should require a majority voting in favor of the act before it became operative on any reservation. We can see here a bit of cunning on the part of Collier and the bureau. From his long experience with Indians, the commissioner knew, or should have known, that a majority of the full-blood or traditional people would automatically refuse to participate in any election called by the secretary of the interior. Many traditional people regarded themselves bound by treaty to respect the sovereignty of the United States by refusing to participate in its elections and expected the United States to return their respect by not intruding into their traditional way of doing things. It was a certainty, therefore, that by adding the number of people failing to vote or deliberately boycotting the election, the IRA could be extended over a few more tribes. There is little doubt that Collier and the bureau knew exactly what they were doing in this arrangement. Not even the agreements reached under the General Allotment Act had counted boycotting Indians as voting in favor of the agreement. Collier was clearly determined to see that as many Indians as possible come under the provisions of the law, even if it meant a game of legal sleight-of-hand, and he clearly used his knowledge of Indians to gain a victory over Wheeler without Wheeler even understanding the nature of the conquest.

The idea that Indians could exclude themselves from the application of a federal statute that otherwise would have applied to them made it seem as if the Indians had a veto power over Congress, and the bureau would later cite this provision approvingly as one of its overtures toward Indian self-determination.

Thus the burden for rejection of the law was to rest with the tribe, and disapproval required any opponents to pit themselves against the rather formidable strength that the bureau could muster to gain approval of the law. The tribes had only one chance to vote to accept or reject the law. Once an Indian community had rejected it, the people could not reconsider their decision at a later date. This provision also played directly into the hands of the bureau, since many Indians would be confused about their decision, and pressure could be put on them to accept it because there would not be another chance to gain the benefits the law promised. Section 18 raised the first question among outside observers as to just how much flexibility Indians would be given under the Collier administration to vary from the course he had laid out for them.

The additional provisions that the special-interest groups were able to insert into the Indian Reorganization Act did not materially affect the philosophy that constituted the underpinnings of the original version of the Collier Bill. What is most significant when comparing the original proposal with the final law is the large amount of substance that Collier was able to salvage from his early measure. Many of the suggestions that emanated from the Meriam Report and the Cosmos Club meeting in Washington in early 1934 ultimately found a home in the Indian Reorganization Act. The termination of the old policy of allotment, the acquisition of land for landless Indians, the development of a system of credit for Indian economic development, endowment of tribal governments with greater responsibility and powers of self-government, the preservation of Indian lands under the control of Indian nations—all became legitimized policies with the passage of the IRA.

There were, of course, major disappointments. The transfer of "homerule" powers to tribal governments fell far short of what was desired. The attempt to consolidate fragmented lands into productive economic parcels was lost. No attempt was made to resolve the problems surrounding property inherited by Indian heirs. Perhaps the most important omission from the new law was the absence of a provision creating a Court of Indian Affairs. The existing system of tribal justice, along with the federal attempt to deal with Indian legal problems, left much to be desired. The local tribal court system needed stability and some semblance of form. It did not get it. The creation of a national Court of Indian Affairs would have gone a long way in correcting the neglect and inattention that federal courts extended to Indian issues. The Anglo-American courts seemed both incapable and unwilling to address themselves to these Indian needs.

Unfortunately, the IRA did nothing to remedy this situation. Much of the responsibility for this omission must be laid at the feet of John Collier. The Indian commissioner came to the conclusion very early in the congressional hearings that the Court of Indian Affairs was not a salable product. It thus became the sacrificial lamb. The price paid for passage of other major parts of the Collier Bill was high. The jettison of the Court of Indian Affairs, along with other compromises, served a noble cause. One cannot help but wonder, however, how devoted Collier was to this particular provision. Certainly the Court of Indian Affairs would have made it possible to focus all litigation dealing with Indian matters in one court, which would have expertise in such topics. The court, however, was not central to either self-government or economic development. It was a wholly superfluous institution that would have become an intrusion on the general organization of the federal court system.

The Cosmos conference had dealt briefly with Indian claims, but Margold and Collier had drawn up draft proposals for an Indian Claims Commission several times while they were working for the American Indian Defense Association. Collier may very well have seen in this proposal a means of settling some of the claims through equitable and legal theories consonant with his philosophical preambles that articulated the new congressional Indian policy. He was certainly aware of the deep Indian feeling that the Court of Claims was not handling their complaints with the measure of justice they believed they deserved. If the claims for land, education, and other services were made the subject of this court, for example, the spirit of the treaties could certainly be revived. Whatever the reasoning, Collier's submission on this point indicated a wise political move. He had to take what he could reasonably get at that time.

Bringing
the Law to Life

Although statutes are significant statements of congressional policy, they rarely provide a philosophical framework within which administrative decisions can be made. Administrators, when they are confused about the interpretation of a statute, have a variety of remedies they can take. They can go back to Congress for additional instruction, a course that is rarely used because it can make the administrator look incompetent, even though his directions from Congress are less than coherent. An administrator can also promulgate a complex set of rules and regulations for the administration of the act, publish these instructions in the *Congressional Record* or *Federal Register*, wait for some response and reaction, and then adjust his course accordingly. He can also wait for a new Congress and then propose amendments to the statute that he believes will clarify the meaning of obscure phrases, hoping that new members of the committee before which he will appear will tip the balance in favor of his position. Or he can have the solicitor of his department issue an opinion concerning the manner in which the statute is to be interpreted. Unless there is a violent objection, this opinion will be recognized as a legal interpretation of the law until the Supreme Court or the Congress speaks to the contrary.

Today most federal statutes contain an elastic clause that instructs the executive agencies to make such rules and regulations as may be necessary to carry out the intent of Congress as expressed in the statute. On the whole this catchall phrase really surrenders necessary legislative powers to the executive branch and enables the federal bureaucracy to sort out the various provisions of the statute to its best advantage. If the executive agency is far afield of the original congressional intent in administering the law, complaints will usually arrive at the committee chairman's desk, and he will call for oversight hearings and investigate why the federal agency is administering the law in the manner it is. Amendments will usually be offered to the original bill to make certain that the federal agency follows the wishes and intent of Congress. Since many federal statutes are only authorizations of agency activities for a short period of years, oversight hearings enable Congress to keep a closer monitoring eye on what the federal agencies are doing.

There is a vast difference between what a statute *means* and how it is *interpreted* in a programmatic sense. Determining what a statute means is often the task of the solicitor, who makes his best judgment as to what the congressional intent might have been in passing the statute. Translating the statute in terms of program directives is another entirely different process. While it also involves grappling with the language of the statute, there is usually considerably more flexibility in dealing with the statute. Unlike modern legislation, the Indian Reorganization Act had no elastic clause that directed the secretary of the interior to promulgate rules and regulations spelling out how the act was to be administered. Therefore Collier himself had immense latitude in fleshing out the IRA, and he made the most of his opportunity. Undaunted by the fierce and tenacious bureaucratic and legislative opposition he met, Collier rose to the occasion in a magnificent and sophisticated performance as an administrative virtuoso, demonstrating a talent that no one had suspected he possessed.

Collier had originally tried to fix his ideological program permanently by inserting, in section 1 of the self-government and land titles, a prolonged expression of philosophical principles he hoped Congress would endorse. His fear was that administrative actions by one commissioner might be overturned by later occupants of that office. Changing a clear statement of policy made by a previous Congress would prove a much more difficult task, hence the extensive preambles that spelled out the theoretical base he saw beneath the Indian Reorganization Act. Senator Wheeler objected violently to this effort to declare the mind of Congress, and the offending language was removed from the final version of the bill.

Without the policy statement the new statute would have to be interpreted on the basis of statements made during the hearings, and the executive branch would have to tread cautiously in administering the statute. The final version of the Indian Reorganization Act had only one clear policy statement of any significance. In the first section it declared "that hereafter no land of any Indian reservation, created or set apart by treaty or agreement with the Indians, Act of Congress, executive order, purchase, or otherwise, shall be allotted in severalty to any Indian."[1] This cryptic prohibition referred to the allotment experiment, of course, but it did not admit the great damage that the policy had already done to Indian communities. Nor did the prohibition disavow assimilation as a federal goal for Indians. It only made one possible avenue of assimilation a historical curiosity.

The final version of the IRA, with its nineteen different and basically unconnected sections, granted the secretary of the interior the discretionary power to take the necessary steps to accomplish the goals of each section. But there was no general directive under which the bureau could formulate an attitude toward the Indians and against which it could judge its accomplishments—or which others could use to evaluate it. Sections 16 and 17, which dealt with tribal governments, were particularly vague in wording. Collier had originally spelled out the new powers the tribes would be authorized to exercise once they had adopted a constitution and bylaws, granting the new corporations a wide variety of specific municipal powers depending upon their ability to negotiate with the secretary of the interior to assume them. He also closed the door on traditional Indians by including language to the effect that the new corporation would replace as successor any existing native political organization.

Collier had attempted to force Wheeler's hand on the troublesome matter of tribal corporations while the Senate hearings were still in progress. On May 15, 1934, the acting solicitor gave an opinion on the pending legislative proposal, a move that was virtually without precedent in legislative history. *Indian Corporations—Federal Charters* described the bill as "in effect, a general incorporation law for a defined class of Federal corporations, to wit, incorporated Indian tribes or communities." The opinion cited various previous proposals to incorporate tribes and suggested that these bills had failed because "Congress could not devote sufficient time to working out the administrative details of the 'legislative charters.'" Therefore, the opinion concluded, "the present Wheeler-Howard Bill puts the responsibility for working out these details upon the Secretary of the Interior and the Indians seeking the charter."[2]

The Senate Indian Committee's response was predictable. Collier got none of the language he desired dealing with the status of the newly organized Indian tribal corporations. Instead the final version of the bill contained the language of congressional caution: In addition to "all powers vested in any Indian tribe or tribal council by existing law, the constitution adopted by said tribe shall also vest in such tribe or its tribal council the following rights and powers." The section then went on to spell out three basic powers that the Congress intended the new organizations to have: *to employ legal counsel, to prevent the sale of tribal lands and assets without the consent of the tribe,* and *to negotiate with other governments.* If these three powers were all that Congress intended new corporations to have, they could hardly expect the Indians to make much progress. It was obvious that no one in Congress had thought much about what powers the tribes might have existing in law. So the phrase was used simply to distinguish (but not define) the vague area in which then-existing tribal governments might be active and to add to those powers some basic authority that would allow the tribes to contract with the bureau and with state and local governments. An echo of the old Klamath proposal is seen here, since the Klamaths had informed Congress that their corporation, as proposed, would simply contract with state agencies for services.

Section 17, the only part of the final bill that described the content of the tribal charters to be issued under the act, spoke primarily of the economic functions of the new organization:

> Such charter may convey to the incorporated tribe the power to purchase, take by gift, or bequest, or otherwise, own, hold, manage, operate, and dispose of property of every description, real and personal, including the power to purchase restricted Indian lands and to issue in exchange therefor interests in corporate property, and such further powers as may be incidental to the conduct of corporate business, not inconsistent with the law.

This section quite clearly contemplates that tribal corporations would be engaged primarily in the business of consolidating its land base and developing its economic resources. No other mention is made of corporate enterprises, and no mention whatsoever is made of any political powers that tribes would have, apart, of course, from the vague wording regarding "powers under existing laws."

After the passage of the act, when the bureau began to get the tribes moving toward organization and actual constitutional powers were being discussed with tribal delegations, a number of unanticipated questions began to arise. Was the act limited to those tribes that had a historical relationship to the federal government? What about families living on government lands who wanted to organize themselves into a separate community? Could bands of a tribe organize together? What was the status of reservations that had two or more tribes living on them? Could the secretary purchase lands for landless Indians and then allow them to organize as a tribal corporation on them? What were the powers of a tribe as distinguished from the powers vested by existing law? When the cumulative impact of these questions became apparent, the bureau recognized that the Indian Reorganization Act had become their greatest problem, not the Indians. How was one to write a constitution and bylaws for a tribe with no clear indication what powers and activities the corporation had or could exercise?

By late fall of 1934 there was no question that something was needed to clarify the dreadful situation that existed in administering the statute. It was Collier's golden opportunity to bring back to life the original set of powers he had described in his legislative proposal. Collier and Nathan Margold then began to devise a solicitor's opinion that would spell out the powers of Indian tribes in no uncertain terms. Freed from the necessity to convince Congress, and responsible primarily to Harold Ickes, who had given them a relatively free rein in developing the Indian programs, Collier and Margold came up with a masterpiece of reasoning and cleverly finessed Congress with an exhaustive tract that purported to interpret the vague phraseology of the Wheeler-Howard Act—"in addition to all powers vested in any Indian tribe or tribal council by existing law."

"Powers of Indian Tribes" was issued on October 25, 1934, and was some thirty-two pages in length, hardly a casual commentary on the wording of the statute. The opinion adopted the theory that "those powers which are lawfully vested in an Indian tribe are not, in general, delegated powers granted by express acts of Congress, but rather inherent powers of a limited sovereignty which has never been extinguished."[3] The theory of tribal political powers was that Indian tribes had at one time been fully sovereign and that in embracing a relationship with the United States they had, from time to time, allowed some of those powers to be changed, modified, or surrendered. They had, however, a vast reservoir of inherent powers, which any political entity had, and they could exercise these powers in addition to the three new powers given to them by Congress in the Wheeler-Howard Act.

The reasoning of the opinion, therefore, simply reversed the first draft of Collier's original proposal in that it assumed that tribes already had certain powers and needed only to surrender those powers, or at least some of them, to the new tribal corporation that the IRA authorized. Among the "inherent" sovereign powers that Margold was able to identify were the right to adopt a form of government; to create various offices and prescribe their duties; to prescribe the procedures and forms through which the will of the tribe was to be expressed; to define conditions of membership; to provide or withhold suffrage; to regulate domestic relations; to prescribe rules of inheritance; to levy fees, dues, and taxes; to remove or exclude nonmembers; to regulate the use of property; to administer justice; and to describe the duties of federal employees insofar as such powers were delegated by the Interior Department.

Some of these powers were undoubtedly of historical origin, and some of these powers can be found in treaty provisions or negotiations. Other powers were simply Margold's projections of rights he believed accrued to the tribes once their basic sovereignty had been established. The only limitation on this inherent sovereignty, according to the opinion, was the previous action of Congress insofar as it had limited tribal sovereignty. Since Congress had never presumed that tribes had this astounding set of powers, it was unlikely that they would have thought to limit them specifically. Margold's opinion worked steadily in one direction: buttressing the political powers of the tribe that had not been previously acknowledged by any organ, agency, or branch of the federal government.

Of all the areas of tribal powers that Margold described, none was so extensively covered as the power of an Indian tribe to administer justice. "If an Indian tribe has the power to regulate the marriage relationship of its members," he wrote, "it necessarily has power to adjudicate, through tribunals established by itself, controversies involving such relationships. So, too, with other fields of local government in which our analysis has shown that tribal authority endures. In all these fields the judicial powers of the tribe are coextensive with its legislative or executive powers."[4] This part of the opinion completely reversed the basic posture of the Bureau of Indian Affairs on the subject of tribal courts. Less than a decade before, the bureau had timidly introduced a measure to make the courts of Indian offenses a part of the federal judicial system, thereby giving them some kind of status as judicial forums. Now Margold was creating a tribal court system that existed, or could exist, in isolation apart from the federal courts and the Bureau of Indian Affairs. This court system derived its authority from the enduring sovereign powers of the tribe, not from a congressional delegation of power or from a decision of a federal court.

The scope of this revolutionary opinion cannot be underestimated. Less than a year before, Collier had come to Congress with a forty-page legislative proposal in which he had wanted to vest these same powers in federal municipal corporations that would be authorized by Congress. Section 4 enumerated a list of powers that these new corporations could exercise, and when the list of Margold's "inherent powers" is compared with section 4 of the bill Collier submitted to Congress, it is apparent that in the opinion, Collier had finessed Congress and simply declared that the powers that Congress would not grant were inherent from the very beginning. Collier had pulled an administrative coup of the first magnitude. If tribes already had these powers, why did Collier need to get them authorized as part of the activities his federal municipal corporations would be able to perform?

The shift in emphasis must be understood as precisely as possible. Had Collier's original legislative package been approved without amendment, tribes would have been able to exercise these same powers, except that they would have been *delegated* powers, and delegated by Congress in an experiment in social engineering. A future Congress might have radically changed the powers, or it might have canceled them altogether. With the opinion as the basis of authority, tribal governments could exercise powers of self-government, but these powers were regarded as *inherent* powers, powers that could only be surrendered on the initiative of the tribe or changed, but not abolished, by the Congress. Delegated powers would have made tribal government a part of the federal government; inherent powers preserved an area of political independence for the tribes across which the United States could not venture. Modern tribal sovereignty thus begins with this opinion, although it would be another generation before Indian tribes would understand the difference and begin to talk in the proper terms about their status.

In order to further gauge the scope of Collier and Margold's administrative revolution, we must look at the concluding sentence of the solicitor's opinion. With the exception of specific qualifications imposed on any particular tribe by its treaties, special statutes, or unique historical relationship with the United States previous to the Indian Reorganization Act, Margold wrote that "the conclusions advanced are intended to apply to all Indian tribes *recognized now or hereafter* by the legislative or the executive branch of the Federal Government."[5] This broad language meant that if and when the federal government recognized an Indian group as a distinct entity having the necessary political characteristics, that Indian group acquired, or the federal government recognized that it had always possessed, all the attributes of a sovereign political power *whether the group had previously exercised those powers or not.*

The New Dealers loved this idea, and it certainly made administration easier to have a clear guideline when writing tribal constitutions and bylaws, but they soon had to contend with its implications. Under the provisions of the IRA the secretary of the interior could purchase lands for landless Indians, gather together families and groups of Indians who had not previously been associated with each other, move them onto these lands, and then call an election and have them adopt a constitution and bylaws. Thereafter, if they approved their organic governing documents, they acquired a vested set of political powers that theoretically originated in the mists of history before the coming of the white man. Here indeed was the most revolutionary interpretation of federal law ever attempted—and it was accepted by Congress with nary a murmur.

As the bureau began to organize groups of Indians, it had to face the question whether or not it was possible to distinguish between tribes who had preserved their aboriginal sovereignty and those who had become related to the federal government through the administrative actions of the Interior Department during or prior to the IRA. There were a great variety of situations in which the bureau had to determine the status of groups of Indians. For example, in 1938 the solicitor was asked to render his opinion on the powers that the Lower Sioux and Prairie Island Sioux communities in Minnesota possessed. These two groups were not historically independent tribes or bands, but did live in reserved lands. They constituted the remnants of Sioux groups who were moved or forced from the state after the conflict of 1862. In the opinion of April 15, 1938, the solicitor stated that "the group may not have such of those powers as rest upon the sovereign capacity of the tribe but may have those powers which are incidental to its ownership of property and its carrying on of business, and those which may be delegated by the Secretary of the Interior."[6] The bureau did not publicize this substantial difference in tribal powers, however, but simply advised the assistant commissioner of Indian affairs that articulation of these powers should not appear in the tribal constitution then being considered for ratification. Consequently, as far as either Congress or Indians in general knew, the two groups did acquire the same powers as other tribes, but chose not to include them in their constitutions.

A more difficult question, and one that has not been easily resolved even today, concerned the status of a reservation government where there were two tribes inhabiting the same reservation but having different ethnological roots. A question arose concerning the proper title in which land purchased for the Indians of the Fort Belknap Reservation in Montana should be held. An opinion of March 20, 1936, found that "The Fort Belknap Indians have in fact organized as a single tribe and adopted the name 'Fort Belknap Indian Community.' Title to any land acquired for this tribe should be vested in 'The United States of America in trust for the Fort Belknap Indian Community.' "[7] Presumably the aboriginal sovereign powers of each tribe were contributed to the new political entity, and it enjoyed all the status that its two predecessor entities had possessed. This particular reservation is important, because a later federal court decision had to deal specifically with this question.

The bureau often worked backward in determining tribal existence and vesting it with sovereign powers. On August 31, 1936, the solicitor rendered an opinion regarding the purchase of lands for the Mississippi Choctaws. After reciting their history, which included the Dancing Rabbit Creek Treaty of 1830 and the allotment of Oklahoma Choctaw lands in the first decade of this century, Nathan Margold advised the secretary of the interior to take the titles to the lands being purchased as follows:

> The United States in trust for such Choctaw Indians of one-half or more Indian blood, resident in Mississippi, as shall be designated by the Secretary of the Interior, until such time as the Choctaw Indians of Mississippi shall be organized as an Indian tribe pursuant to the act of June 18, 1934 [48 Stat. 984], and then in trust for such organized tribe.[8]

It is difficult to determine the chicken and the egg in this situation. Was the secretary purchasing lands knowing that he would be able to find Choctaws in the neighborhood? Or did the Choctaws appear when the land had been purchased for them, knowing that they could organize as a tribe? The question here is not whether these people were Indian but whether or not the secretary was in fact creating a formally recognized tribe from a group of Indians who had formerly chosen to live as individuals under state laws without any federal relationship.

Compare the Mississippi Choctaw land purchase opinion with the opinion rendered with regard to the Nahma and Beaver Island Indians in Michigan issued on May 1, 1937. These groups had essentially the same history as did the Mississippi Choctaws. They had once constituted bands of the Chippewa Indians, and in fact tracts of land had been set aside for them under the treaty of 1855. But that treaty provided that the tribal organization be dissolved, each band thereafter being on its own to deal with the government. Although there was clear evidence that the political organization of the separate bands continued until the present, the solicitor insisted that the Chippewa were simply individual citizens and not groups that were eligible for organization under the IRA. He suggested that the Interior Department determine which Indians were one-half Indian blood, purchase lands for them, and then help them organize. Since even tribal groups recently organized under the IRA were presumed to have the power to determine their own membership, this procedure turned the usual manner of securing recognition on its head.

The problem of determining which Indians were in fact eligible for the benefits of the IRA was a continuing dilemma for the bureau because of the extreme position taken in the original opinion dealing with the powers of tribes. The memorandum opinion of March 6, 1937, concluded that the Winnebagos of Wisconsin could organize themselves as a tribe even though they consisted of individuals who had fled from the Winnebago reservation in Nebraska and took public-domain allotments under the act of March 3, 1875.[9] The opinion suggested that they could obtain all the benefits of the act except organization and would have to have a reservation in order to become eligible for that provision. The same question arose in 1947, and the opinion rendered on December 7 of that year found that the Nooksacks of Washington State, who had also taken public-domain allotments under the same statute, could not receive the benefits of the IRA because they lacked a reservation. The problem was that the Nooksacks had already enjoyed the benefits of the IRA before the bureau ruled that they were not eligible for it, receiving education, health, and revolving loan funds.

We have already touched on another major problem that the solicitor's opinions attempted to resolve—the question of the conduct of the elections to ratify a constitution and bylaws or charter. Indians never forgave either Collier or Margold for their blatant attempt to stack the deck in favor of ratification by assuming nonvoters were approvals. The opinion also attempted to resolve other thorny questions regarding eligibility, again using language to the benefit of the Collier program in deciding that those eligible would be "those Indians who reside on the reservation and at the same time have some legal interest in the affairs of the reservation."[10] This narrow construction was given to the election to vote for or against the application of the act. When it came to the election to ratify the constitution of the tribe, however, Margold changed the qualifications, finding that

> It is clear that the act contemplates two distinct and alternative types of tribal organization. In the first place, it authorizes the members of a tribe (or of a group of tribes located upon the same reservation) to organize as a tribe without regard to any requirements of residence. In the second place, this section authorizes the residents of a single reservation [who

may be considered a tribe for purposes of this act, under section 19] to organize without regard to past tribal affiliations.

So, Margold concluded, "in the former situation, tribal affiliation is essential, and residence is immaterial in the determination of voting rights. In the latter situation, residence is a necessary condition of the right to vote, and tribal affiliation is not necessary."[11] It is not difficult to see that here we are talking about two distinct groups of Indians. To refuse the act, one needed to be a resident and have a legal interest in the reservation—both. But to vote on the adoption of the constitution, one needed to be either a resident or a member of the tribe; suddenly the legal interest was not important.

Margold also considered how to determine which Indians belonged to the tribe. The Indian Service had assumed that tribal membership could be determined from the official rolls of the tribe. This assumption would seem to be proper and common sense. Margold argued, however, that

in the absence of any statutory provision to the contrary, the descendants of enrolled members of a tribe who are not themselves enrolled but who are recognized as members of the tribe, in accordance with tribal custom and usage, have the right to vote on the adoption of a tribal constitution. Similarly, recognized members of the tribe who were, through accident or mistake, omitted from the tribal rolls have the same right to *vote* (a right which does not carry with it any claims to tribal property) as other members.[12]

The interpretation of tribal membership represents a pernicious effort by Collier and Margold to ensure the reception of the IRA by the Indians. At the Rapid City congress the Sioux had bitterly complained of Collier's plans to organize a government for the reservations and turn the institution over to those Indians who had already sold their lands and were no longer considered members of the tribe. Collier reassured the full-bloods that he would never entertain such a plan. In this particular part of the solicitor's opinion the Interior Department broke this solemn pledge and opened tribal government to those Indians who had little to recommend themselves except an Indian ancestor, and sometimes a rather dubious Indian ancestor at that. Today when popular writers describe the Indian Reorganization Act as a government plot to disenfranchise the full-blood Indians, they are referring to this particular ruling and the impact it had on the constituency of the tribal governments.

In essence Collier and Margold made the Indian Reorganization

Act function in the following manner: A majority of Indians who lived on the reservation and owned property—and these people were primarily full-bloods—had to come in and vote against the application of the Wheeler-Howard Act to their reservation. If they did not have a clear majority of all eligible voters, they had the act extended over them. Once the reservation was declared to be under the IRA then a majority of the people in the vicinity who could trace their ancestry back to a member of the tribe could adopt a constitution. They would naturally also be eligible to vote for the officers of the new tribal government, thereby installing themselves in office, sometimes permanently. In insisting on this interpretation of the IRA Collier placed the reservations in the hands of Indian politicians, whose only loyalty was to their own political careers. Margold then interpreted the provision for the adoption of a charter to include as eligible voters only those Indians who were resident upon the reservation, thereby again narrowing the qualifications for voting to approve the charter.

The solicitor's opinion did contain one interpretation that, unfortunately, not many Indians knew about or understood. Under the sixteenth section of the act it appeared that a group of Indians could organize without the consent of a majority of the adult Indians living on the reservation if they occupied a definite geographical area and desired to have an organization to deal specifically with their own property. Theoretically this provision could have provided a means for fullbloods to protect themselves from the possiblility of a reservation-wide tribal government being imposed upon them. Margold ruled that smaller groups, separate tribes, or bands did have this right of organization under the act, and if organized, they were entitled also to receive a charter. This part of the ruling was not highly publicized, however, and almost all Indians thought that they had to accept a tribal government that represented the whole reservation. Collier might have avoided a considerable amount of the difficulty he experienced on the Navajo reservation, for example, had he publicized this interpretation more. He would, however, have seen widespread use of the provision in the northern plains, where the IRA was extended over most of the reservations, and he would have found the natural contentiousness of Indians in the political arena expressing itself by frequent use of this power, thus fragmenting any semblance of unified reservation government.

When it appeared, by the beginning of 1935, that some reservations were not even achieving a 30-percent turnout in ratification elections, Collier knew he needed another interpretation of elections where the required number of voters failed to cast ballots. Again Margold came to Collier's rescue and ruled, on February 5, that if the required number of Indians did not vote, the act nevertheless applied to the reservation. Congress finally became outraged at the bureau's tactics and on June 18, 1935, it amended section 16 to provide that a majority of Indians *voting* could accept or reject the application of the act. In a solicitor's opinion dated September 13, 1935, Margold replied that if the required 30 percent did not vote in the election, the secretary could hold another election at his option regardless of the outcome of the first vote. This new interpretation was a two-edged sword, which could be used to extend the act over a reservation or force another election with the hopes of doing so.

Two solicitor's opinions were rendered on the subject of tribal courts—one on February 28, 1935, entitled *Secretary's Power to Regulate Conduct of Indians,* which dealt with the status of the old courts of Indian offenses, and one on April 27, 1939, entitled *Law and Order—Dual Sovereignty—Powers of Indian Tribes and U.S.,* which dealt with jurisdictional questions involving the new courts established by tribes under the IRA. In the first opinion Margold reviewed the establishment of the courts of Indian offenses and noted that Indian offenses were generally those cultural practices that appeared to disrupt the smooth functioning of the reservation. Twice, in 1911 and 1926, the department had made an effort to update and standardize the regulations that might be enforced in these courts, but both these efforts failed. "Because this revision and standardization of the law and order regulations never occurred," the opinion noted, "it is almost impossible to tell exactly what at present is the body of instructions under which the superintendents, Indian police and judges are operating and it is difficult, therefore, to ascertain precisely the legality of their actions."[13]

The opinion found legal authority for the courts of Indian offenses in two distinct but contradictory sources. The first source was the secretary's general power to regulate the conduct of Indians derived from his authority to create administrative courts, an argument that seemed circular at best. Administrative courts are not designed to provide municipal law for American communities. If anything, they are specialized avenues of appeal for individuals to use against rulings made by government officials that they consider detrimental to their interests or constitutional rights. There were, further, no existing Interior regulations that could have been used to justify the cultural oppression that courts of Indian offenses inflicted upon traditional Indians—other than the naked assertion of power that is always a distasteful claim in a democracy.

The second source Margold discovered and described was the

"manifestations of the inherent power of the tribes to govern their own members."[14] As Margold related the early history of the reservations,

> as tribal activities were weakened by the other policies of the Federal Government, it became necessary for the Federal Government to stimulate tribal judicial action by the appointment of tribal dignitaries as judges where no tribal courts existed any longer. It was a recognition by the Interior Department, and by Congress, that Indian offenses, perhaps more than any other Indian problem, must be handled by the Indian tribes but that such was no longer possible without the active cooperation of the Indian Office.[15]

When this opinion is measured against the historical facts involving Indian self-government, it is sadly lacking and is mostly a fictional justification for vesting tribal courts with powers they had neither possessed nor exercised. The only tribes to have well-developed courts were the Five Civilized Tribes of Oklahoma, and their court system was abolished in the preliminary move by Congress to prepare them for allotment and the dissolution of their governments. The *Crow Dog* case also illustrated how eager the government had been to intervene in instances where traditional customs had already resolved the dispute. Of all Frederic Kirgis's opinions, this one seemed the least defensible historically and one of the most important administratively.

The other opinion relating to tribal courts, issued by Frederic Kirgis as acting solicitor, dealt with four basic issues, two involving the jurisidiction of tribal courts and two covering the power of an Indian police officer to make arrests on unrestricted lands inside a reservation and outside the boundary of a reservation. Kirgis framed the two tribal court questions in terms of the authority by which an Indian court acts. The courts of Indian offenses were charitably described as vehicles for the education and civilization of Indians, an administrative convenience when considered from the government's viewpoint, rather than a judicial forum. Kirgis skirted the issue of the historical treatment of tribal judicial forms again and concluded that "the analysis of Federal laws applicable to the situation under consideration indicates that the right of Indian tribal authorities to punish errant members of the tribe for offenses, no matter where committed, has not only never been denied but has been positively recognized."[16] Kirgis then cited the Act of June 30, 1834,[17] which organized the Department (later Bureau) of Indian Affairs, as his authority for making this statement. That act certainly deals with some aspects of jurisdiction, but it cannot possibly be cited for the proposition that Indian tribal courts or traditional ways of resolving disputes could be enforced everywhere by the tribal authorities.

Why, we may well ask, did the Solicitor's Office go to such lengths to establish a historical precedent for some of the powers it wished tribal courts to exercise? Here the reality of Indian political problems is informative. A number of tribes had rejected the IRA but wanted self-government anyway. They organized themselves and adopted a constitution and bylaws and submitted these documents to the secretary of the interior for approval. Since Collier's basic philosophical position was that of encouraging self-government, he could hardly turn these tribes away simply because they had rejected his version of how Indian communities should perceive themselves. So constitutions were approved and in some of these constitutions were provisions for tribal courts, in line, of course, with the theories articulated in Margold's opinion, *Law and Order—Dual Sovereignty—Powers of Indian Tribes and U.S.* (1939).

The bureau had to locate some ground for authorizing tribal courts for those tribes who rejected the IRA but established themselves as self-governing entities. The old courts of Indian offenses, whatever Kirgis might say of them, and no matter how charitably people might now describe their activities, were still perceived by the rank and file of reservation people as the bureau's courts. Hence there had to be an outside authority whereby the bureau could justify the creation of tribal courts as a natural part of the Indian revival. Actually, when we begin to look at the real shift in emphasis away from the specific wording of the IRA to the accommodations Collier made to tribes that rejected his overtures, we discover that he located an external authority for doing what he wanted to do—either in the tribe's inherent sovereignty or in some obscure power of administrative remedy that the secretary of the interior possessed. One can conclude, finally, that Collier left the IRA and simply began to do what he wished.

With rare exceptions, Collier, with the assistance of Margold and other members of the Interior legal staff, put considerable flesh on the resurrected idea of tribal sovereignty. They were not foolish enough to broadcast the idea too widely, however, and they rarely spoke of anything resembling sovereignty—it would have alerted the Indian committees of Congress and created a political fight they would undoubtedly have lost. Rather, they spoke always of "inherent powers" of a tribe, so that in reading the opinions of the period, one is struck by the fact that a large and unexplored reservoir of powers existed somewhere beyond the reach of mortals that readily provided whatever was needed to authorize a course of action.

Collier was safe in his position and secure from any real congressional interference as long as he did not articulate what he was doing in such a manner as to alert the Congress of the vast philosophical changes he was creating. Fortunately two things worked together to direct people's attentions away from his administrative revolution until it was a *fait accompli.* Tensions in Europe attracted the attention of Burton K. Wheeler and other of the western senators, and they paid little attention to Indian matters after the preliminary hearings authorizing the IRA. Appropriations committees before which Collier appeared were concerned only with his expenditures and his efforts to improve the economic situation of the Indians by helping them become more self-sufficient. Since the most promising aspect of the Collier years was the rapid increase in Indian cooperatives and economic development projects, no one bothered to check the shift in political philosophy that was occurring.

The second thing that assisted Collier, oddly, was the personal abuse he suffered: It provided a badly needed stalking horse to shelter Collier's more ambitious projects and programs. Indians might demand hearings on Collier's programs, but they would almost always discredit themselves by accusing him of being a socialist or communist, using the flimsiest of evidence to substantiate their claims. Churches and other groups that attacked Collier did so on the basis of old and outmoded ideas, so that they looked ridiculous to the members of Congress when they complained about what Collier was doing. Since few people could understand the difference between inherent and delegated powers, and no one really cared to understand that distinction, the substance of Collier's revolution went unchallenged.

Traditional Indians understood what Collier was doing for the most part, but they were not a united force by any means. Each tribe had its little group of chronic critics who were not in favor of any changes, and traditionals frequently aligned themselves with these people when they wished to criticize the tribal governments that Collier had helped to establish. Some tribes made great efforts to incorporate old traditions, such as the chiefs, in their constitutions. The bureau allowed the tribes to include the chiefs on their councils because they recognized the fact, even if the Indians themselves did not, that the chiefs were largely an honorary society, the people no longer clinging to them as they had during the early reservation days. Hence allowing some flexibility in the form of the constitutions tribes could have was a small price to pay for the peace it seemed to guarantee on some reservations.

An observer of the Collier years might well have asked whether or not this fundamental shift in emphasis was sufficient to allow Indians to recapture the essence of their communal life. Collier certainly thought he was accomplishing that end and saw the corporation and cooperative as simply modern versions of the old tribal consensus he admired. The generation of Indians who adopted the IRA and attempted to work within its confines were not the traditional Indians who had intimate knowledge of their own past and the social customs that had bound them together. Generally these Indians of the New Deal were familiar enough with the modern world to realize that they had to adopt new organizations and ways if they were to preserve anything of the reservation life they had known. One might describe these Indians as quasi-traditional. They remembered the tranquillity of their childhood and wanted to preserve the social customs of the people. But they were ready to experiment with new ways of doing things, believing they could do as well or even better than the government had done in managing their own resources. Hence the revolution that Collier had wrought, when it reached the reservations, manifested itself in new economic activities, not political sophistication.

The Collier years, we must remember, were the years of Depression. America was in great economic distress, and Indians suffered great hardships. The demand in the Roosevelt administration was for innovation, with the hope that some program could be found that would turn the country's economic fortunes around. Hence Collier was given great latitude in his experiments. That he was clever enough to build a theoretical foundation under the practical changes he was making testifies to the genius of the man. But each power that tribal councils received during the Collier years was subject to the superior power of approval of the secretary of the interior, exercised, of course, by the commissioner of Indian affairs. Self-government was a process of community control, but only in the sense that communities followed the basic ideological guidelines the bureau established. It would take another generation before Indians realized the difference between self-government and the freedom of nationality for which they deeply yearned.

Ratification
and Its Aftermath

When the Collier Bill had become law, many casual observers probably thought the books were now closed. In fact the enactment of the Indian Reorganization Act was only the beginning of the struggle for self-government. Congress had passed a law, but it still needed to be ratified by the Indians and implemented by the bureau before it could affect life on the reservation. The forces of opposition were still ready to meet the Collier administration in battle. If the New Deal administrators in the Indian Bureau were not aware of the resolve of this opposition when the IRA was passed, they would soon learn of it.

Ratification was Collier's first priority. Section 18 of the act provided that the secretary of the interior, within one year after passage, had to call a special election on each reservation to afford the tribes an opportunity to accept or reject the act. As we've noted, the IRA was to be considered adopted unless a majority of the adult Indians voted against its application, the vote being structured so that the majority of Indians had to vote *against* its application, placing the burden of action on those Indian factions that opposed the law's application. Collier's work was further lightened with the Solicitor's Office additional—and controversial—opinion in 1934 that all eligible voters who failed to vote would be counted as being in favor of adoption.[1] For seventeen tribes, comprising a total population of 5,334, this ruling reversed an otherwise negative vote.[2] That is, in each instance the actual vote cast indicated that the majority of those Indians who participated in the election had opted to reject the act, but when the votes of the Indians who did not participate were added in favor of adoption, the act was construed as having been accepted. On the Santa Ysabel Reservation in California, for instance, 43 Indians voted against the Indian Reorganization Act and only 9 voted for it. Still, the Santa Ysabel tribe came under the act because the 62 eligible tribal members who did not vote were counted as being in favor of adoption. Hence, the final tabulation was viewed as 71 in favor of adoption, 43 opposed.[3]

One troublesome element in the ratification process was the requirement that elections be held within one year of the date of passage. Having been told that the Indian Reorganization Act was a momumental turning point in their lives, Indians were hard pressed to understand why an issue of such magnitude had to be decided with such haste. The impracticality of the one-year requirement soon became apparent, and in 1935 Collier was able to get Congress to amend the IRA, extending the time period for holding elections for an additional year.[4] Incidentally, this same amendment also authorized the bureau to count only the votes of those tribal members who actually participated in the election, thus finally neutralizing Collier's attempt at a legal hedge.

In conducting the ratification elections, Collier had to rely heavily upon the agency superintendents, who acted as his pipeline of information to the various reservations. And while the bureau was supposed to be neutral in its position, there is little doubt that it subtly campaigned in favor of the bill whenever possible. Some of the agency superintendents, however, remained proassimilation and were not in sympathy with the new law. Collier therefore had to be careful during the early phase of ratification to select tribes that he knew would be supportive of the new law. By holding the elections on reservations that would vote in favor of the Indian Reorganization Act, he hoped to develop a "bandwagon" strategy. If they heard that a number of large reservations had decided to come under the act, other tribes might follow suit.

For the most part, Collier's strategy was successful. Ultimately 181 tribes, with a population of 129,750 Indians, voted to accept the Indian Reorganization Act. Seventy-seven tribes, with a population of 86,365, rejected the act.[5] But there were major disappointments. The Klamath Indians, a relatively large tribe, voted against adoption. So did the Crow Indians in Montana. The most significant rejection, however, came from the Navajos. Almost 98 percent of the eligible Navajos participated in the election. The tribe rejected the act by 419 votes; 8,214 members against, 7,795 in favor, a bitter defeat for Collier.[6] He had enlisted the assistance of a number of organizations to convince the Navajos that adoption would be to their benefit, but to no avail. Navajos living in the western part of the reservation supported the measure, but the hostility that had grown up in the northern and eastern regions over the stock reduction program, as well as pressure from the Christian missionaries and white businessmen, was too much to overcome.[7]

While the ratification elections were being conducted throughout 1934–35, the Indian Bureau was beginning to address itself to the problem of policy implementation. Once a statute is passed, a program must be initiated to put that policy into effect. In confronting this task, Collier brought into the bureau a number of anthropologists to assist in the planning and coordinating of the new IRA programs. Ultimately, an Applied Anthropology Staff was established, headed by H. Scudder Mekeel, a nationally prominent scholar, formerly of Harvard University.[8] This group of Indian experts not only conducted "social" surveys of reservations but functioned in an advisory capacity in the drafting of tribal constitutions. This drafting itself was done by the attorneys within the Department of the Interior. A model tribal constitution was drafted to assist tribes, and teams of lawyers were dispatched to reservations to help in this endeavor.[9] Though local tribes were given the opportunity to write their own constitutions, too often the lack of expertise and experience meant that local Indian communities relied heavily on the legal experts from Interior. Is it little wonder that so many of the newly established constitutions had a distinct Anglo-American flavor? Or that they resembled one another so much?

Meanwhile, the forces of opposition were not idle. A number of congressmen who had become increasingly disenchanted with the New Deal programs continued their attacks upon Collier, the Indian Reorganization Act, and the Bureau of Indian Affairs in general. Collier had to appear before Congress several times to defend the bureau and his policies. Many of his problems could be traced directly to the American Indian Federation, a group organized immediately following the passage of the IRA by proassimilationist Indians. The president of this association was John Collier's old adversary Joseph Bruner. Bruner had shown the Indian commissioner no mercy during the congressional hearings on the Collier Bill. He had accused Collier of attempting to blanket Indians with a communist system of government. Bruner was joined by Alice Lee Jemison, a mixed-blood Seneca, who questioned Collier's fitness for office, since he belonged to such organizations as the American Civil Liberties Union. Jacob Morgan, a Navajo who was active in the Christian Reform Church, criticized Collier for attempting to close Indian boarding schools. Collier, not one to stand by and accept attack without some type of rejoinder, characterized the American Indian Federation as an "audacious humbug."[10] He felt that the AIF did not speak for most Indians and that the intemperance of their attacks spoke for itself.

Collier became quite concerned over the continued opposition in Congress, particularly since many of the IRA's provisions still required Congress to appropriate funds in order to be put into effect. It had been passed in June 1934, and Congress had adjourned before money could be appropriated. When Congress came back into session, the real battle began. The House Subcommittee on Interior Appropriations, led by Congressman Jed Johnson of Oklahoma, provided only about one quarter of the $12.5 million authorized by the IRA. In the following years, Johnson was instrumental in cutting the revolving credit fund to $2.5 million, the annual land purchase fund to $1 million, the funds allocated for tribal organization to $150,000, and educational loans to $175,000.[11] This dampening reception that Collier received in Congress was a preview of coming attractions.

Despite the appropriation setbacks, the Indian Bureau continued to push ahead with its implementation program. Early efforts to get tribes to adopt constitutions and corporate charters were somewhat disappointing. Of the 181 tribes that voted to accept the IRA, only 96 drafted constitutions that were approved by the secretary of the interior.[12] Furthermore, only 73 tribes received corporate business charters.[13] Though it was not necessary for a tribe to adopt a constitution prior to taking advantage of certain benefits under the IRA, it did limit the Indian community from functioning as fully and freely as it might otherwise have. The failure to establish a business corporation, however, inhibited a tribe rather significantly. Without a corporate charter from the secretary, Indians could not receive benefits from the revolving credit fund.

When the Indian Bureau failed in its attempts to get tribes to vote in favor of the IRA, it did not simply ignore the plight of those Indian communities. They continued to receive federal benefits and services under other existing governmental programs. The bureau also moved forward and encouraged local groups to draft constitutions, even though they did not fall under the auspices of the IRA. Thirteen tribes responded to this encouragement and began to operate as duly organized communities.[14] Unfortunately, they could not participate in any of the programs authorized under the IRA, since they had not voted to accept the act.

Seeing the Indian Bureau hamstrung in trying to implement the act, Collier began looking to other federal programs for funds. For example, when Collier could not get appropriations for land purchases, soil conservation, and road building, he turned to the Civilian Conservation Corps and the Public Works Administration, where he received more than $100 million. As Lawrence Kelly described it, from the Resettlement Administration and the Farm Security Administration he obtained over a million acres of submarginal lands for Indian use. Through the Federal Emergency Relief Administration, the Civil Works Administration, and especially the Works Progress Administration he obtained relief funds that kept Indians on the reservations and stimulated their involvement in industries devoted to traditional arts and crafts.[15] This circumvention of Congress did not win Collier a lot of friends, but it did keep the money flowing into Indian country. And Collier felt that the programs initiated by the New Deal were not designed for the white man only. The Indians needed and should receive a share of the bounty.

During the congressional hearings, successful attempts had been made to exclude Oklahoma and Alaskan Indians from most of the benefits of the Indian Reorganization Act. Indeed, Senator Elmer Thomas of Oklahoma was one of the bill's most vociferous opponents. Collier, however, never gave up hope to bring the IRA to Oklahoma. Immediately following the passage of the IRA, the Indian commissioner promoted his vision of Indian reform in a series of articles that reached throughout Oklahoma. Senator Thomas finally decided to take a second look at the situation himself, and Collier accepted an invitation to accompany him on tour. The sojourn through Oklahoma provided a lively exchange between the two old combatants, and by the time the tour ended, they agreed that something had to be done. Though Collier admitted that the existing legislation was probably not right for Oklahoma Indians, they both accepted the need to purchase land for tribes and afford the Oklahoma Indians access to more credit.[16]

When Congress returned to its work in 1935, Thomas assumed the chairmanship of the Senate Committee on Indian Affairs, and Will Rogers of Oklahoma became the head of the House committee. With two native sons from Oklahoma in these powerful positions, it appeared to be the optimum time to pass legislation helping the Indians of Oklahoma. The resulting Thomas-Rogers Bill divided Oklahoma Indians into two categories. Those of one-half Indian blood or more would be permitted to hold their property in trust. Those of less than one-half Indian blood would be released from their restrictions as soon as they were able to manage their own affairs.[17] In order to deal with the delicate problem of Indian wills and heirship, the secretary of the Interior was to be given exclusive jurisdiction over the probate matters of deceased Indians.[18]

The bill further provided for the government to assist Indians with education, medical, and other welfare measures. Indian communities could organize at the local level, and the secretary was authorized to issue corporate charters to Indian groups that would enable them to participate in the IRA revolving credit funds.[19] In essence, many of the benefits of the IRA were extended to Oklahoma Indians, but only under this separate act. The Thomas-Rogers Bill, unfortunately, ran into a good deal of opposition. The proassimilationist forces, led by Congressman Wesley E. Disney of Oklahoma, together with white business groups and the Oklahoma state legislature, was successful in killing the bill.[20]

But this time Senator Thomas was committed to the passage of some type of Indian legislation. Collier and Thomas therefore drafted a new version of the bill, designed to meet some of the more vociferous objections to their initial proposal. In order to accommodate the concern of a number of hostile Indians who had testified in opposition to the Thomas-Rogers Bill, the amended measure eliminated the provisions relating to the degrees of Indianness.[21] The portion of the bill vesting exclusive control of Indian probate matters in the hands of the secretary was also jettisoned to placate the feelings of the Oklahoma state legislature, which felt that this provision constituted an intrusion into the province of its state courts. In a spirit of true compromise, the amended version of the legislation eliminated the New Deal welfare services that would have provided Oklahoma Indians with needed educational and medical benefits. This minimized the attacks coming from the conservative anti–New Deal critics. As a final gesture, the measure included a provision that permitted the state to tax the gross receipts from oil and gas leases located in Indian country.

As in the case of the Indian Reorganization Act, this willingness to compromise saved the day. After a stormy session the Oklahoma Indian Welfare Act became law on June 26, 1936.[22] The final version of the act not only included the adjustments just mentioned, it made Oklahoma Indians eligible to participate in a program of self-government. They could already establish corporate business organizations and obtain federal credit under the Indian Reorganization Act.[23] Unlike the IRA, however, the Oklahoma act permitted groups of ten or more Indians to organize into cooperatives that could draw on an appropriation of two million dollars, administered by an Oklahoma Indian Credit Corporation. This fund was also to be made available to individual Indians who lived in the state.[24] Finally, the secretary of the Interior was authorized to acquire restricted lands of "good quality" to be held in trust by the United States government and exempt from state taxation.[25] Eventually, twenty tribal constitutions and fifteen corporate charters were adopted under the Oklahoma act.[26] The number of Indians that came under the act, however, was relatively small. None of the Five Civilized Tribes, with the exception of three Creek towns and the Cherokee Keetoowah band, adopted either a constitution or a charter under the law.[27]

The success in bringing the philosophy of the Indian Reorganization Act to Oklahoma also found its way into Alaska Territory. Alaskan Indians had been excluded from all but five provisions of the IRA. They could take advantage of the tribal organizations provision, the funds to assist in the development of self-government, the revolving credit fund, the Indian education loans, and the Indian preference in employment section. It had been difficult to argue that the IRA should apply to Alaskan Indians because there were no reservations in the territory. Most Indians lived in small, isolated villages, but these Indians still clearly needed assistance in their quest for governmental and economic development. On May 1, 1936, Congress passed an act extending to Alaskan Indians all of the remaining sections of the IRA except those pertaining to tribal lands and reservations.[28] The 1936 act also corrected an embarrassing omission in the original IRA. Though Congress had stipulated in the IRA that Alaskan Indians could have access to the revolving credit fund, it failed to permit them to apply for a corporate charter. Unfortunately, tribes could not apply for loans from the credit fund until they had received a corporate charter. Alaskan Indians had therefore been effectively prohibited from gaining access to the credit fund due to this congressional oversight. The 1936 law corrected this perplexing problem. Ultimately, sixty-six Indian groups adopted constitutions and corporate charters under the Alaskan Indian Welfare Act.[29]

Within three years after the passage of the IRA, or Wheeler-Howard Act, Burton Wheeler introduced a bill to repeal the very act that bore his name. Wheeler had been one of the Collier Bill's most vigorous opponents during the 1934 congressional hearings, and even the compromise he finally struck with Collier never entirely satisfied the senator from Montana. Wheeler was still principally concerned with the fact that the IRA, as he interpreted it, was philosophically designed to preclude Indians from becoming self-sufficient and operating within the mainstream of white society. Tribal corporations, not individual Indians, controlled the economic resources of Indian communities. This arrangement not only went against Wheeler's commitment to the idea of "rugged individualism," but it also placed enormous power in the hands of the Indian Bureau, the federal agency that so many of the tribal corporations relied upon. The senator's dislike for the bureau has been documented several times over.

This initial attempt to do away with the IRA never really got off the ground. There were a number of alienated Indians ready and willing to oppose John Collier again, mostly on personal grounds, but most of the organized Indian interest groups came to the defense of the act, even the Indian Rights Association, which had originally opposed it. While the Indian Rights Association did not agree with all of the act's provisions, it acknowledged that the law had a number of financial provisions that would benefit Indians throughout the country and eventually joined forces with the National Association on Indian Affairs and the American Indian Defense Association to stop the repeal movement.[30] Their efforts were successful.

Two years later, in 1939, members of the Yankton Sioux tribe had a bill introduced in the House of Representatives designed to amend the Wheeler-Howard Act in such a way that they would be excluded from its coverage.[31] The tribe had originally voted to accept the act 248–171. But when a constitution was drafted and submitted to them for approval, it was defeated. They were now greatly confused about the status of their tribe, and another constitution was in the process of being drafted at the time the 1939 hearing was commenced. As the first witness before the House Committee on Indian Affairs, John Collier pointed out that whatever their grievances, by excluding themselves from the act, the Yankton Sioux would be jeopardizing all of the benefits they were now receiving under the act. About $60,000 had already been spent on land purchases for the tribe, and there were options on another $60,000 worth of land. Sixteen young tribal members had received educational funds amounting to $4,544. Furthermore, the tribal members would lose access to potential governmental employment.[32]

Clement Smith headed up the delegation of Indians that appeared before the House committee with a petition supporting "exclusion," signed by 397 members of the tribe. Tribal membership at that time was 1,951. Will Rogers, the chairman of the House committee, showed Smith a telegram from the officers of the Yankton tribe indicating that Smith and his group did not represent the tribe nor were they connected with any official tribal organization. The petition appeared to be evidence of an intratribal political conflict that the Smith faction felt might be resolved by the House committee. Though his testimony was clouded by the fact that he was personally involved in a land dispute on the reservation, Smith still used this opportunity as a vehicle for condemning the IRA as well.

While the main issue before the House Committee on Indian Affairs was excluding only the Yankton Sioux from the coverage of the Indian Reorganization Act, it was clear that the critics of the law were using the hearing to launch a general attack on the statute. John St. Pierre, another Yankton delegate, argued that under the legislation Indians could not "rebuild the practice or the right of individual enterprise or private enterprise."[33] He noted that Indians wanted to be intermingled "with white people and associated with them and kept there. We do not want to be segregated and kept off by ourselves because that tends to lead the development of Indians back toward the blanket, and that will not be the solution of this Indian problem."[34] St. Pierre then focused attention on the fact that the Bureau of Indian Affairs would only do business with four communal organizations it recognized. As it turned out, these organizations were simply four co-ops that had been organized to gain access to federal funds because the Yankton Sioux had not yet adopted a constitution and established a recognized organization to represent them. The newly organized co-ops enabled the tribe to receive money from the CCC, the WPA, and other federal agencies. They had no connection whatsoever with the IRA.

The April meeting at which the complaints of the Yankton Sioux delegation were presented to the House committee came to an abrupt end without any action being taken. The Indian critics had attacked the IRA but had scored few points, largely because their main thrust was not really related to the IRA. The Yankton Sioux dispute did not disappear, however. On May 29, 1940, the dissident tribal members were back in Washington replaying their scenario. Clement Smith again acted as spokesman for the tribal faction. Like his testimony the previous year, Smith's general assault was directed toward the philosophy of the Indian Reorganization Act. Equally important, however, was Smith's contention that the bureau was too authoritarian and discriminated against those Indians who had opposed the law. "I wish to state . . . that the tactics and methods used out there, we believe, are un-American, and we also know that we have absolute, pure dictatorship on the reservation. We have substantial evidence to show that the Indian Bureau is in absolute control as dictator over the Indians."

Will Rogers still had difficulty understanding how the Indian grievances were in any way connected to the Indian Reorganization Act. Smith responded by indicating that the act "sets up the practice of communism. Everything is done under a communistic set-up. There is no such thing as private ownership of private property under the act."[35] Rogers finally gave up, remarking that "frankly the Chair will state that he is of the opinion that the witness does not know what he is talking about."[36] Unfortunately, other committee members, including Usher Burdick of North Dakota, James O'Connor of Montana, and Francis Payne Bolton of Ohio, seized upon this trivial issue as a basis for urging repeal of the Indian Reorganization Act.

Representative John Murdock of Arizona presided over the subcommittee meeting that continued to hear the Yankton Sioux complaint on the next day. Murdock, a dedicated foe of the IRA, joined forces with Llewellyn Selwyn, an Indian witness, to criticize the Indian legal codes and courts established under the IRA. Murdock and Congressman Burdick questioned the legality and effectiveness of these local legal operations. Selwyn testified that local Indian courts deprived tribal members of liberty without due process of law, destroyed the home life of Indians through marriage and divorce proceedings, and desecrated religious liberty.[37] John Collier was not present at the meeting, and so the testimony at this session went largely unrebutted. Collier later sent several letters to Will Rogers, responding to the charges and defending the legality of local Indian courts. Ultimately, the Yankton Sioux issue quietly faded away but not before congressional critics of the IRA had a field day attacking the law.

Throughout the New Deal period, John Collier not only had to defend himself and the Indian Reorganization Act against congressional opponents, but he also had to fend off attacks from dissident Indian groups. The most vocal of these Indian opponents, of course, was the American Indian Federation, led by Joseph Bruner. Kenneth Philp has described the activities of the AIF in some detail elsewhere.[38] The AIF never wavered in its attack on Collier and his policies as being communistic and anti-Christian. Ultimately, it joined forces with pro-Nazi groups in the United States to fight the IRA. The German government had decided that Indians rightfully belonged to the Aryan race. Hence, a coalition with these disgruntled Indians seemed to be a natural alliance. Elwood A. Towner, a mixed-blood attorney from Oregon, toured the West attacking Collier and heaping praise upon Nazi organizations. Towner referred to Collier as a "Jew-loving Pink Red" and accused President Roosevelt of being a Jew whose real name was Rosenfelt.[39] The tragedy of it all was that Senators Wheeler and Thomas cloaked the American Indian Federation with an air of legitimacy in permitting its members to testify at congressional hearings as a basis for attacking the Indian Reorganization Act and embarrassing President Roosevelt.

The year 1944 witnessed the final attempt to repeal the IRA during

Collier's administration. The Senate Committee on Indian Affairs, by now strongly opposed to both Collier and the New Deal, approved a bill recommending that the Wheeler-Howard Act be repealed.[40] The report on the bill noted that ten years after the passage of the IRA, there was no more self-government than before the act. Land had not been given to landless Indians but to those tribes that had more land than they needed. Furthermore, poor Indians could not get access to the revolving credit funds. The BIA had simply used the law to centralize power in the hands of the bureaucrats. In assessing the achievements of the IRA, the report listed eight specific conclusions:

- Stopping the allotment program perpetuated governmental supervision over Indians and was incompatible with the American system of land tenure.

- The indefinite extension of the trust period has caused many inheritance problems.

- The return of surplus lands to tribes has been futile and expensive. It simply placed tribal land under BIA control.

- The communal land set up under the IRA simply did not work. Indians possessed no land individually, and this was contrary to their wishes.

- The land purchase program was grossly mismanaged. What land that had been purchased went into tribal ownership and had not been given to landless Indians.

- The reservation system remained obnoxious and should be terminated.

- The revolving credit fund had placed too much power into the hands of the Indian Service. The bulk of the loans had gone to few tribes and only to those tribes that had sufficient security to handle their own affairs.

- Loans to Indian students were no longer needed, since these students could obtain funds from general sources.[41]

The Senate Committee on Indian Affairs report was probably the most comprehensive criticism yet directed toward the IRA and its operations. Abe Fortas, the assistant secretary of the interior, did submit a supplement to the report, indicating many of the IRA's achievements to date and urging the Senate not to repeal the act. Like so many other congressional reports, this one got lost in the legislative shuffle, and the Indian Reorganization Act remained intact. This hearing was the last formal defense of the IRA made during Collier's tenure as commissioner. He resigned from office in the spring of 1945.

Collier's departure from the commissionership seemed to take the steam out of the opposition to the IRA, suggesting that perhaps he himself had become the real subject of controversy and that the idea of self-government had become secondary in the complaints of both Indians and congressmen. It is not difficult to trace the increase of personal attacks against Collier during these later hearings; apparently the innovations Collier had made were not nearly as controversial as he was himself. A prophet never has honor in his own land, and Collier recognized that fact of human social life as much as he understood other aspects of community life and politics.

The Barren Years

Although later commentators have praised Collier for his efforts in achieving a measure of self-government for Indians, the New Deal Indian policy as implemented was basically aimed at restoring the economic fortunes of Indians. Collier might use glowing terms in describing the Indian cultural revival to Congress, and in emphasizing the benefits that would accrue to the United States by allowing the Indians a measure of local municipal control, but his lasting achievements were in the area of economic development. He recognized that many Indians were spiritually and emotionally depressed because they could not use their own lands in ways they wanted and that tribes had lost a considerable amount of land during the first part of this century. So much of the work of the New Deal was to bring the necessary resources to the reservations to help Indians reconstitute an economic base for themselves.

Collier's approach to funding reservations programs was a radical departure from that of his predecessors. Previous commissioners had taken the position that Indians stood separate from other Americans and were therefore not eligible for programs enjoyed by the rest of American society. Collier saw things in an entirely different light. He reasoned that Indians were American citizens, even if some of the traditionals vehemently denied it, and that they were therefore entitled to participate in all public programs available to other Americans. The services that Indians received from the Bureau of Indian Affairs, Collier believed, were special services that had been promised to Indians in treaties and agreements and therefore did not separate Indians from the rest of America as much as they provided the additional assistance that Indians required to bridge the cultural gap that existed between them and other Americans.

Collier was never popular with the congressional appropriations committees. Many of his best programs were perennially underfunded, and he continued to answer irrelevant and unwarranted questions about communism and socialism during the hearings on Indian appropriations. But he was a skillful administrator and even more skillful at bringing the resources of other agencies into the field of Indian affairs. During his time as commissioner, he was able to get the Resettlement Administration, the Farm Security Administration, the Civilian Conservation Corps, the Works Progress Administration, the Soil Conservation Service, and the Federal Emergency Relief Administration to fund Indian projects and using these agencies and their programs enabled him greatly to expand the scope of federal services available to Indians. In this respect Collier was a generation ahead of his time and foreshadowed the attitude of Lyndon Johnson toward Indians during the War on Poverty, when tribes were recognized as eligible sponsoring agencies for the poverty programs.

Collier would frequently write later that one of his most important interests upon taking office as commissioner, and throughout his life, was to help Indians rebuild their land base. He believed that Indians were able to derive substantial spiritual sustenance from their lands and could not survive without a homeland. The Pueblo struggle to prevent wholesale forfeiture of their lands had brought Collier into the field of Indian affairs in 1922. Later in the 1920s Collier had assisted the Navajos of Arizona and the Kootenai and Salish of Montana in maintaining control of important resources on their reservations. And Collier praised the Klamath corporation proposal as a farsighted effort by the Indians to make better use of their resources. So Collier's record when he became commissioner was already exemplary in this respect.

The land restoration program of the IRA was a resounding success, considering the handicaps under which the bureau worked. Harold Fey pointed out that by 1950 "for the first time in 80 years, Indian holdings of land increased—from 48 to 52 million acres."[1] The Indian Bureau spent over one and a half million dollars to purchase four hundred thousand acres of cropland to be used by Indians.[2] In addition, tribes regained control of seven million acres of grazing land that had previously been held by white cattlemen under leases made by the Bureau of Indian Affairs.[3] Almost one million acres of surplus land was returned to tribes under the IRA.[4] Collier might have been even more successful in restoring lands to tribes, but the Interior Department was forbidden from returning surplus lands to those tribes that had rejected the IRA without special legislation, and it was very difficult to get approval from Congress for this kind of proposal.

The land ethic extended to conservation and the preservation of wilderness in addition to land consolidation. Problems of overgrazing on some reservations, most notably the Navajo, were brought under control, although at a fearful price. The reduction of the Navajo herds fell unequally on the small herder, and the Navajos never forgave Collier for forcing this program on them. But when all was said and done, the program did save the Navajo lands from total desolation. Water development and flood control programs were also initiated, and land nutritional programs were promoted. One report indicated that "the Indian estate that a few years ago was being dissipated and destroyed is today being conserved, amplified, and improved for the benefit of the Indian people today, and for the unborn Indian generations."[5]

Collier also anticipated the idea of setting aside a wilderness area, and he was particularly proud of his achievements in this respect. He established roadless areas on eleven reservations, with a total acreage of 4,745,000 acres. "The roadless areas were *administratively* created," Collier wrote in *From Every Zenith,* and he noted that "they could be abolished altogether if this or that tribe, after genuine consideration, might want them abolished. Across some twenty years, no tribe did want them abolished."[6] This program, more than any other, recognized the Indian relationship with the land and encouraged some of the traditional Indians to support Collier's efforts in other areas of reform.

Economic development under the IRA was a success in most instances. Prior to the passage of the act, only a handful of livestock associations were in existence on Indian reservations, and these groups operated informally for the most part. The bureau improved existing cooperatives and helped begin new ones. About 160 cooperative livestock associations were operating by the end of the thirties.[7] Breeding and range management were also improved, and feed production and co-op sales of cattle were initiated.[8] The increase in Indian ownership of domestic stock rose dramatically. In 1932 Indians owned 171,000 head of beef cattle; by 1941 this number had increased to 361,000. In 1932 Indians owned only 11,300 head of dairy cattle; by 1944 this number had risen to 50,700.[9] Unlike the social programs of the sixties, which tried to bring industry to the reservations, the New Deal sought to emphasize those activities that were native to the lands the Indians owned, and in this respect they were very successful.

The major source of funds for reservation development was the revolving credit loan fund established as part of the Indian Reorganization Act. Although the act called for an appropriation of $10 million, during the Collier administration only $5,245,000 was allocated.[10] Thus, though Congress authorized the bureau to help tribes develop their resources, it did not provide the funds to enable them to do the job. Still, loans were made to eighty-two organized tribes and to thirty-nine Indian credit and cooperative associations.[11] In spite of this handicap, the variety of cooperative enterprises that was initiated during this period is unique and impressive. In addition to the great number of fishing cooperatives started in Alaska native villages and the many stores and trading posts operated as cooperatives on reservations in the western states, a tractor and machine cooperative was established at Catawba in South Carolina, a cranberry cooperative at Lac Court Oreilles Chippewa in Wisconsin, and a ferryboat was purchased at Fort Berthold in North Dakota.

Recent studies of the Indian Reorganization Act have been somewhat critical of Collier's performance, but on the whole these accusations have not been well founded. Lawrence Kelly, for example, suggests that there existed quite a "disparity between the number of Indians eligible for benefits under the Indian Reorganization Act and those who actually received . . . benefits."[12] Though admitting that it is difficult to identify how many Indians actually came under the provisions of the act, Kelly identifies a large number of Indians who were clearly excluded. Collier certainly should not be charged with neglect in this respect. Many tribes voted not to come under the act, and once this position was taken by a tribe, there was little that the commissioner could do to extend the benefits of the act to them. On the whole, his manipulation of legal doctrine for administrative purposes provided them with as many benefits as they could expect, given the time and conditions under which Collier labored.

In Graham Taylor's recent examination of the Indian New Deal, he presents an argument that the act, however enlightened, "was fatally weakened by its emphasis on tribal reorganization and the assumptions about contemporary Indian societies which formed the basis for the tribal idea."[13] Collier's concept of the tribe as the most effective vehicle for improving the plight of the Indian was flawed, according to Taylor. By the beginning of the twentieth century, Indian cultural groups varied widely. The old tribal cohesion was only a shadow of its former strength, and factionalism was widespread on many reservations. Dissident groups frequently disrupted tribal affairs for their own purposes. Religious controversies flared between Christian Indians and the traditional people and between traditional practitioners and the practitioners of the fast-spreading peyote, or Native American Church, religion. Full-bloods and mixed-bloods quarreled over both the form of government and the role it should play in their lives. New divisions distinguished by economic status appeared, and the old struggle continued between those Indians who wished to assimilate into American society and those who preferred to remain separate from it.

A more realistic focus on the actual realities of the conditions under which Indians lived, Taylor suggests, might have helped Collier understand Indian bands and villages, where most of the people lived. The Iroquois, the Cherokees, and the Creeks all possessed their own constitutions and formal government, as did the Pueblos, but they generally lacked the formal documents or established forms of government that the federal government would recognize. But the Iroquois had a sophisticated clan system, which was the center of their functioning government, not a village system. The Cherokees and Creeks did have a town system, but their constitutions had not been operative for several decades when the New Deal proposed to reorganize Indian affairs. Even then there were a number of Cherokee groups that chose to organize themselves apart from the tribe and did so under the Oklahoma Indian Welfare Act.

Taylor argues that by focusing on the tribal unit, Collier "in many cases created and sustained an essentially artificial institution in Indian life."[14] Admittedly, the original bill that Collier submitted envisioned more powers for such Indian subgroups as villages and bands on the reservations, and it may be that Collier too easily surrendered this idea when Senator Wheeler rejected it. The Oklahoma and Alaska amendments to the act did permit establishment of Indian organizations below the tribal level. Since the thrust of the IRA programs was economic, not political, Collier can hardly be faulted for the failure of the bureau to organize an increasing number of smaller political units on the larger reservations. Cooperatives and small businesses were established under charters from the tribal government, and these activities were probably more important, given the situation that Indians faced, than an effort to reconstruct the old band or village structure of former days.

Of the ninety-three tribal governments established under the IRA between 1935 and 1945, Taylor's analysis reveals that only thirty-one could be classified as tribes in the true sense of the word.[15] In 1934 it was not possible, according to Taylor, to distinguish tribes in the old cultural-political sense of the word. Many tribes had signed the same treaty and agreed to live on the same reservation. Some reservations were established to provide for the remnants of tribes that had almost vanished, through continuous warfare with the whites or because of losses from disease. Some reservations were small and supported only a few related families, not tribes in any sense. Any effort to reconstitute tribes in an aboriginal sense would have met with stiff resistance from the Indians. People had adjusted to the reservations, and they now sought only to make them fruitful for themselves.

There is no question that other criticisms could be leveled against the Collier administration and the Indian Reorganization Act. The fact remains that the man engineered a complete revolution in Indian affairs. Congress reversed itself on allotments; it then authorized a form of self-government that was suitable for the conditions under which Indians then lived. Congress gave strong support to Indian education and made official the Indian preference in hiring in the Bureau of Indian Affairs, which had been informal and sporadic in previous administrations. And Congress frequently provided funds for badly needed projects on reservations that it had never before contemplated under any circumstances.

The ideological revolution that Collier wrought, as we have seen, was even more profound but hardly noticed by anyone except those few legal experts who helped Collier to shift the ground of tribal self-government from delegated powers to inherent powers. Self-government, as opposed to a nationalistic revival, however, was Collier's own description of what he had wrought; he did not contemplate any revival of traditions except in religion and crafts. Even at Collier's death the Indians had not yet intuited the powerful theoretical framework that the commissioner had prepared for them. If tribal governments were artificial entities, they were no more artificial than the social programs of the New Deal, which other Americans eagerly embraced at the time. Inherent powers of government were hardly artificial and neither Collier nor the Indians understood how fundamental this change really was.

More incisive accusations can be made against Collier, however, in his fascination with the idea of indirect rule. Late in his life, Collier noted that:

the sovereign aims toward a mutual, an organic relationship with the people being governed. This means knowing the social complexities of the governed people. It means striving toward genuine partnership with the governed people. It means confronting the problems of the governed people shoulder to shoulder with that people. It means evocation, the opposite of imposition. Ultimately, it means genuine and ever-deepening, ever more precise democracy, within a total field of forces in which the alien ruler is a minor, and ideally, a disappearing part.[16]

This description of a partnership is hardly equivalent to self-government. It suggests at best a compromise from the very beginning of the relationship so that the governed people do not realize the degree to which they have made or are making accommodations. The traditional Indians saw immediately that the wrong kind of accommodations were being made and much of their opposition to the Collier program was not because they rejected self-government per se but because they wanted free and undisturbed government of their own choosing. No matter how Collier and the bureau might tidy up the facade of tribal government and no matter how many trinkets might be made available to the reservation people, the traditionals did not want a decision-making process in which their ideas were subject to approval by the secretary of the interior or the commissioner of Indian affairs. They wanted independence, and partnership was not independence.

Perhaps the best rebuttal supporters of Collier and the New Deal can muster against criticisms is to point to the barren period, which soon followed upon Collier's resignation from the commissionership. He was not out of office very long before the Senate Civil Service Committee, holding hearings on ways to reduce federal expenditures, inquired of Acting Commissioner William Zimmerman when the Indian tribes would be ready to succeed on their own. Zimmerman was asked to classify the tribes in three basic categories: those tribes who could succeed without federal assistance immediately, those tribes that would be ready for a withdrawal of federal services within a decade, and those tribes that would for the foreseeable future need federal assistance. Collier would have used this occasion to expound on the congressional failure to support the Indian Reorganization Act with solid financial and legislative actions. Zimmerman weakly tried to evade the question by bringing in a number of extraneous factors that should be considered before Congress embarked on such a radical venture. These hearings provided grist for a later congressional mill and gave evidence that Collier's self-government experiment had been but a brief interlude in the continuing misunderstanding that Congress held concerning Indians. The hearings also demonstrated that John Collier provided two irreplaceable ingredients in the movement for Indian self-government: He articulated a philosophy of self-government that was more powerful than any competing policy alternative, and he gave energetic and creative administrative support to his beliefs. When he was no longer in charge, the field of Indian affairs virtually collapsed.

★   ★   ★

We can mark out the two decades from 1945 to 1965 as the barren years. Self-government virtually disappeared as a policy and as a topic of interest. Indian affairs became a minor element in the American domestic scene; Indians became subject to new forms of social engineering, which conceived of them as a domestic racial minority, not as distinct political entities with a long history of specific legal claims against the United States. Like other areas of American life, the most profound influence in these years was the change in perception and conditions created by the experience of the Second World War.

By 1940 America seemed heading unavoidably into the spreading global conflagration. Lend-Lease signaled a solid commitment to support the Allies, and the increase in expenditures in war materials meant a drastic retrenchment of funds for domestic programs. The Bureau of Indian Affairs was moved from Washington, D.C., to Chicago, Illinois, for the duration of the war, freeing office space in the nation's capital for wartime agencies. With the institution of the draft and the expansion of new agencies to prosecute the war, many talented people resigned from the Bureau of Indian Affairs and entered the service or another agency that was closer to the action. The bureau budget was drastically reduced during the war, and agencies and schools were closed on many reservations. The bureau suffered attrition in its ranks throughout the war.

Tribal governments were particularly hard hit by the Second World War. A new generation of Indians was just beginning to enter tribal government when the war began. Educated young men and women immediately enlisted, leaving their homes to fight in the war. As war industries expanded on the Coast, thousands of reservation Indians departed to work in aircraft plants and shipyards. The reservations were rapidly depopulated of the age groups that would have been most involved in tribal government, leaving elders and children who were living with their grandparents while their parents sought work. Many tribal enterprises stopped functioning for lack of any trained people to operate them. Tribal lands were again leased to white farmers and cattlemen who had the capital to expand their operations rapidly and take advantage of the wartime rise in agricultural and beef prices. When the war ended, many Indians remained in the cities where they had jobs; many Indian veterans returned home briefly, realized they would not be happy in what now seemed too restrictive an environment, and after visiting relatives left to find work outside the reservation.

The first year after the war saw several developments that became prophetic insofar as Indian affairs were concerned. Congress reorganized itself, and the two Indian committees were reduced from full standing committees of the Senate and House to minor subcommittees within the larger public lands committees. Congress passed the Indian Claims Commission Act,[17] which allowed the tribes to file in a specially established commission any claim in law or equity that it felt it had outstanding against the United States. The purpose of this commission was not simply to do justice to living Indians but to clear the historical slate so that federal services could be withdrawn from the tribes. In the fall of 1946 the Republicans took over control of Congress and began to talk of dismantling the welfare state that the New Deal had created. Whereas other federal agencies of the Depression era had developed strong constituencies, making their demise unlikely, the Bureau of Indian Affairs was still without a powerful private lobby that could protect its programs and budget. The newly organized National Congress of American Indians was only two years old and was having its growing pains; it did not have national recognition and would not have any status as a representative group for at least another decade.

With some minor exceptions the issues that now became important in Indian affairs dealt with two subjects: control of Indian resources and jurisdiction over Indian affairs. Anti–New Deal senators and congressmen simply preempted the discussion of Indian policy and sounded a continuing theme that grew louder as the years progressed: Big government is inefficient, and Indians need to be freed from it once and for all. Whenever the Indians tried to rebut this one-sided argument—which was more of an authoritarian fiat than a discussion—they were accused of intending to live off the fat of the land if at all possible. Real problems, therefore, were met with the ideological recital that freedom from the federal government would resolve all problems. Like the Reagan administration later, Congress simply cited conservative slogans to respond to the pressing problems of Indians. In this atmosphere it was impossible to discuss the status of tribal governments, the movement toward self-government, or the intangible desire to recapture a sense of nationality. All that mattered was that Indians be made to conform to the norm in American society.

At least a part of the blame for this state of affairs could be attributed to John Collier. His optimistic characterizations of self-government had led some members of Congress to believe that Indians were making considerably more progress than was actually occurring on the reservations. Congressional hearings of these years feature irascible senators and congressmen crossly chastising Indians about the lack of progress they have been making. Almost always the senator or congressman recalled some vague but optimistic report of Collier and inquired why Indians had not done better with their opportunities. No one took into account the real devastation the war had wrought on reservation society.

In 1948 Congress granted the state of New York considerably more civil and criminal jurisdiction than it had ever possessed over the remaining Iroquois reservations and amended the definition of Indian country to allow considerably more leeway to the secretary of the interior in leasing Indian lands at his own discretion. The theory behind these moves was that Indians would eventually integrate into American society and that laws protecting them from the states were simply inhibiting them from making progress in this direction: in other words, assimilation. This ideology got a significant boost in March 1949, when the Hoover Commission, charged with recommending how the federal government could reduce its expenditures, suggested that the states should begin to assume responsibility for most of the services the federal government was providing for Indians. Although the committee report was almost equally divided between those people who felt that any alteration of the federal Indian relationship was outside the commission's scope because it involved important national policy, conservatives in congress tended to take the view that coincided with their own political philosophy and overlooked the series of admonitions the report included.

By 1950 there was a significant head of steam supporting the termination of federal services to Indians. The House Interior Committee authorized a "Domesday Report" on Indians, through which it hoped to gain as complete a picture of Indian resources as William the Conqueror had once obtained of medieval England following his conquest. Not only did conservatives endorse this outmoded pattern of gathering research, they even adopted the tack that Indians were a conquered nation subject to the arbitrary disposition of their lives and property in much the same way William must have dealt with the recalcitrant Angles and Saxons.

In 1953 the move to place Indians under state jurisdiction began in earnest. In August Congress passed a number of preliminary laws that laid the groundwork for transferring Indians to state control.[18] States were given jurisdiction over Indian reservations in five states and parts of other states, and any state wishing to amend its constitution and remove any disclaimer clause it had restricting its reach onto the reservations was given congressional permission to do so. The federal liquor law prohibiting the sale of alcoholic beverages to Indians was repealed under the excuse that Indian servicemen had fought and died for their country but had been unable to get drunk for it. Tribes fought hard against this repeal and managed to get local option at the tribe's discretion for liquor sales on the reservations.

The election year 1954 saw the conservative forces in Congress at high tide in their effort to disentangle Indians and the federal government. For the only time in American history the two Indian subcommittees sat in joint session and considered a number of termination or withdrawal bills. The reason for holding joint sessions was to forestall any effort to sidetrack the terminal legislation. The joint subcommittee could ensure that each house of Congress had identical language in its bill, thereby eliminating the need for a conference to reconcile differences, a step in the procedure where most compromises are made and a place where tribes had traditionally stopped bad legislation.

A number of tribes found themselves the subject of terminal legislation as the subcommittee began its hearings, generally the ones mentioned in Zimmerman's list presented to the Senate Civil Service Committee in 1947. The members of the subcommittee argued vehemently with the tribal representatives that the tribes had been certified as ready to take over their own affairs nearly a decade before and interpreted any reluctance on the part of tribal leaders as an effort to avoid the issue and remain on the federal payroll. Senator Arthur Watkins went to the unusual step of going to the Menominee reservation and telling the Indians that they could not have a claims judgment they had won against the United States unless they agreed to their terminal legislation, which was patently untrue. A rump meeting representing about 8 percent of the tribe reluctantly agreed to accept the terminal proposal, believing it was the only way they could get their funds from the government.

Although the senators and congressmen talked enthusiastically about self-sufficiency and independence, the final versions of the bills they passed gave the tribes neither access nor control over their property. The Klamaths of Oregon, Menominees of Wisconsin, and Affiliated Ute Citizens of Utah found themselves at the mercy of private banking institutions, which became their trustees under the legislation. Considering the ideological statements made by the conservative subcommittee members throughout the hearings, the Indians were greatly surprised and shocked when they learned that they had simply traded one trustee, the bureau, for another, a private bank. Indians enthusiastic about getting out from under the Bureau of Indian Affairs and taking care of themselves found themselves in the grip of trust officers at the bank who had little knowledge and no sympathy at all for the human problems of termination.

Once aware of the magnitude of the disaster that confronted them, the Indians fought back. During the winter of 1954, while the hearings were being held, the National Congress of American Indians (NCAI) called an emergency conference in Washington to protest the work of the subcommittee. The NCAI was able to develop sufficient political pressure to curtail the hearings that year, before more tribes were pressured to accept terminal legislation. When the Democrats again took control of the congressional committees after they had regained the majority in Congress in the 1954 fall elections, the threat of immediate termination was blunted. Nevertheless, the bureau still used termination as a club to hold over the heads of tribes and tribal leaders who might prove uncooperative. The poison that spread during this brief congressional experiment with conservative ideology has not yet disappeared from the field of Indian affairs.

The shortcomings of Collier's mode of organizing tribal governments became apparent during termination. The joint subcommittee made every effort to show that termination was not their idea but was a relief welcomed by the tribe. In order to show Indian agreement, they went to extraordinary lengths to describe the democratic processes that led to tribal approval of the terminal legislation. Senator Arthur Watkins, in particular, would describe meetings with sullen and shocked tribal councils as "enthusiastic," and he would imply that his mission was simply to give voice to the real feelings of Indians. Every tribe had to approve the terminal legislation in one way or another, and traditional Indians, as they had done in the votes to accept or reject the Indian Reorganization Act, refused to vote, allowing the Indians who were in favor of termination to win narrow victories in tribal elections and votes approving the legislative proposal. Sometimes the consent of the tribal council alone was deemed sufficient to enable the subcommittee to proceed. The idea of self-government, of decision making by Indians, was twisted to the purposes of Senator Watkins for termination in much the same way that Collier had forced the IRA on some reluctant tribes. In both instances traditionals refused to participate.

With Democrats in charge of Congress in 1955, the direction of Indian affairs moved slightly toward the left. Termination was still the official policy of the Congress, and there were very few senators or congressmen who dared to oppose it directly. So the notion began to emerge that if the interests of tribes intertwined with those of corporate America and their white neighbors, there would be a sufficient non-Indian interest to prevent any further rapid termination of federal services. The first indication that this approach was being realistically considered was in the passage of the Act of August 9, 1955,[19] which significantly amended the existing laws governing leasing of Indian lands. Under this statute nonagricultural surface lands could be leased for "public, religious, educational, recreational, residential, or business purposes" for a period of twenty-five years, with an option to renew for another twenty-five years—in effect a fifty-year lease of tribal and individual lands. Section 3 of the act prohibited making any lease whose terms might delay or prevent termination of federal services and supervision. The conservatives thus struck directly at the liberal effort to veer away from termination via the long-term lease, but everyone knew that if an important non-Indian lessor had an interest in a reservation, the chances that it would be considered for termination before he had made his money would be negligible.

The termination question certainly made Indians deeply aware of the society outside the reservations and the damage it could do to them. As early as the 1954 national elections, Indians were beginning to think about bringing their voting power in the western states to bear on recalcitrant senators and congressmen who supported termination, and wise politicians saw that a certain way to get Indian votes was to oppose any action of the federal government that did not have Indian consultation and approval. The liberals who represented the western states from 1956 to the liberal debacle in 1978 almost all received an overwhelming percentage of Indian votes when they first ran for office.

Termination also made Indians start to think about the nature of self-government. If it was as fragile as it seemed to be, there must be an appeal beyond Congress to bolster the status of Indian tribes. Much of the ideology of nationhood began to surface in the minds of many Indians as the 1950s came to a close.

The opening of the New Frontier in 1960 did not change Indian policy as much as recent commentators have led themselves to believe. In 1961 President Kennedy established a task force and charged it with making a report to the secretary of the interior regarding the future of Indian policy and programs under his administration. The task force contained a future Indian commissioner, Philleo Nash of Wisconsin, and a future assistant commissioner, James Officer of Arizona, and therefore many of the recommendations the Task Force made were later implemented by members of the group that had originated them, a feat not unlike Collier's four letters under Rhoads's signature a generation before.

The Democrats waffled when it came to termination. Some of the senior members of the Senate Interior Committee—in particular, Henry Jackson of Washington, Clinton Anderson of New Mexico, and Frank Church of Idaho—were strong supporters of termination, having accepted the conservatives' interpretation of past events when they became members of the Interior committee. Since the Kennedy administration wanted to ensure smooth passage of its conservation bills, it was not in a mood to antagonize these powerful members of the Interior committee. So the administration rather lamely described its Indian policy as *preparing* the Indians for termination. In practical terms, many of the programs of the Kennedy administration did reverse the trend in reducing funds for the Bureau of Indian Affairs, particularly in education. A glance at the education expenditures of the Kennedy administration, however, will indicate that much of the money used in school construction went to public school districts bordering the reservations, not to projects in Indian education on the reservations.

In 1961 Congress authorized the Area Redevelopment Administration (ARA),[20] and the bureau under Philleo Nash, like it had under Collier, saw this program as a chance to increase the amount of available funds for the reservations. The tribes were made sponsoring agencies eligible to receive funds under the act, and through the programs of the ARA, later reauthorized as the Economic Development Administration (EDA),[21] the tribes were able to build a number of community centers and tribal headquarters buildings on the reservations.

The ARA-EDA inclusion of tribal governments on the same basis as counties and local governments was a major breakthrough for the cause of self-government and may have been the watershed event of the century. Even the best of the New Deal programs had not regarded Indians as sufficiently responsible to subcontract large sums of money with them. More often the tribes were recipients of programs operated by others. Placing the control of funds and programs directly in the hands of reservation people was a radical change in both legislative and executive perception of tribal governments. Yet, in the context of the time, it seemed the natural thing to do.

Events moved rapidly under the Kennedy and Johnson administrations. The Democrats were still wedded to the idea that the way to save the Indians from termination was to vest enough interest in a reservation's resources in a large corporation so that the tribe could not be terminated without disrupting the plans of corporate America. The long-term leasing act seemed the most likely place to begin changes, and during the sixties a parade of tribes arrived in Washington with the bureau's encouragement seeking to obtain ninety-nine-year leases on tracts of their reservations that might have unique potential for development. A ninety-nine-year lease was in effect a sale of the reservation because it meant a heavy investment by non-Indian developers with the almost certain result that the lease would be renewed a century later. The reservations were seen in Democratic eyes as resources that could and should be developed, not as homelands where Indians lived.

The House Subcommittee on Indian Affairs, led by Congressman James Haley of Florida, refused to authorize a blanket lease and insisted on hearing each tribe present its reasons why it should be allowed to lease its lands for the longer term. On the other hand the Senate Indian subcommittee generally favored long-term leasing, and Secretary Udall encouraged this manner of using Indian lands. This conflict considerably inhibited legislation affecting Indians. Had Haley not stood firm against the policies of the Democratic administrations, there might be few Indian reservations today in the hands of Indians.

The War on Poverty, under the Office of Economic Opportunity,[22] featured a special "Indian Desk," which channeled federal poverty funds directly to the tribes and reservations. In general, this effort inspired other federal agencies to take another look at tribal governments, and before long, when Congress was considering educational and economic development programs, tribes were becoming accepted as eligible sponsoring agencies. The civil rights movement made the employment of minorities a major federal priority, and the doctrine of the Office of Economic Opportunity was that the poor themselves should conceive and manage the programs that were designed to lift them out of their dire economic straits. When these two ideas were combined, as they generally were when Indian programs were being considered, the result was to make enormous sums available to tribal governments from a wide variety of federal agencies.

Almost all Indians were enthusiastic about the poverty programs, and many of the reservation people adopted the bureaucratic shorthand to describe themselves. In former days when a person might have identified himself as coming from a certain village or group of people on a reservation, he now proudly related that he worked for "Title IV" or "Neighborhood Youth Corps," or any of the major programs that were operating on the reservations.

The passage of time has given us some new perspectives on the poverty programs. The programs the Indians received were standard activities that almost all poor communities received, and reflected little self-governing power. Tribal governments simply acted on behalf of the federal agency with whom they had contracted. Though Indians might administer the programs they received from the federal government, almost all important decisions, including the population to be served and the guidelines for employment and operation of the programs, were determined by bureaucrats in Washington or in a regional office.

Tribal governments became surrogates for the federal government during the sixties, and this trend extended into the seventies, clothed ironically not as termination but in the new language of self-determination. Federal bureaucrats began to speak in hushed tones about the "government-to-government" relationship they enjoyed with the tribes. The fact of the matter was that the tribes were almost totally dependent upon the federal agencies for their funds and program ideas. Few really innovative activities were begun on the reservations by the people. In almost every instance a new program could trace its ideological roots to someone in the federal government and its funds to a consortium of federal agencies that had sponsored the activity at the urging of interested bureaucrats. Collier the pragmatist rather than Collier the theoretician had become the programmatic father of the Indian renewal of the sixties.

In the private sector, however, very interesting things were happening. As part of the general Indian effort to influence the new Kennedy administration, the anthropologists at the University of Chicago and some of the leaders of the National Congress of American Indians worked to call a national conference of Indians to draw up a statement of purpose, which they hoped would be adopted by the incoming administration. Several hundred Indians met in Chicago for a week in June 1961 and finally agreed upon a poetic document that rather sentimentally reminded the president, and by extension other Americans, of the Indian role in the history of America. The statement emphasized the "good citizenship" aspect of Indian people and prayed for a new federal policy that would fulfill longstanding federal commitments to Indians. For the time, and particularly for that generation of Indians, the statement was rather daring and innovative. It did not assert rights as much as it played upon the reservoir of sympathy that is always present in American society when history is recited in nostalgic, friendly terms. Though it was good publicity for Indians, the statement did not voice the real concerns of most Indians on the reservations.

This disparity between what most Indians felt and what the Chicago conference allowed the delegates to express was noticed by the Indian young people who attended. Following the conference, they decided to organize themselves and push for a "Greater Indian America." Thus the unintended result of the Chicago conference was the organization of the National Indian Youth Council (NIYC), with its program of resurrecting the sense of national pride among Indians. Although the NIYC began slowly, its message to Indians was unmistakeable: Indians were no longer to bow their heads in humble obedience to the Bureau of Indian Affairs or the institutions of white society. The NIYC called upon Indians to look back at their own great cultural traditions and make decisions based on the values they had always represented. The Indian counterpart to Collier's idea of self-government had finally found its voice and was beginning to develop its ideology.

Beginning in 1964 with a series of "fish-ins" on the rivers in Washington State, the NIYC began to assume an increasingly militant posture toward institutions and individuals who had traditionally dominated Indian affairs. The impact of the NIYC was all out of proportion to its actual numbers. Once the ideology of traditionalism was accepted by Indian youth, it slowly made its way across the age spectrum of Indian society, creating an exceedingly more aggressive edge to Indian relations with non-Indians. In 1968 a separate group formed the American Indian Movement, initially to patrol the streets of Minneapolis to prevent police brutality against Indians. With antiwar and civil rights protestors becoming increasingly shrill in their demands, Indians had to appear as angry and disillusioned as their competitors on the left, and the road to Wounded Knee and a direct armed confrontation with American society became inevitable.

The expansion of tribal governments to perform federal administrative functions and the increasing demand by Indian militants for recognition of the fundamental national status of Indian tribes were changes both in the Indian perception of their own status and in their attitude toward non-Indian society. A third and very important movement, which began to develop during the barren years, was the Indian effort to preserve tribal jurisdiction in the face of federal determination to place Indians under state jurisdiction. The basic federal statute (Public Law 280), as we have seen,[23] allowed most western states to assume jurisdiction over civil and criminal matters on the reservations without the consent of the tribes. This statute was detested by both Indians and non-Indians alike because it was exceedingly vague and seemed to promise (or threaten) more than could actually be accomplished.

Indians saw the wording of Public Law 280 as a direct interference with tribal governments. States felt they could not take jurisdiction over reservations without some kind of subsidy from the federal government—or in lieu of that kind of support, the right to tax Indian lands. Congress would not give the states power to tax the reservations, and the federal courts zealously protected Indian tax immunities from state intrusions. In many instances states would simply refuse to provide law enforcement over the reservations, leaving the tribe helpless and without any recourse. When Indians began complaining about their nebulous status in the practical aspects of law enforcement, federal officials could do little except join their complaints to those of the tribes. Finally the Subcommittee on Constitutional Rights in the Senate determined to begin holding hearings on Indian civil rights—including the situation with respect to Public Law 280 and state jurisdiction in general, and these hearings led directly to the American Indian Civil Rights Act of 1968.[24]

The Indian
Civil Rights Act

Civil rights is an old and familiar topic to most Americans. Our social contract theory of government limits the exercise of arbitrary and capricious authority over individuals by the civil rights protections of the Bill of Rights. We expect the equal protection of the laws and the protection of due process in any proceeding that affects our liberty or our property. At least part of our fear of government intrusion is based upon the fact that we are not personally related to or responsible for those who exercise political authority over us. Each citizen is presumed to stand on an equal footing with every other citizen, and it is the state that guarantees us its institutions and procedures to remedy real and even sometimes imagined wrongs.

Indian tribal societies had no concept of civil rights because every member of the society was related, by blood or clan responsibilities, to every other member. There was no pretense that the state existed to prevent injuries to its members by other members. Indians understood fully that injury is personal, even if committed by a stranger, and that only when the personal hurt is compensated could society relax its sanctions. Therefore remedies were made personal in the sense that families were required to resolve their disputes in an orderly fashion that would not allow any hurt, real or imagined, to continue to disturb the body politic. In many tribes the only occasion when society needed to act as an integral unit was when a tribal member had committed a crime so heinous as to warrant expulsion and exile. In that instance the shame to the family involved was so great as to make the decision of the council virtually self-operating: The culprit usually fled, to alleviate further harm and ill will against his family or clan.

As Indian tribes began to adopt different aspects of the white man's way of governing themselves, they found that political institutions operated with a relentless neutrality, which precluded many of the old ways of reconciling disputes. After the Cherokees had moved to Oklahoma, for example, it was decided that those leaders who had signed the removal treaties had violated the tribal laws against selling the lands of the people, and assassination squads hunted down most of the treaty signatories and killed them. Although the penalty was severe, the decision-making process that led to this radical punishment was definitely cast in the procedures of the white man's way of doing things. The assassins were simply regarded as carrying out the laws of the Cherokee nation, not as clansmen performing a savage and personal retaliation in accordance with precontact customs.

The Seven Major Crimes Act, although it specifically stated that it was applicable to all Indian reservations, did not apply to the Five Civilized Tribes. Under the treaties of 1866,[1] the tribes were allowed a measure of self-government, which included a full and complete code for law and order in tribal courts with appeal to the federal district court of Arkansas. The Five Civilized Tribes retained complete civil and criminal jurisdiction over their membership until the act of June 28, 1898[2] prohibited the enforcement of tribal laws in the special federal court having exclusive jurisdiction over the Indian Territory and abolished their tribal courts.

During the period in which the Five Civilized Tribes did have jurisdiction over all offenses committed by their members against another tribal member or against the tribe itself, an important case was decided by the United States Supreme Court, which contributed significantly to the idea that Indians constituted a distinct and sovereign nation, on the one hand, and to the idea that there should be some articulation of the political relationship between an Indian tribal government and the tribal members it governed that was more specific than simply the appeal to tribal custom, on the other hand. *Talton* v. *Mayes*[3] involved a determination of the status of the Cherokee nation as a self-governing political entity and the constitutional protections the Cherokee nation owed its membership.

In making the transition from their traditional ways of handling crime to the white man's way, which included courts, prosecutors, sheriffs, and juries, the Cherokees had proceeded cautiously, trying each step out before they went on to another. In May 1892 the Cherokee legislature established a grand jury of five persons and required the judges of the circuit and district courts of the Cherokee nation to furnish the sheriff with the names of the jurors selected two weeks before the beginning of the term. In December 1892 the Cherokee legislature passed another law that increased the number of jurors to thirteen, the statute to take effect at the beginning of the term that started on the second Monday of May 1893.

Talton, a Cherokee, killed two other Cherokees in 1892 and was swiftly brought to trial and convicted on December 31 by a five-person grand jury acting under the old statute of May 1892. He appealed his conviction with a writ of habeas corpus to the Circuit Court for the Western District of Arkansas and then to the Supreme Court of the United States. Talton claimed that his constitutional rights under both the United States and Cherokee constitutions had been violated because the five-person grand jury was not proper under United States law and it would not be proper in May 1893 under Cherokee law. Talton argued that the Cherokee grand jury of five persons violated the Fifth Amendment, which he claimed was still operative on the Cherokees in any legislation they might pass dealing with purely local matters. The Supreme Court faced a dilemma. Congress was at that point contemplating the complete allotment of the lands of the Five Civilized Tribes, and the Court knew that it was merely a matter of time before the Cherokees, as well as the other Indians of that region, would be regarded as United States citizens or at least subject to the Constitution of the United States and protected by the Bill of Rights.

The Supreme Court, in deciding the case, relied heavily upon the Cherokee treaties with the United States and concluded that "the crime of murder committed by one Cherokee Indian upon the person of another within the jurisdiction of the Cherokee nation, is . . . not an offence against the United States, but an offence against the local laws of the Cherokee nation."[4] In distinguishing between offenses against the Constitution of the United States and those offenses against the laws of the Cherokees, the Court characterized murder as a matter for local self-government, a position wholly without support when viewed in the light of the *Crow Dog* case and the Seven Major Crimes Act of 1885. The Court declared that

the case in this regard therefore depends upon whether the powers of local government exercised by the Cherokee nation were Federal powers created by and springing from the Constitution of the United States, and hence controlled by the Fifth Amendment to that Constitution, or whether they are local powers not created by the Constitution, although subject to its general provisions and the paramount authority of Congress.[5]

Never before had the Supreme Court attempted to distinguish between inherent and delegated powers of government that tribes might exercise, because it was presumed, until *Crow Dog,* that the tribes were fully capable of determining in what manner they would govern themselves. A tribal decision was regarded as an Indian matter, and the cultural overtones to this belief overshadowed any concern with political institutions and proper jurisprudence. The Court described in amazingly clear language precisely how it saw the distinction between inherent and delegated powers:

[The] existence of the right in Congress to regulate the manner in which the local powers of the Cherokee nation shall be exercised does not render such local powers Federal powers arising from and created by the Constitution of the United States. *It follows that as the powers of local self government enjoyed by the Cherokee nation existed prior to the Constitution, they are not operated upon by the Fifth Amendment.*[6]

Under this interpretation Congress had the power to limit self-government but not abolish it. The reasoning falls well within the domestic dependent nation end of the political spectrum described by John Marshall in the *Cherokee Nation* cases. It avoids the idea of wardship vigorously, since any exercise of powers under the concept of wardship would have to be delegated powers.

Talton probably does not support the contention of traditional Indians that the IRA and other Interior-sanctioned tribal governments were not legitimate and were impositions by the white man on existing tribal governments. The question in *Talton* is whether the Constitution of the United States can, through the political relationship between Indians and the federal government, affect and/or authorize the exercise of powers of local self-government. In reaching this question, however, the court departs completely from the question raised in *Crow Dog*—whether or not the tribe has preempted certain powers and subject areas for its own exclusive use—and sees Indian tribal governments as a transitional form of organization to which it then attributes the kinds of political powers that non-Indian governments are presumed to possess and exercise. Insofar as the federal courts, the Congress, and the executive branch are concerned, therefore, *Talton* stands for the proposition that Indian tribes possess certain forms of self-government; it does not mean that Indian tribes possess any residual sovereignty or nationhood that might be burdensome to the United States and the administration of Indian programs.

Within a decade of the *Talton* decision there were no tribal courts functioning except the traditional courts of the Iroquois, which had been maintained, and the practices of the Pueblos, which were both religious and political in nature. The agents created the courts of Indian offenses, but these institutions, as we have seen, were not concerned with the relationship of the individual Indian to the larger tribal society. They were simply devices that enabled the agent to function efficiently and control a large Indian population. The 1926 movement, sponsored by the Bureau of Indian Affairs, to make the courts of Indian offenses part of the federal judiciary was not concerned with the civil rights of tribal members with respect to tribal governments but with the rights of Indians vis-à-vis the Bureau of Indian Affairs, particularly the superintendents of agencies. Hence the subject of civil rights was not seen within the context of tribal governments at any time prior to the Indian Reorganization Act or in the first few years during which tribes operated according to its provisions.

The question of individual Indian civil rights arose in the 1950s primarily because of the development of case law that sought to articulate the list of inherent powers possessed by the tribes. Cases involving the power of tribes to tax, to lease lands, to consolidate lands within the reservations, to give rights of way, and to other functions that were necessary to expand the economic activities of the tribe began to shed light on the question of arbitrary actions by the tribal government. Inevitably the progress of the tribes raised the question of membership, and one of the first modern cases dealing with the power of tribes to determine its own membership, *Martinez* v. *Southern Ute Tribe*,[7] involved the question of the power of the IRA tribal government to determine the right of an Indian woman to membership in the tribe. The case was heard once at the district court in March 1957 and at the circuit in November of that year.

The district court attempted to establish a framework within which the question of membership could be resolved. But it fell back upon a procedural gimmick to turn Martinez aside, ruling that membership in an Indian tribe "is not a right created by the Constitution, laws or treaties of the United States, but solely by the terms of the Constitution of the Southern Ute Tribe."[8] Hence the district court felt there was no federal question involved. The circuit court tried to recast the case, remarking that "Congress at no time intended to provide for federal supervision of private civil actions by Indians."[9]

Tribal membership, however, was hardly a matter of private civil action. Martinez argued that tribal membership meant economic benefits, and therefore a real interest was involved. Since the tribe had organized under the Indian Reorganization Act and the Interior Department had described tribal governments as federal agencies for some purposes, Martinez saw no reason why the courts denied the federal question. The circuit court, however, ruled that the tribe was not "a federal instrumentality within the various statutory and constitutional restrictions upon federal instrumentalities" and stated that this rule had not been diminished since *Talton*.[10] It was not necessary, in retrospect, for the circuit court to have resurrected *Talton* in order to decide *Martinez*; in doing so, it enhanced the idea held by many Indians that tribal sovereignty constituted a special reservoir of powers different in kind and importance from what tribal governments were then exercising.

A confrontation between two groups of Navajos in 1958 brought the question of civil rights even closer to the top of the Indian agenda. The Navajo tribal council enacted an ordinance making it an offense to bring peyote onto the Navajo reservation. The ordinance was a direct slap at the Native American Church, which used the substance in its ceremonies, and the Navajo followers of this religion promptly filed suit against the tribe in federal court, seeking to enjoin enforcement of the ordinance. The district court dismissed the case, citing four grounds: The ordinance was a valid exercise of police powers; the Navajo tribe could not be sued without the permission of Congress; the court was without jurisdiction, since the seat of government was in Window Rock, Arizona (a very curious reason indeed); and there was a misjoinder of the parties—each would have to sue separately.

Apart from the technical reasons given for dismissal, the important ground for the district court's decision, for our purposes, was the immunity of the tribal government from suit because Congress had not given permission for anyone to sue the tribe. This ground effectively precluded tribal members from seeking any relief from arbitrary and oppressive ordinances and actions perpetrated by the tribal government. It was this particular assertion that was to lead to agitation for congressional intervention. The circuit court, in excluding the tribe from the application of the First and Fourteenth Amendments—which brought state action under the scrutiny of the federal courts—declared that *"Indian tribes are not states. They have a status higher than that of states. They are subordinate and dependent nations possessed of all powers as such only to the extent that they have expressly been required to surrender them by the superior sovereign, the United States."*[11]

This language is exhilarating to lawyers and traditional Indians alike. No one could miss the message signaled by the circuit court, but the importance of the case and the interpretation given by the groups who read this decision demonstrated that the Indians and the Congress were proceeding down (at least) two completely separate tracks in their thinking. For some congressmen the decision suggested that tribal members should have some guaranteed form of civil rights against the actions of their own governments. The idea that a tribal government could prohibit the free exercise of an Indian religion on a reservation was abhorrent to them. To tribal officials the decision seemed to mean that they were badly underestimating the actual powers they possessed as sovereign nations and that they could be considerably bolder in their actions before either Congress or the courts would rein them in. Traditional Indians saw the decision confirming their long-cherished belief that they constituted nations as surely as France and England constituted nations. Although these paths of theory were quite divergent, they had occasion to intersect in the years ahead in completely unexpected ways.

Civil rights for individual Indians might have remained a nebulous subject, fit primarily for speculation by liberals who saw all minorities as constituting the same domestic "problem." The *Brown* decision of 1954 had buried the old separate-but-equal doctrine of segregation, and three years later Martin Luther King had led the Birmingham bus boycott, triggering the modern civil rights movement. The Southerners fought back with great tenacity, and one of their tacks was the argument that Indians were even more oppressed than blacks, yet Indians remained calm and dignified on their reservations, causing no trouble and certainly not demanding equal access to education with white children. But these arguments and the stalling tactics failed to inhibit the movement toward national involvement with civil rights, and it was but a matter of time before Indians were dragged into the civil rights discussion.

The National Congress of American Indians went to extravagant lengths to distinguish Indians from blacks during the late 1950s so as to keep the issues clear. Whether the leadership did not like blacks or whether they saw the danger in supporting integration at a time when members of the Senate Interior Committee were busy trying to terminate the tribes, or whether they simply didn't understand the depth of revolt represented by the burgeoning movement in the South, the fact remains that the NCAI studiously avoided involvement in civil rights issues. But the membership of the NCAI demanded one major change in Indian legislation and was determined to get it at any price. Conditions on some reservations where state jurisdiction was allowed by Public Law 280 were bad and getting considerably worse. The states refused to provide decent law and order, and there was no sympathetic federal ear in the executive branch that could take the initiative and straighten the situation out. So Indians had to approach Congress to seek amendment of 280.

Frustrated in their efforts to get the Senate Interior Committee to call hearings on the repeal or amendment of 280, the NCAI then approached members of the Senate Judiciary Committee. Senator Sam Ervin of North Carolina agreed to consider the subject of Indian constitutional rights in his subcommittee, and after some preliminary planning the subcommittee held field hearings in Los Angeles in November and December 1961, after the Democrats were in control of the White House. Senator Ervin did not attend the first hearings, leading some Indians to become suspicious of his motives in sponsoring the hearing, and Senator John Carroll of Colorado chaired the sessions. Carroll, like many of the other senators on the periphery of Indian affairs, completely accepted the idea of Indian tribes as sovereign nations as a rhetorical point that made for good relations with the Indians. In his opening speech Carroll sounded the familiar refrain:

> Notwithstanding the law of 1924, which made all American Indians citizens, there is still the basic problem of authority of the tribal council over the members of the tribe on the reservation. Tribes are not looked upon as States, generally speaking. They are looked upon as independent nations, and therefore, have jurisdiction over the people on their reservations. I think one of the most interesting and perplexing problems we are going to have to face is bridging the gap and getting Indians to recognize, although within the jurisdiction of tribal council, they are American citizens and may be entitled to greater protection under the Constitution.

It was clear, therefore, that the price of amending 280 to provide for Indian consent before states could extend their civil and criminal jurisdiction over the reservations was to be the extension of constitutional protections to individual tribal members in relation to their own governments. The "independence" of the Indian nations vanished rather quickly in this context.

Senator Ervin conducted both field hearings and hearings in Washington, D.C., but seemed in no hurry to bring his study to a close. One reason for Ervin's reluctance was that the hearings did not present a simple picture of the Indian situation. Three distinct areas of concern began to emerge: First, Indians were very concerned about the arbitrary actions of the Bureau of Indian Affairs and other federal agencies that had responsibilities for their welfare. Numerous instances of violations of civil rights were cited with respect to federal agencies. Second, state governments came in for their share of criticism. States would either take wholly unwarranted steps in extending their laws over Indians, or they would deliberately turn their backs on situations in which Indians needed assistance of law enforcement personnel. Finally, some problems individuals were having with tribal governments were cited. The bulk of the evidence obtained from the hearings, however, favored strengthening the federal role in protecting Indians, not in tampering with the powers and activities of tribal governments.

In the first session of the Eighty-ninth Congress, beginning in 1965, Senator Ervin finally introduced a series of bills he felt would adequately meet the needs of Indians. Eight bills and one Senate joint resolution were introduced on February 2, and hearings on these proposals were held in mid June 1965. The legislative package represented a compromise between the various competing interests. The protections of the Bill of Rights were extended to members of Indian tribes, the right of appeal from a tribal court ruling to a federal district court was allowed, and the attorney general was authorized to receive and investigate complaints filed by Indians claiming a violation of their civil rights by state or local agencies. Provisions were also made to develop a model law-and-order code for the reservations, for concurrent federal and state jurisdiction over offenses committed by non-Indians against non-Indians on Indian land, and for the amendment of Public Law 280 to provide Indian consent. The major crimes were to be expanded under the Ervin proposals to include aggravated assault. Changes in the manner of approval of attorney contracts by the Bureau of Indian Affairs were also proposed. Finally the resolution authorized the revision and publication of Kapplers's *Indian Affairs: Laws and Treaties.*

The first proposal was regarded as the most hazardous, and the Pueblos almost unanimously opposed the extension of the Bill of Rights to their governments. The other proposals reflected some of the problems experienced by a few of the tribes but sought to make major revisions in federal law that some tribes felt were too broad. Unfortunately, the Ervin bills did not distinguish clearly which of the problems uncovered by the field hearings they were attempting to solve, and many tribes were puzzled at the changes the senator wanted. It seems certain that Ervin believed he should advance his legislative package as quickly as possible, for even then the federal courts were taking a hand in the resolution of tribal judicial problems. If Congress was to have its say in the matter, it would have to act with some dispatch.

★   ★   ★

In 1964 Mrs. Madeline Colliflower was denied a renewal of her leases on tribal lands. She was certain that the change in lessors was politically motivated, and there was some evidence to this effect, so she refused to remove her cattle. The tribal court issued an order removing her cattle and ordering her arrest. She pled not guilty to the charge of "disobedience to lawful orders of the Court" and was found guilty and fined twenty-five dollars or five days in jail. Unable to pay the fine, Mrs. Colliflower elected to serve the jail sentence and was committed to the custody of the Blaine County sheriff, who provided jail space for the tribal court under a mutual working agreement.

Mrs. Colliflower sued on a writ of habeas corpus, claiming that her confinement violated her constitutional rights because she was not afforded the right to counsel, was not afforded a trial, and was not confronted by any witnesses against her. The federal district court followed then-existing law and denied Mrs. Colliflower's petition, and she appealed to the Ninth Circuit Court of Appeals. The circuit court reversed the district court and remanded the case, cutting through the symbolic fictions it felt had surrounded Indian tribal courts and obscured the practical realities of the situation.

In spite of the theory that for some purposes an Indian tribe is an independent sovereignty, we think that, in the light of their history, it is pure fiction to say that the Indian courts functioning in the Fort Belknap Indian Community are not in part, at least, arms of the federal government. Originally they were created by the federal executive and imposed upon the Indian community, and to this day the federal government still maintains a partial control over them.[12]

If Congress wanted to deal with Indian civil rights, therefore, it had to act before the federal courts established a new interpretation of the impact and meaning of the Indian Reorganization Act. Although few people understood it at the time, Collier's clever ploy with Senator Wheeler was in danger of being unraveled.

The questions raised by Mrs. Colliflower were civil rights issues that had not previously been addressed by any court, but they were anticipated by S. 961, the first of the Ervin proposals. It seemed certain, therefore, that extending the Bill of Rights to the relationship between individual Indians and their tribal governments was a certainty to become law; the other Ervin proposals were less immediate and somewhat less controversial. Little progress was made, however, in getting the Indian civil rights package through Congress. Just when everyone assumed that the Indian bills would die, Senator Ervin acted with dispatch, partially revealing one of his motives in spending time and energy on Indians.

In April 1968 Martin Luther King was assassinated, and in the furious aftermath the Fair Housing Act of 1968 was being rushed through the Senate. Ervin waited until later in the afternoon, and then, with few senators on the floor, he attached the Indian Civil Rights Bill to the housing bill as an amendment. The strategy that Ervin seemed to be adopting was to use the Indian amendment to kill the housing bill. When the legislative package passed the Senate and reached the House of Representatives, Wayne Aspinall, a conservative western Democrat, and a bevy of southern congressmen demanded that the housing bill be sent to the House Interior Committee for hearings on the Indian proposals. Once buried within the Interior Committee, the housing bill would be dead for that session of Congress.

At that point, as might be expected, the unexpected happened. Congressman Ben Reifel, a South Dakota Republican and a Sioux Indian, led the opposition to Aspinall's demand that the bill be committed to the Interior Committee. The liberal Democrats rallied, freed of the onus that they would be opposing civil rights for American Indians, and the bill was sent to the House Judiciary Committee, where Congressman Emanuel Celler, a New York Democrat, safely guided it through to become Public Law 90-284 or, as it is popularly known, the Indian Civil Rights Act. The language of the Indian portion of the act was primarily the last language that had been discussed in hearings on the proposals and hence did not represent the final deliberations of the Senate Judiciary Committee or the Subcommittee on Constitutional Rights. Indian leaders at the National Congress of American Indians, consulted on the bill, urged its passage with the language intact, fearing that any effort to make the bill more suitable for Indian purposes might derail its major objective, the amendment of Public Law 280.

The Indian Civil Rights Act (ICRA)[13] radically changed the substance of tribal courts. It incorporated the First Amendment and Fourth through Eighth Amendments into a package of enumerated rights that tribal governments were forbidden to abridge. But the language of the amendments was changed somewhat to reflect the Indian complaints raised in the field hearings. Thus the establishment of religion was not prohibited—to placate the Pueblos of New Mexico, who governed themselves in a quasi-theocratic manner. The right to counsel, a critical point in Mrs. Colliflower's successful writ of habeas corpus, was provided, but at the defendant's own expense, not at the tribe's expense. The right of indictment by grand jury was not guaranteed, but tribal courts, restricted to misdemeanors, really had little occasion to use a complicated device such as a grand jury. Equal protection of the laws was guaranteed as well as due process of law. Double jeopardy was prohibited and bills of attainder and *ex post facto* laws were also banned. The original provision for appeal from a tribal court judgment to a federal district court was not contained in the final version of the bill, but, significantly, the remedy used by Mrs. Colliflower, the writ of habeas corpus, was included.

Passage of the Indian Civil Rights Act alleviated the problem of Public Law 280, but it greatly complicated the lives of Indians. No one knew exactly what effect the statute had on the authority of tribal courts, and a period of groping and grappling ensued, which has not completely abated. Some tribes feared that skilled non-Indian practitioners would soon dominate tribal courts now that Indian defendants had a right to counsel, and so, to protect the informal processes that people had appreciated in the tribal judicial setting, some tribes authorized a tribal bar or required that anyone practicing before the tribal court speak the native language or have as co-counsel a tribal member licensed to practice in tribal court.

The American Indian Tribal Court Judges Association was founded in 1970 to assist tribal courts in meeting the new procedural requirements that many people believed the statute instituted. The training of judges and court personnel emphasized federal substantive and procedural law almost to the exclusion of older tribal traditions. Court personnel in many tribes expanded to meet all the new duties that tribes believed they had. The most important movement within the tribal courts was training personnel to keep the proper records so that the decisions of tribal courts would be seen in their proper light and the courts would be regarded as courts of record, whose judgments would be respected by non-Indian courts.

Law review articles streamed out of printing presses in the years following the act, as non-Indians attempted to draw conclusions regarding the impact of the statute on tribal sovereignty. Most analyses verged on speculation, since it was entirely too early for anyone to discern what course tribal judicial systems would take once they began to feel the restrictions of the act on their activities. In a more theoretical sense, the act had to be related to past statutes and decisions in such a way that there would seem to be some continuity between the act and the cumulative body of federal Indian law. One commentator suggested that the act rejected the line of reasoning issuing from *Talton*,[14] in that it gave review on the merits to controversies within the tribe. This point of view is possible only if one conceives of judicial and political power flowing from one source. In practical terms this description is accurate, but historically and at least in theory Indian tribes derived their basic powers from that primordial precontact era when they enjoyed perfect political freedom.

The problem with this line of reasoning and analysis is that it projected backward into remote period of time a curious and unwarranted assumption that Indian political organizations would have followed the cultural evolutionary ladder upward until they arrived at Anglo-Saxon jurisprudence, and both the substance and procedure of law would strongly resemble what we have today in the non-Indian legal world. In fact, *Talton* attempts to define what source of power Indian tribes have and decides that Indians have an inherent power to establish local laws, not a delegated right. In that context, then, the Indian Civil Rights Act transforms the aboriginal sovereignty by objectifying it in institutions designed by non-Indians. The ICRA thus stands within the Collier tradition of transformation, but the act is exceedingly premature in attempting to provide a judicial system that can be of constructive service to Indian reservations.

Civil rights depend first of all upon a social contract theory of government, which Indian tribes do not possess, but they also depend upon a kind of government that allocates the sovereign powers to branches and then separates the branches of government to act as a checks-and-balance protection for the citizenry. Thus, we believe that even with an administration we abhor or a congress we believe is inept and incapable of solving problems, we have in the court system a means of blunting the malevolent actions of the government. By the same token, an aggressive congress can force the other two branches to respond to perceived needs of American society, and an active president can motivate the other two branches of government to deal with social and political problems through his own initiative in bringing issues to their attention.

If we remember Collier's original perception of tribal governments, we find that there is no separation of political powers because the intent of the tribal governments is to manage Indian resources, not to act in a national capacity. When they realized that failure to include aspects of nationality, traditional Indians rejected Collier's institutionalizing of the tribe out of hand. The tribal judicial system, under the Collier conception, and certainly under the solicitor's opinion *Powers of Indian Tribes,* was a creature of the tribal government and therefore could never stand on an equal footing with the tribal council itself. The ICRA's premise was the belief that with the inclusion of certain protections derived from the Bill of Rights, tribal courts would have the same relationship to both tribal citizens and the tribal government as did the federal courts to the American citizen and the federal government.

The real impact of the Indian Civil Rights Act, therefore, was to require one aspect of tribal government—the tribal court—to become a formal institution more completely resembling the federal judiciary than the tribal government itself resembled either the state or federal governments. The informality of Indian life that had been the repository of cultural traditions and customs was suddenly abolished, and in its place came the rigid requirements that were necessary to identify those instances in which the actions of the tribal government impinged upon the rights of tribal members. The ICRA basically distorted reservation life because it meant the imposition of certain rules and procedures with respect to the tribal courts that did not exist and could not exist in any of the other reservation institutions—the tribal government, tribal schools, and tribal economic enterprises.

In philosophical terms it is much easier to describe the impact of the Indian Civil Rights Act. Traditional Indian society understood itself as a complex of responsibilities and duties. The ICRA merely transposed this belief into a society based on rights against government and eliminated any sense of responsibility that the people might have felt for one another. Granted that many of the customs that made duties and responsibilities a serious matter of individual action had eroded badly in the decades since the tribes had agreed to move onto the reservations, the impact of the ICRA was to make these responsibilities impossible to perform because the act inserted the tribal court as an institution between the people and their responsibilities. People did not have to confront one another before their community and resolve their problems; they had only to file suit in tribal court.

The Indian Civil Rights Act was understood by most people as a major step toward the fulfillment of Indian self-government and, if we continue our analysis with consistency, it was certainly a step toward more self-government. But was it what Indians really wanted? A glance at the occupation of Wounded Knee will certainly give us an indication of the direction that Indian affairs went emotionally after the ICRA. As tensions built up on the Pine Ridge Indian Reservation, the tribal government was consistently used by one group of Indians to harass and oppress another group of Indians. When the violence erupted, there was no role for the tribal court except to echo the sentiments of one side of the intratribal dispute. The tribal court was virtually helpless as an institution that could assist in resolving the conflict. But—because the tribal court was there and available as an institution—it became a competitor with the more traditional way of resolving Sioux disputes. Thus, the introduction of the sacred pipe was not understood in its cultural context but was seen as a political weapon in the hands of one group of Indians. When we compare sacred pipe and tribal court as two competing means of reconciliation and problem-solving, the two sides in the conflict become readily apparent. The accusations by the American Indian Movement that the tribal government was a tool of the white man's colonial mentality take on real substance and significance.

It is probably very early in the life of modern tribal courts to issue a final judgment on the effect of the Indian Civil Rights Act. Tribal judges themselves have recently begun to recognize that customary law has been sadly neglected. In the fall of 1983 a committee was established by the American Indian Tribal Court Judges Association to study the idea of traditional or custom law with the view toward including the concepts of the respective tribal traditions in reaching decisions. Indians themselves have seen the imbalance and are seeking to remedy it. The mere fact that traditional law has become important and is recognized as forming the integral "Indian" dimension of the rights of Indians demonstrates that the movement toward nationality cannot be underestimated—even if it can frequently be misunderstood and thwarted.

The Cry for
Self-Determination

If we are to believe John Collier, his administration gave Indians self-government and laid the groundwork for the modern revival of Indian fortunes. However the arguments about its potency are resolved, the fact remains that emotionally the IRA and John Collier were a watershed in federal Indian policy. Recent evaluations of the IRA suggest that even limited self-government was a mirage. Every decision that an Indian tribal government made was subject to the approval of the secretary of the interior. Economic development rather than political and social progress was Collier's real achievement. Nevertheless, many Indians believed that they had been given self-government and in that spirit were able to accomplish a great deal before they realized how constricted and narrow their political powers actually were.

By the same token, the late sixties and early seventies will always be remembered for the great expansion of tribal activities under the new policy of self-determination. Beginning with the ARA in 1961 and continuing until the last years of the Carter administration, Indian tribes were the beneficiaries of numerous federal programs that invested millions of dollars in the reservation and its programs. Industrial parks were established, resort motels and recreation areas were constructed, Indian-controlled schools were established, thousands of new homes were built by tribes for homeless tribal members, and tribal courts were significantly expanded, giving the local people some more reliable form of local control of domestic affairs.

When the dust finally clears away and people evaluate the most recent period of Indian history, they will realize that the progress of the sixties and seventies was purchased at an enormous price. In order to attach themselves to national social welfare legislation, Indians had to pose as another American domestic racial minority. Few of the funds and programs that Indians received during the sixties and seventies were given to them because the government felt responsible to fulfill treaty obligations long withheld and due them. National policy sought to abolish poverty, and all low-income groups and areas were eligible to receive funds to accomplish this purpose. Indians happened to be a group that fell well within the identifiable guidelines of the poverty program, and they therefore qualified as recipients.

The cry for self-determination came at a favorable time because it coincided with the prevailing slogans of the administration that advocated the War on Poverty. In the spring of 1966 Secretary of the Interior Stewart Udall determined to remove Indian Commissioner Philleo Nash, who had terrible relations with Senator Henry Jackson, chairman of the Senate Interior Committee. Jackson wanted to revive the termination policy long enough to rid himself of the Colville Reservation in the northeast corner of his state. Nash successfully blocked this move, and Jackson then pressured Udall to remove Nash or face a hostile committee in other areas of interest to Interior. Nash was replaced by Robert Bennett, an Oneida Indian and career employee of the Bureau of Indian Affairs.

Udall called together the important personnel in the bureau at Santa Fe, New Mexico, to determine how he could get out of the trap that Jackson had thrown around Indian legislation. Udall believed that if he threw some tribes to the Senate committee in exchange for development plans for the remaining Indians under federal supervision, he could resolve the deadlock that had settled over the legislation proposed by the Interior Department. The National Congress of American Indians held a meeting concurrent with the bureau at Santa Fe in an effort to thwart Udall's plans to continue termination; as a countermeasure to his suspected program, the NCAI coined the phrase "self-determination." Real self-determination, if anyone had cared to think about it, was indeed termination, but under conditions established by Indians instead of Congress. Nevertheless self-determination was passed off in the language of the poverty wars to mean that the government should provide the funds and transfer the responsibility for administering the programs to the tribes—the same program that Collier once envisioned—except that the trust and its services would also continue unhampered and undiminished.

It took more than two years before the administration responded to the Indian demand in a formal manner. In the spring of 1968, as the election neared, President Johnson announced the formation of the Vice President's Council on Indian Opportunity, which was charged with the responsibility of overseeing the funding and administration of Indian programs and making them more responsive to Indian needs. Several cabinet members and some nationally prominent Indians were named to council membership. A staff was hired and a series of meetings were scheduled, designed to highlight the benefits Indians had received from the Democratic administration. Self-determination, which initially meant consultation with Indians prior to any initiative by the federal government, became the replacement of non-Indians by Indians in the basic policy-making positions. Since no one trusted Indians nor believed they could reach the proper decision, policy making more or less vanished and the practical policy emerged of giving Indians whatever they wanted, providing that they did not cause embarrassment to the administration. Before things broke down completely, however, a great many changes were wrought in Indian affairs that provide the context within which Indians live today.

The poverty programs emphasized education almost to the exclusion of other areas of interest. The kinds of programs that tribes received from the Office of Economic Opportunity sought to create a competitive educational system outside the normal institutional setting in which education had traditionally taken place. Head Start, Follow Through, A Better Chance, Neighborhood Youth Corps, and Job Corps were all designed to give students an extra boost in their educational opportunities. Tribes welcomed these programs because they provided a large payroll for the reservations and held forth the hope that Indian children could better themselves through acquiring the skills needed to compete in the outside world.

Compensatory educational programs had the benefit of showing Indians just how poor an education their children were receiving in bureau and public schools. If students were encouraged and given additional skills in Head Start, they were soon discouraged and held back by the attitudes of the regular educational institutions they attended. Once Indians recognized that they had to improve all education if their children were to succeed, they went about seeking a way to highlight that problem. By 1968, when the poverty program began to encounter great difficulties in Congress, Indians realized that they would have to make their educational programs a permanent and continuing part of federal services or they would not be able to preserve the progress they had made and expected to make in the future.

Coincidence again played an important role in determining the Indian posture toward federal programs. In 1967 Robert Kennedy, seeking to stake out a position for his presidential ambitions, had the Senate Education Committee sponsor a special subcommittee on Indian education. Using this committee to highlight failures of the federal government in Indian affairs, Kennedy could preempt administration relations with the liberal community, which was rapidly turning away from civil rights following Martin Luther King's speech against the Viet Nam War. Indians had been relatively quiet—in the liberal view, the "deserving poor," who were not expected to bite the hand that fed them.

With Robert Kennedy's assassination the chairmanship of the subcommittee drifted for a while until his brother Edward, another presidential aspirant, assumed the chairmanship and finished the work that Robert had begun. The subcommittee held numerous field hearings and authorized several studies, compiling a massive body of literature about Indian education and Indian aspirations in education. In November 1969 a final report was issued by the subcommittee, entitled "Indian Education: A National Tragedy—A National Challenge." In then-popular liberal rhetoric the report declared, "We are shocked at what we discovered." Then followed sixty recommendations that the subcommittee felt would enable Indians to have "unfettered opportunity to grow to their full potential." [1]

The recommendations varied considerably in terms of the problems the subcommittee sought to address. Any comprehensive educational study should of course comment on the social and economic environment in which children live and seek to learn, but it is apparent from reading its sixty recommendations that the subcommittee was primarily concerned not with education itself, but with using education as an excuse for a complete and critical analysis of the status of Indians. Among the recommendations were the need to establish a national policy in Indian education, national goals for health, housing, and employment needs for American Indians; and a White House Conference on American Indian Affairs—suggestions that encompassed everything Indians might want from an administration. The other recommendations, apart from the suggestions for technical adjustment of existing laws, were in sum threefold: Indians should control their educational institutions; Indians should have more education; and educational funding should dramatically increase. In short: Do more, faster.

Indians loved the Kennedy Report, as it was popularly known, because it provided an authoritative congressional voice to bolster the complaints they had made over the years. The report encouraged Indians to demand that they be given control of educational institutions wherever located and to be funded to experiment with model school programs. Unfortunately, the emphasis in the report was on the reformation of institutional life, and a glaring absence was any discussion of the quality of education, the content of learning that Indians might want for their children. Subcommittee staff members simply assumed that Indians wanted the same kind of education *they* had enjoyed as middle-class Americans, and they believed that control of the school board would ensure that result. Following the publication of the report, a number of national Indian educational organizations were created, with funds from the Department of Education and some of the larger foundations, to work on recommendations of the report. These groups promptly began to lobby to ensure that the minor recommendations of the report be implemented by federal legislation.

Kennedy was regarded as the presidential heir apparent, and consequently his recommendations did not receive support from the Nixon administration nor from some of the Democratic senators who regarded themselves as rivals for that party's nomination. Three years passed before Kennedy was able to secure passage of his Indian education package. With strong Indian support the Indian Education Act of 1972[2] became law as a result of election-year maneuvering. The act did define a national policy for Indian education, but it had the same basic flaws as the previous poverty legislation. Instead of a new and comprehensive organization of Indian educational programs, the statute simply amended existing national educational legislation to provide an Indian component. The ideological framework of education was not changed; Indians were simply given more direct access to funds for operating their school programs.

Among the important provisions of the Indian Education Act was the creation of the National Advisory Council on Indian Education. The legislation anticipated a skilled and experienced body of people who could exercise an oversight function and provide direction for the future of Indian education. Unfortunately, membership on the council became an Indian political issue, and various Indian educators promptly began to line up support to secure an appointment to the council. In addition to the Indian politics, national politics influenced selection of council members, and the administration reviewed hundreds of Indian nominees, trying to find a group it could trust not to embarrass it. The council was always in a political turmoil, and staff members came and went as if in a revolving door. Members of the council could not decide whether they represented the federal government or the Indian community and so adopted a middle course and rewarded those groups that had helped to secure their nomination.

Indian education now seemed to be the central focus around which other legislative proposals revolved. In 1975 Senator Henry Jackson, his presidential ambitions now tempering his approach to Indian policy, secured passage of his version of Indian education legislation with the Indian Self-Determination and Education Assistance Act.[3] John Collier must have smiled from his perch in bureaucratic heaven as he noted the provisions of this act. Section 2 contained what amounted to an admission of guilt by Congress for its complicity in allowing Indian programs to languish, and it pronounced education to be the key to any meaningful policy of self-determination. Section 3 defined a new federal policy of self-determination through Indian involvement, participation, and direction of educational service programs. The impetus for passing the legislation might have been the violence at Wounded Knee, which had taken place about a year before Jackson introduced his proposal, but the theoretical framework the act embraced left no doubt that it was the final offering of the liberal era in Congress.

The act was divided into two basic titles: the Indian Self-Determination Act and the Indian Education Assistance Act. Title I provided for subcontracting of federal services to tribal organizations, authorized discretionary grant and contract authority, provided for tribal government participation in the Intergovernmental Personnel Act programs so that civil service employees could work for tribal organizations without losing their benefits, and allowed the secretary of the interior to waive federal contracting laws and regulations if he determined they were not appropriate for the tribal contracts. Congress was thus taking the lock off the barn door and inviting Indians in to seize whatever they could pry away from suspicious bureaucrats.

Title II was basically derived from some of the problems that were identified during oversight hearings on the Indian Education Act. They involved a complicated set of amendments to the old Johnson-O'Malley Act (JOM), primarily of importance in two areas: Section 5 provided for the establishment of a local committee of parents of Indian children in schools served by a JOM contract, and section 6 authorized the secretary of the interior to pay the full per-capita cost of educating Indian students in public schools if the students were residing in BIA boarding facilities and were not regularly residents of the state. Some of the other sections spoke to the question of "quality" of education but merely required certification that Indian students were receiving equal services.

When hearings were held on the proposal,[4] in the House Interior Committee, Congressman Lloyd Meeds of Washington, who was chairing the hearings, presented his understanding of the development of the idea of Indian self-government. Meeds believed, as did Senator John Carroll before him during the hearings on Indian civil rights, that the theoretical framework for self-government had been worked out during the New Deal, presented by Collier, understood by the Senate Indian Committee, and made a part of the regular philosophy of the federal–Indian relationship. His statement is singularly enlightening as an indication of how firmly the folklore of self-government had become entrenched in people's minds:

> the Meriam Report of 1928 . . . made recommendation for administrative and legislative action to move away from paternalism to eventual Indian self-determination and self-government. In response to these findings, the Congress enacted the Indian Reorganization Act of 1934. Some have viewed this legislation as conferring powers of self-government on the tribes and imposing an outside form of government to implement these "new" powers. The legal effect of the act, however, was to restrict the extra legal administrative curtailment of tribal sovereignty and to facilitate tribal governments to implement those sovereign powers which had not been specifically limited by the Congress and, in some areas, to define these powers.[5]

Myth had finally overtaken political reality. Meeds spoke not out of his own ignorance but from a consensus of congressional minds that had begun to see the underlying Indian desire for more than simple municipal control of local activities.

Meeds cited two "ancient Indian laws," which, he argued, the bureau had attempted to use to effect its policy of self-determination. The laws were section 23 of the Act of June 25, 1910,[6] which authorized the secretary of the interior to employ Indian labor and purchase products of Indian industry, and the 1834 statute that reorganized the Department (later Bureau) of Indian Affairs and provided in section 14 that:

> where any of the tribes are, in the opinion of the Secretary of War, competent to direct the employment of their blacksmiths, mechanics, teachers, farmers, or other persons engaged for them, the direction of such persons may be given to the proper authority of the tribe.[7]

Indian Commissioner Morris Thompson was less enthusiastic about the proposal. Challenging the origins of the ideas in the Meriam Report and the Indian Reorganization Act, he announced that the title of Indian self-determination had actually derived from three proposals made by President Nixon in his 1970 message on Indians:

A proposal providing for Indians to assume control of Federal programs established for their benefit; a proposal whereby Federal employees who accompanied programs transferred to the tribes could retain their civil service benefits; and a proposal to amend the Johnson-O'Malley Act by adding Indian tribes to the list of parties with whom the Secretary of the Interior can contract out the education of Indians.[8]

Meeds had the better of the argument by reminding everyone that these promises were originally made during the treaty-making period and were reinforced as the agreement-making era was ending.

Indians were enthusiastic about the education proposals of the seventies because they meant that the tribe would be gaining control of one of the most important institutions on the reservations. Indian politicians saw this development as a new way by which they could control patronage and enhance their position as incumbents. The rank-and-file tribal members seemed to like the proposals because it meant having some power over the people who taught their children. Major problems were not discussed or mentioned, and there were other clues to the limits of the reform's significance. For one thing, Indian education was now split among the tribe, the bureau, mission schools, and the public school system, and no single party had a superior responsibility for what happened in Indian education. Responsibilities for funding sources were again divided; the Department of Education had a considerable amount of money designated for Indian education, but the bureau still controlled the Johnson-O'Malley funds and contracts. The public schools had to work out financial arrangements as best they could, providing from their own sources a considerable percentage of their annual budgets.

In the move to quality education, the progress of the seventies was hardly a step forward. Indians became so concerned about their annual funding cycle that they spent most of their time at conferences inquiring about waivers of rules and regulations that would allow them some measure of flexibility. Indian education came to be considerably more complicated than it had been because it now involved determining the proper relationships between competing institutions and sponsoring agencies. A few "freedom schools" were established during the height of the Indian-controlled school drive, but these programs were generally in the remedial rather than the innovative category. Contracting was a hazardous endeavor. Most tribes simply did not have enough free money to meet all the contingency expenses that arose in the course of a school year, and the Office of Indian Education (OIE) in the Department of Education did not help matters. OIE was perennially behind in approving grants and authorizing expenditures, so tribal and public schools often arrived at the opening of school without knowing whether or not they would have funds to complete the academic year.

Indian-controlled education was not actually self-determination because Indians did not determine what kind of education their children would receive; they only replaced non-Indian bureaucrats and educators in institutions that changed very little with the shifting of personnel. Nevertheless, Indians believed that they were directing their own fortunes because they were at least visibly in charge in the only place where such visibility counted, on the reservations. Even with the onerous task of securing refunding of programs, most Indian educators could work their way through the bureaucratic maze of Washington successfully.

Indian education encountered reality when the matter of credentials arose. Tribes might arrange to assume control of public or bureau schools and they might establish community colleges on the reservations, but in order for these institutions to have any meaning they had to meet the standards of a regional accreditation organization, which many of the Indian schools could not. Indians began to realize that though they might get rid of the bureau through subcontracting and might even take over some functions of public schools through a complicated contracting system, they could not subcontract the substance of education; for better or for worse, Indians were still connected to the larger American society. Since no one had any idea how to construct a competing school system after the manner of the Amish, another group that sought isolation from the mainstream of American education, Indians sought to bring their schools into some kind of conformity with the rest of American education. Thus ended, at least for the moment, the movement toward schools specifically designed to service Indians as Indians.

Tribal court expansion and assumption of educational institutions required a considerable amount of free money that could be used to supplement grant funds. For most projects the tribes had to match a certain percentage of the grant with cash and services. At the beginning tribes might dedicate some tracts of land to serve as their matching share of the project, but after a while it became necessary to find additional moneys in order to keep the larger grant sums coming to the reservations. Claims moneys could not generally be used because the tribal members usually wanted these funds distributed on a per-capita basis. A faster rate of exploitation of existing reservation resources became the only ready source of funds to meet the ever-increasing demands for administrative matching funds.

A few tribes had some valuable resources. The Navajos had oil, gas, uranium, and coal. The Yakimas and Quinaults had timber. The Laguna Pueblo had uranium. The Fort Hall Shoshone-Bannocks had phosphate reserves. The list is deceptive, though, for in fact most of these reserves are owned by a very small number of tribes, and even they are not unlimited. Exploiting them rapidly only means advancing the time when the tribes are completely helpless before the larger economic forces in the land. For the many large tribes, who had primarily grazing and agricultural lands, the idea of increasing tribal income to amounts that were needed to continue the expansion of social service bureaucracies on the reservation was simply an impossible task. Farmland simply does not return enough money to sustain anything except a continuing agricultural operation.

Secretary of the Interior Stewart Udall in 1966 suggested that Indians might consider mortgaging their lands in order to get enough money to embark on development schemes. The problem with Udall's suggestion was that technical assistance would be given by the Bureau of Indian Affairs, and if the project did not succeed, the bureau could walk away from its responsibilities, leaving the tribe not only bankrupt but potentially landless. Indians rejected Udall's proposal immediately, and consequently economic development during the sixties took a different tack. Tribes did not do much in the way of development of industries, but rather the bureau sought to bring industries to the reservations, hoping to provide a wage economy where there was great unemployment. Generally industries received either a tax benefit or subsidies for training Indians to do certain jobs of an industrial–light manufacturing nature. When the benefits expired, the industries generally closed down, leaving empty buildings and a disrupted community. The problem with mortgages and wage industries as avenues for bolstering the Indian economy was that Indians did not respond like non-Indians to the opportunities that were made available to them. Most people simply did not understand what such activities involved and abhorred the impersonality that seemed to go with these developments.

Indian tribes became eligible for revenue-sharing money in 1972, when the revenue-sharing act was passed.[9] Some tribes with a large population received good-sized sums, but these moneys were not exactly free and could not, in most instances, be used to meet the growing tribal deficits. Most of the funds had to be spent for such municipal purposes as safety programs, transportation, recreation, health care, and financial administration. Participation meant that many tribes had to spend additional funds in order to receive their revenue-sharing funds, and this requirement only drove some tribes further in debt. Revenue sharing was useless for many small tribes, which did not have a sufficient population to make the sums realistic. Conservative critics of the program took great glee in pointing out the completely inadequate funds some small tribes received. Though inadequate funds did make the program irrelevant to some tribes, the basic problem was that reservations were not municipalities in the traditional sense and programming the funds was very difficult, considering the distribution of population on the reservations. Since the agency town usually had a big population, funds were spent there, and the people in the back country felt they had been deliberately neglected when it came to spending the money.

In 1974, in an effort to generate more capital for use by the tribes, Congress passed the Indian Financing Act.[10] The act was applauded as a major step forward in financing reservation development, but it was more a cosmetic reordering of existing loan programs administered by the Bureau of Indian Affairs. All funds were consolidated, and authority was given to add fifty million dollars to the fund. The secretary of the interior was authorized to pay interest subsidies and to guarantee or insure loans from private lenders. Guarantee was important because some tribes wanted to pledge their lands, and there was no way under existing federal law that such lands could be foreclosed should the loan fail. Some programs were initiated with loans from this source, but in important areas, such as land consolidation, the fund was not very useful.

Tribes got an emotional but not a capital boost when the Tribal Governmental Tax Status Act was introduced in 1982. For years Indian leaders had emphasized their national status to little avail. The purpose of the bill was to amend the Internal Revenue Code to place tribes in a favorable position with respect to the various definitions of the code. Section 202 of the act established the conditions under which a tribal government would be treated as a state and as subdivisions of a state. These exceptions amended a long list of definitions and basically gave tribes the same status as states for the purpose of excise taxes, charitable contributions, and contributions to candidates for public office, and they made them eligible for benefits associated with pension and annuity plans. Section 203 allowed tribes to issue bonds for industrial development purposes, with certain territorial and subject matter restrictions.

The idea was certainly worth merit, but when it was finally passed, the tribes lost most of the privileges and retained only a very restricted power to issue bonds for some municipal purposes—which power they might have possessed all along.

Education and industrial development were but parts of the larger Indian demand for self-determination. In both instances the effort to come to grips with the substance and institutional framework of the field led to larger considerations that would have drastically altered the nature of the federal-Indian relationship. Few people understood how complicated the situation was getting, and since the Congress and the respective administrations only received response from the Indians who worked in national organizations and from a select group of tribal leaders, the tempo of Indian affairs was not often represented at the policy-making levels. Indian response to some proposals was favorable, out of proportion to the seriousness of the suggestion; other overtures fell on deaf Indian ears when it was anticipated that they would be eagerly embraced. Consequently, no one was really prepared for the continuing escalation of activism in Indian country. The occupation of the Bureau of Indian Affairs during election week 1972 caught everyone by surprise by its violence and seemingly unreasonable demands.

The response of the Nixon administration to the occupation of the Bureau of Indian Affairs was to seek a confrontation with the American Indian Movement at a remote place in the West, where it would be difficult to capture and hold headlines, as the Indians had done while occupying federal buildings in the nation's capital. When AIM announced it would go to the Pine Ridge Reservation after returning home from its adventures in Washington, the administration provided additional funds to the tribal government of that reservation. Confrontation was almost inevitable. We will deal with the activist movement in the next chapter because it forms an integral part of the Indian drive for nationhood. It is important at this stage to recognize that activism drove the administration much closer to tribal governments, underscoring the feeling that tribal governments were merely arms of the federal government and that true self-determination would have to occur outside the regular channels of institutional life.

Wounded Knee produced a strong reaction in Congress and may have provided some impetus for Senator Jackson's decision to move forward with his Self-determination Act. The occupation did inspire Senator James Abourezk of South Dakota to take a more active hand in Indian affairs, and during the summer of 1974 he introduced S.J. Reslution 133, which established the American Indian Policy Review Commission.[11] The original intent of the commission was similar to the 1928 Senate investigation of conditions of Indians in the United States. Unfortunately the resolution was radically amended prior to passage, creating ten (later eleven) task forces to do the field hearings for the commissioners. The commission was to be composed of three senators, three congressmen, and five Indians. The resolution provided two years of study before the final report was due, and the commission started its work in January 1975.

The Abourezk Commission, as it was popularly called, responded to long-standing Indian requests that Congress take a good, hard look at the conditions under which Indians live and then adjust federal policy accordingly. It represented one of the best opportunities in this century for Indians to affect the manner in which the Congress and hence the federal agencies understood Indian problems. Unlike the Meriam Report, which had a few minor Indian consultants; the Committee of One Hundred, which had some token Indian members; and Secretary Udall's 1961 task force, which had an affluent Indian as a member, the Abourezk Commission was packed full of Indians of every persuasion at every level. In addition to the five Indians who were commissioners, thirty-one out of thirty-three task force members were Indians, Indians dominated staff and secretarial support positions, and a significant number of contracted consultants were Indians.

The commission from the start was plagued with behind-the-scenes Indian politics, as various individuals saw an opportunity to use commission participation as a means of enhancing their own careers. The congressional representatives knew so little about Indians that they frequently made glaring errors in identifying the Indians they wanted on the commission and in its task forces. Jake White Crow, a Quapaw from Oklahoma, was nominated as "Jack White Cow." He was approved as a member of the commission before anyone checked to see what his correct name was. The record of proceedings was later changed to save both Mr. White Crow and the senator who nominated him embarrassment. Various cliques of Indians sought control of the different task forces, and the final membership of both staff and task forces reflected the relative strength of the different Indian interests rather than expertise in the subject matter.

No plan for either research or field hearings was designed to assist the task forces in their mission. The various groups would meet and decide what their work involved and proceed without much idea of what they were supposed to be gathering as data or what present policy they were critiquing. Procedures for reimbursing the task forces were not established until very late. As a result many task forces did not even begin to work until the end of the first year, making their investigation of conditions almost perfunctory. The report was due in the early months of 1977, and by the fall of 1976 the staff of the commission gave up all pretense of working with the task forces. It simply borrowed employees from the Bureau of Indian Affairs and had them help write up the final report. Unlike the Senate investigation of 1928, the field hearings were never published, so it was impossible to tell if the final report bore any relationship whatsoever to what the task forces had found in the field. Unused was the subpoena power given to the commission for use in investigating difficult areas of inquiry.

The final report of the commission followed the line of the Indian militants, who had generally been excluded from positions on commission and its task forces, which made the orientation of the final statement difficult to understand. "The relationship of the American Indian tribes to the United States is founded on principles of international law," the report stated. "It is a political relation: a relation of a weak people to a strong people; a relation of weak governments to a strong government; a relationship founded on treaties in which the Indian tribes placed themselves under the protection of the United States and the United States assumed the obligation of supplying such protection." With this powerful statement the commission then recommended two fundamental concepts, which it said should guide all future federal policy determinations affecting Indians:

1. That Indian tribes are sovereign political bodies, having the power to determine their own membership and power to enact laws and enforce them within the boundaries of their reservations.
2. That the relationship which exists between the tribes and the United States is premised on a special trust that must govern the conduct of the stronger toward the weaker.

It was not the first time in the history of Indian–white relationships that such conclusions had been offered—but they had nonetheless never become the guiding principles of administration. They give content to John Marshall's phrase "domestic dependent nations," but, when viewed in the context of Nathan Margold's solicitor's opinion of 1934, a panoply of powers, ordinarily exercised by Western political systems, is attributed to Indian tribes. Though the commission sought to restore the original political status of tribes, it refused to acknowledge subsequent changes that had occurred in American history which had made the exercise of some powers of self-government obsolete.

Congressman Lloyd Meeds, co-chairman of the commission, was outraged at the language of the final report, which he considered, and rightfully so in the context, unnecessarily inflammatory. He hired an Arizona lawyer named Frederick Martone to write a dissenting opinion for him, in which he opposed almost all of the commission's findings on the grounds that they were impractical in a land in which Indians were greatly outnumbered. Meeds's harsh dissent provoked an additional statement by Senator Abourezk denying that the report was inflammatory and a separate statement by the Indian commissioners thanking Congress for allowing them to serve on the commission, an exceedingly strange way of rebutting Meeds.

The final report also contained 206 specific recommendations, which ranged from the terribly abstract philosophical notions regarding Indian sovereignty that the staff believed should become part of congressional rhetoric and technical language, on the one hand, to very practical changes in particular sections of various federal statutes, on the other. A substantial number of recommendations required additional funds from Congress; a large number of recommendations involved amending the Internal Revenue Code to make various kinds of Indian income virtually immune from any form of state or federal taxation. Some of the recommendations suggested amendments in the Indian Civil Rights Act that would limit the power of federal courts to review and intervene in the proceedings and decisions of tribal courts. In specific reference to the Bureau of Indian Affairs, the commission wanted the commissionership elevated to the status of assistant secretary of the interior and various kinds of model training institutes for better management created.

The recommendations dealing with self-government are very interesting in light of the extensive history of self-government efforts by both the Indians and the Congress. The commission wanted section 16 of the Indian Reorganization Act amended to read as follows:

The right to choose their natural form of government is the inherent right of any Indian tribe. Amendments to tribal constitutions and by-laws adopted pursuant to the Indian Reorganization Act shall be ratified and approved by the Secretary to protect the trust assets and resources of the tribe.[13]

When taken with the recommendations that followed, restricting the authority of the secretary of the interior to intervene in the decisions of the tribe to those instances involving the use or disposition of resources, this amendment showed considerable promise in restoring a balance between the demands of the traditional Indians and the practical realities of the contemporary Indian situation.

Unfortunately, the recommendation to secure permanent status for tribal governments was buried under the list of recommendations involving federal administration and was theoretically linked to changes in the perceived status of Indian tribes as eligible recipients and sponsoring agencies for the administration of federal programs. It declared the real threat of a return to the termination policy to be depriving tribes of access to federal funding sources, not a dangerous alternative to federally sponsored and assisted development of the reservations. The section covering recommendations on federal administration also sought to include tribes in eligibility sections of the federal laws that recognized the political status of states as agencies designated to carry out certain federal policies and administer certain kinds of federally funded programs. If anything, the final report made Indian tribes seem like an intimate, functioning part of the sprawling federal administrative apparatus.

Although the commissioners divided along rather sharp theoretical lines, there was much to commend the final report of the American Indian Policy Review Commission as a positive program that Congress could embrace. Had some of the major recommendations been introduced in legislative form during the life of the commission, when it had considerable leverage in Congress, a good number of the more controversial recommendations might have been written into law before they stirred up antagonisms. Placed in the context of a strident militant language in the final report, however, provisions that were essentially housekeeping chores became ominous and appeared to be going beyond the mandate of the original resolution establishing the commission.

No study has been made to determine how many of these recommendations of the Abourezk Commission have become a part of federal policy. Indians were given an assistant secretary position within Interior in addition to the commissionership of the Bureau of Indian Affairs within a short time after the publication of the final report. Additional funding was rejected by the Carter administration, and subsequent administrations substantially reduced federal funding, which badly hampered the continuation of reservation programs in those areas where tribes received funds from federal agencies other than the Interior Department. Most important, perhaps, was the elimination of the Indian subcommittees in the Senate and House Interior committees. A Senate Select Committee on Indian Affairs was established on a continuing basis as a courtesy to Senator Abourezk, but when he left Congress, it had to be renewed every session of Congress, making any significant legislative program to realize some of the recommendations of the commission exceedingly difficult.

Perhaps Congressman Meeds was correct in his dissenting opinion. Perhaps times had changed and Indians could not demand a radical revision of their status that would guarantee them a permanent place in the American domestic political landscape. A good deal of the motivation for the policy review commission had been generated by the occupation of Wounded Knee, and by 1978 the activists had been quieted by prolonged criminal trials and FBI harassment. There no longer seemed to be much urgency in resolving Indian problems. The American Indian Policy Review Commission lacked the single factor that had made the Indian Reorganization Act such a profound revolution in federal policy. There was no energetic person within the Interior Department or the Bureau of Indian Affairs who could, like John Collier, take the reins of administration and use them creatively to put the new program in place. Instead the bureau cautiously and hesitantly proceeded to review the recommendations, finding very little of worth in them and seeking to preserve wherever possible the prerogatives and privileges it considered to be its own.

The Abourezk Commission provided the theoretical framework within which the reforms in education, tribal courts, and economic development would have found a comfortable home. Its task was to translate long-standing Indian desires into a programmatic format that would be acceptable in Congress. Unfortunately, no one on the commission recognized the fact that Indians themselves had to create much of the change in viewpoint by reconsidering how they saw themselves. The commission placed too much blame on the federal government and spoke not at all to the Indian community of its own responsibilities in governing and managing. Self-determination was regarded as something of substance, which Congress might bestow on Indians, not a goal, which Indians might achieve for themselves.

16
The Emergence
of Indian Nationalism

The traditional Indians, as we have already noted, by and large boycotted the Indian Reorganization Act elections. Some felt that the elections were for the benefit of the secretary of the interior and voting in them would reduce them to mere citizens. Others felt that only those people who had kept their lands should be regarded as tribal members and that the elections were therefore designed to put non–tribal members in control of the new tribal government. The strongest feeling expressed by traditional people, however, was that they already had a government of chiefs and headmen and that allowing any other kind of government on the reservations would prove injurious to their rights.

During the termination policy years traditionals would not vote to accept or reject the provisions of the terminal legislation, nor would they discuss any scheme that would change the way that they were accustomed to doing things. The results often backfired on them. In the sixties the failure of traditional people on the Colville Reservation in Washington State to participate in tribal affairs allowed a protermination tribal council to be elected for several years. This council then passed a resolution purporting to express the wishes of the tribe to support Senator Jackson's termination legislation. Even in the face of such clear evidence, it was extremely difficult to get traditional Indians to understand the need to defend themselves using the procedures the federal government would recognize.

The traditional stance in these cases is not difficult to understand intellectually. Most of these people believed that the government was honor-bound to respect the integrity of their little nation and therefore believed that any compromise they might make would be thrown back at them later. If they didn't vote, then the Congress would be unable to terminate them, since it didn't have their consent. The moral conviction, however, was not taken seriously by tribal politicians and tribal attorneys, who knew all too well the cynical and expedient decision-making process to which Indians were subjected. Try as they might, they could not often budge the traditionals and make them realize the peril to which they were subjecting themselves. The traditionals' reasoning, however, greatly appealed to younger Indians, who rejected the morality of the actions of both the tribal and the federal government. Needing something substantial to believe in, these young people generally sided with the traditionals until the situation seemed so dangerous that they had to surrender in order to salvage anything from the debris.

Traditional Indians could usually be identified by certain characteristics that made them a formidable party to be reckoned with on the reservations. They were generally able to trace their ancestry back to the last chiefs and headmen to surrender and agree to go onto the reservation a century before. These chiefs chose isolated places far from the agency headquarters for their villages so that they could stay away from the influence and control of the agents and Indian police. Their descendents usually still lived in the most isolated parts of the reservation. The traditional people followed most of the social and religious customs of the tribe, and they were the most reliable source of information on these things. Consequently, the mixed-bloods at the agency town, who were often uncertain of their own claims to Indian identity, were hesitant to clash with the traditionals for fear they would reveal their ignorance and become an object of scorn.

Traditionals knew the tribal language extremely well. Even in 1960 there were many who had only a smattering of English and preferred to use the native tongue when speaking at community and tribal meetings. Traditional people knew that language was a powerful political weapon in a public forum, and they frequently used it with great effectiveness, cowing helpless opponents who knew few words. There is nothing as embarrassing as being ridiculed in a language a person barely understands, and no astute tribal politician would dare confront a traditional who could bring such evidence of real Indianness to bear.

The oral tradition was almost an exclusive possession of the traditional people. They knew considerably more about the treaties than did the other Indians and remembered the slightest nuance of meaning in every treaty promise. More acculturated tribal people relied upon the tribal attorney to give them information on the status of the treaties—unreliable sources, as most of the tribal attorneys thought that the treaties were useless historical curiosities and preferred to cite current statutes and case law to the tribe when they were discussing legal rights. Even without such training, most of the traditional leadership could carry on a savage dialogue with the tribal attorney on the fine points of federal Indian law. They might not cite the proper case as precisely as an experienced lawyer would, but they knew considerably more about their legal rights than any other group living on the reservation. They simply did not understand nor did they respect the niceties of legal procedure that might ensure that their case would be presented properly in the courts and before Congress.

By the early sixties definite political positions had been drawn between the traditionals and the other Indians in the tribe. Traditionals were by and large very suspicious of federal grants. They had been working most of their lives on Court of Claims cases in which the United States had claimed, as offsets against their claims, money and gratuitous services that the government had given the tribe during early reservation days. Almost the first question a traditional would ask when the subject of receiving federal grants was raised was whether or not the government would come back to the tribe decades later and demand to deduct from a claims award the sums it was giving them under the poverty and other social programs. Tribal officials had to reassure people dozens of times that no offsets would be later deducted if they took the money the government was offering.

Many times traditional Indians would equate the programs of the Office of Economic Opportunity with the treaty promises and argue that there should be no controls placed on the manner in which the tribe administered these grants. Housing was a particularly difficult point to explain because the government negotiators had promised the tribe houses if they moved to the reservation and had not fulfilled this provision of the treaties. When the housing programs began, the traditionals would encourage the people to believe the houses were theirs without any strings whatsoever, making it exceedingly difficult for tribal officials to administer self-help and mutual help housing programs.

Tribal identity was another strong point of the traditional Indians.

They did not, in many instances, even bother to use the word *Indian* unless they used it in a derisive manner; it was too broad and generalized a definition. Uninformative about social and kinship responsibilities, it seemed only an ethnic label that the whites had pinned on their tribe. Anyone could act like an Indian; it took a certain amount of self-discipline and knowledge of the customs to act like a Lakota, a Navajo, a Nez Perce, or a Crow. A tribal Indian—and this appellation is certainly better than simply "traditional" in many respects—did not want to associate with people outside the tribal community unless he or she was forced to do so. An "ethnic" Indian, on the other hand—and this label is most apt, in view of the subsequent developments—welcomed participation with others and looked beyond the boundaries of the reservation to see both opportunities and dangers the tribe might encounter.

Indian activism was certainly an invention of the tribal Indians. They devoutly believed that whites in positions of authority would give them justice if they only knew the conditions under which the tribe lived. They were absolutely fearless in exercising their treaty rights and believed implicitly in the neutral operation of a kind of abstract justice they believed would uphold them. They did not believe in an "Indian cause" but in the specific rights given them under treaty. If a right or privilege was not articulated in a treaty, they did not believe it was theirs, regardless of what laws Congress might have passed vesting rights and privileges in them. The first activist events of the sixties were the "fish-ins" in the Pacific Northwest. Although there was an obvious connection with the "sit-ins" conducted by young blacks in the South, the traditionals made this connection only for publicity purposes; it was easier to explain to the rest of the world what they were doing. They never for a moment believed they were fighting for the rights of an ethnic group; they were fighting for a particular article of a treaty and they intended it to be upheld by the United States.

The fish-ins attracted more publicity than anyone expected when Marlon Brando and Dick Gregory attended and brought national press people with them. When news of what was happening reached Indians in other tribes and other parts of the country, a transformation of no small importance began to take place. Other Indians saw the struggle to preserve treaty fishing rights as simply another example of federal failure to guarantee treaty rights, and the conflict in the Pacific Northwest became a personal affront to many other Indians. As incident followed incident, it became increasingly obvious that tribal rights in many parts of the country were being trampled under foot, and these incidents, representative of the general condition under which many tribes had to live, turned the issue of Indian rights in part into the struggle of a domestic American ethnic-racial group.

The young Indians who formed the National Indian Youth Council in 1963 adopted the slogan put forth by their charismatic leader, Melvin Thom of the Walker River Paiutes: "For a Greater Indian America." Indian rights and conditions became an ethnic issue, but specific treaty rights and particular situations involving Indians remained a tribal concern. Hence it was exceedingly difficult for either the NIYC or the National Congress of American Indians to rally the tribes beyond a certain point of political participation. Indian leadership might agree on the general statements that could be made to the United States government or the press, but they would almost always look at their own tribal condition before they would take action. This distinction was instinctive rather than self-conscious and therefore represented to the whites irrational behavior. Many well-meaning whites hammered at the national Indian organizations to "unify" the tribes, and the national spokespeople did their best to comply. But unity beyond a certain consensus on issues was virtually impossible as long as traditional people preached the doctrine of tribal integrity.

The consolidated Indian movement probably emerged in the urban areas, where Indians of different tribes were coming together for mutual help and support. Cut off from their own communities by great distances, these people preferred to be with other Indians rather than other racial groups including whites. Hence, to articulate the conditions existing all over the country as an "Indian" matter was not only natural for concerned Indians in the cities but wholly justified in terms of their understanding of their situation. It was better in the cities to forego tribal differences in order to gain some kind of identity than simply to disappear or to associate only with people from their own tribe or reservation.

The merging of many tribal identities and histories in the urban setting meant the adoption of a common, albeit artificial, heritage. The 1868 Sioux treaty became regarded as the common property of all Indians, and when the Indian college students of varying tribal backgrounds invaded Alcatraz Island in San Francisco Bay and later Fort Lawton near Seattle, they laid claim to these pieces of federal surplus property under that treaty. The claim was mythological and depended primarily upon the memory and oral tradition carried forward by the traditional people among the Sioux. No article existed in the 1868 treaty that gave the Sioux (or any other tribe) rights to federal surplus property. Traditional people had told younger people that after the soldiers had departed from the forts along the Bozeman Trail, Red Cloud had burned the forts. From this memory came the belief that Red Cloud had negotiated a treaty promise dealing with surplus property. Since Red Cloud had kicked the United States out of northern Wyoming, he was the law and could do almost anything he wanted.

Further evidence of the ethnic nature of the urban-originating movement was the nomenclature adopted by the Indian activists. The students at Alcatraz and the protestors at Fort Lawton called themselves Indians of All Tribes, implying the universal nature of their appeal and of their constituency. In the San Francisco Bay area the United Native Americans was formed around the time of the Alcatraz invasion. The American Indian Movement was organized in the Minneapolis area around 1968, and in that year a number of urban Indian centers organized as American Indians—United. Here we have no tribal affiliation but a strong ethnic flavor. In view of the times—the sixties were filled with various groups emerging and demanding various forms of redress—Indian was more appropriate than tribal identification because it enabled people to cite incidents as symptomatic of the conditions under which Indians lived. The public could deal with Indians; it was never quite certain about tribal affiliations.

The March on Washington during election week 1972 was a major turning point for both ethnic and tribal Indians. Caravans began on the West Coast and worked their way through Indian country on the way east. At every reservation stop speeches and rallies were featured as caravan members tried to explain the purpose of the march. Although the rhetoric was styled in liberal sixties terminology, tribal peoples could immediately identify with specific issues because they had local examples of the callous attitude of government. Consequently, many tribal peoples, including elders and religious leaders, decided to join the caravans. The presence of these people reminded everyone that Indians shared a great tradition of independence and nationhood, which the years had not erased. Many of the marchers now began to consider the specific traditions of their own tribe in addition to the general issues that affected all Indians.

The caravans met in Minneapolis to hold workshops to prepare a platform that they could present to the White House officials when they arrived in Washington, D.C. Many of the marchers had been attracted to the movement by the demonstrations that tried to symbolize the oppression felt by Indians all over the country. The workshops now forced people to be specific about their complaints. What were they going to tell the government? What solutions would they recommend? The participants remembered the general plea of the NCAI half a decade before for "self-determination" and how the federal bureaucracy had turned that demand against the tribal leaders by appointing pliant Indians to serve on advisory committees and in administrative posts. Conditions had not substantially improved, and in some instances they had gotten worse. Hence it was necessary to be precise about remedies and to outline just what steps would be acceptable to the people.

The workshops produced the famous Twenty Points, which were presented to White House officials in the midst of the great confusion that occurred when the headquarters of the Bureau of Indian Affairs was occupied. Unfortunately, the issue soon became whether or not the Indians could be removed from the bureau without unnecessary violence and injury, then how the people would get home (the government finally provided the money for most protestors to return) and how they would get back government records that had been removed from the building during the occupation. The Twenty Points were never given a real hearing by federal officials. They nevertheless form one of the most remarkable documents ever presented to the federal government by an Indian group.

The mark of the traditional Indian is stamped all over the Twenty Points. The first eight points dealt with the restoration of a functioning treaty relationship with the United States. They included:

1. A restoration of a constitutional treaty-making authority.
2. The establishment of a treaty commission to make new treaties.
3. An address to the American people and a joint session of Congress.
4. A commission to review treaty commitments and violations.
5. The resubmission of unratified treaties to the Senate.
6. The provision that all Indians be governed by treaty relations.
7. Mandatory relief against treaty-rights violations.
8. Judicial recognition of the Indian right to interpret treaties.

These points form a coherent whole and describe a process that the Indians wished to initiate. The treaty relationship would be flexible and enable both the federal government and the tribes to alter their stance toward each other when the occasion arose. The address to the American people and the joint session of Congress was necessary to ensure that a small group of technicians did not derail or deadend the treaty process in a morass of bureaucracy.

The remaining points dealt with lands, religious freedom, repeal of oppressive state laws, rehabilitation of Indian prisoners, and finally an appropriation of fifteen billion dollars in specifically programmed funds. They sought to eliminate areas of friction that had been identified as issues that could be remedied by federal legislation, eliminating the need for a large bureaucracy to administer the problem areas. Most of the points can be traced directly to traditional values and beliefs, and the provision for rehabilitation of prisoners spoke to the continuing problem of Indians convicted because of their inability to understand their rights under existing federal and state laws. On the whole, the realization of these points would enable tribal societies to begin to repair the damage that had been done during the previous century.

The Twenty Points stand in stark contrast to the 206 recommendations made by the American Indian Policy Review Commission in response to Wounded Knee (or was it to the BIA occupation?). The Abourezk Commission did not seek to advocate a new institutional framework in which future Indian progress could and would take place. Rather it suggested tightening the rules and regulations governing existing institutional arrangements, hoping to make them more efficient so they could deliver services faster. The Twenty Points made better financial sense than the nebulous requests by the Abourezk Commission for "more money." The Twenty Points based its financial estimates on the fact that if some of the points were realized, many existing financial expenditures of the federal government would not be necessary. A real change of policy would encourage Indians on the reservations to take charge of their lives in a more secure environment. The Abourezk Commission sought to make Indians better Americans; the Twenty Points sought to allow Indians to become functioning tribal members once again.

Wounded Knee followed too quickly on the heels of the occupation of the bureau headquarters to enable the Indian activists to begin to lobby for the acceptance of their programs. AIM announced that it would hold a victory celebration on the Pine Ridge Reservation in South Dakota when people from that state returned home. The federal government rushed additional funds to Pine Ridge to bolster the tribal police force, and border-town toughs began to find their way to the tribal headquarters. Soon the tribal police were brutalizing and harassing tribal members who were suspected of being members of AIM. The people protested this treatment and sought the impeachment of the tribal chairman, Richard Wilson. The bureau not only supported Wilson but allowed him to sit as chairman during his impeachment. Finally, the people believed they had had enough and a meeting was held to determine what to do. Believing they had exhausted all legal remedies, the people got into their cars and headed for Wounded Knee to make their stand.

Traditional people at Pine Ridge formed the backbone of the occupation of Wounded Knee, even though federal and state officials attempted to make it seem as if urban Indian guerrillas had invaded the reservation. Medicine men came and participated in the camp and conducted ceremonies for the people. They also were an integral part of the negotiations with the government, which finally led to the surrender of the village and church. After the occupation was over and the White House sent representatives to talk with the people of the reservation, Chief Frank Fools Crow hosted the meeting, and a strong contingent of traditional people attended the session to air their grievances. This meeting resembled the old negotiating sessions of a century before, with men, women, and children attending and participating in the activities.

A comparison with the role of the Christian clergy in the civil rights movement may help us better understand the involvement of traditional people in the Indian movement at that time. The black clergy were instrumental in initiating the civil rights movement in the South. The Montgomery bus boycott was organized and sustained by the leadership and participation of the black ministers of the city. They developed strategy and were critically important in formulating demands and negotiating settlements. And the black clergy were able to motivate the white Christian clergy by pointing out the great similarity between what the black community wanted and what the white churches had been preaching. When the white clergy finally became involved, they devoted considerable energy to marches, raised immense sums of money, and acted as important spokespeople to the larger American society, calling the nation to account for the treatment of blacks.

Tribal Indians, particularly the religious leaders, cast a jaundiced eye on the first activist demonstrations in the Indian movement. They supported individual efforts by people of their own tribes but looked with contempt on the spectacular and largely symbolic invasions and occupations of federal lands and buildings. The first response of tribal peoples toward the expanding Indian movement was to proclaim that "Indians don't act that way." Many of these people still had hopes that the federal government would come to its senses and sit down and negotiate seriously about tribal problems. Tribal Indians spent a great deal of time deliberating on what was happening in Indian country. When the March on Washington arrived at their reservations and they heard the speeches of the marchers and saw the earnestness of the people taking part, they finally decided to join the caravan.

Generally the traditional Indians did not perform the same function as the clergy had in the civil rights movement. They did not plan strategy, raise funds, or participate as negotiators in the sense of arguing demands and making counterproposals. The traditionals saw their role was to ensure that the protest became a responsible expression of the people's feelings, not merely a recitation of liberal slogans. Indian elders thus put their imprimatur on movement activities as a validating act; they were rarely initiators. Federal officials, accustomed to negotiating a list of demands with activists, were never able to understand the poetic flow of traditional people's language and what seemed to be minor demands for integrity and morality in government. Unable to deal with the larger moral issues at stake, they frequently dismissed the positions taken by the tribal peoples as romanticism, failing to realize that the people were describing a process of national interaction, not adjustments in the existing institutional framework.

The tribal peoples decided to create a vehicle for the expression of their program, and in 1974 the first International Treaty Council was held on the Standing Rock Reservation in South Dakota. Elders from all over the continent attended these sessions and held workshops and discussions in which they enunciated the principles they believed should be followed. The general theme of these discussions was the importance of acting as a nation, and they emphasized the necessity of taking their case to other nations, with the hope that by creating a favorable image of American Indians in the larger world, the United States would be forced to respond to some of their requests. This program was attractive to many Indians because it enabled them to begin to translate immediate political demands into the language of diplomacy and elevate their vision to a larger stage.

The International Treaty Council was finally given the status of a nongovernmental organization with rights as an observer in the United Nations. In 1977 the International Treaty Council and the Indian Law Resource Center coordinated a trip of traditional elders to Geneva, Switzerland, to appear before a United Nations Nongovernmental Organization Conference on Discrimination Against Indigenous Populations. A sizable delegation of Indians from the United States as well as Central and South America testified. The American Indian delegates focused on specific wrongs that some of the tribes had suffered at the hands of the United States. In these impressive presentations we see the melding that the tribal peoples had achieved. There was, to be certain, discussion of the general treatment of the American Indians, but it focused on tribal complaints and never remained simply generalizations about conditions.

Buoyed by the good impression they felt they had given to the other nations at Geneva, the tribal elders decided to keep working on the international scene. In 1980 another delegation made statements concerning several well-documented cases of deprivation of tribal rights by the United States to the UN Commission on Human Rights and the Subcommission on Prevention of Discrimination and Protection of Minorities. In the fall of 1980 another group of Indians, again coordinated by the International Treaty Council, appeared at the Fourth Russell Tribunal with more evidence of federal callousness and neglect. All these conferences helped to keep the spirit of traditional people high because they showed that there was a forum in which ideas of culture and tradition could be discussed.

If traditional and tribal people want self-determination and elected tribal officials also want self-determination, one might well ask why they can't get together, at least on the definition if not on the form and content of self-government? Both groups use the same language, and many Indians move back and forth between the two groups so that the fine distinctions we have made do not always appear as clearly in the reservation setting. The cutting edge of criticism that is exchanged between the two points of view can be described as the conflict between realism and idealism. Tribal peoples tend to vest entirely too much trust in the ability of American institutions to perform the moral acts that would be necessary to secure what they want. Ethnic Indians regard the tribals as an unrealistic and overly romantic group that looks backward to old days and glories, not forward to new programs and experiences. Tribal peoples often regard their ideological opponents as wholly without principles, pragmatic to the point of having no moral stance at all, and claim they regard the tribal government, not the people, as the tribe.

One major and continuing distinction between the two points of view is the manner in which they conceive their opposition. The tribal peoples see the United States as one nation subject in some sense to the trends and movements of history and sensitive to the perceptions of other nations. Their drive for nationhood imagines a time when each tribe will have some kind of parity with the other nations of the world, as each tribe believes it had prior to contact with Europeans. Tribal concerns relate to the absence of the red race in the deliberative bodies of the world, and this larger perspective has overtones of history, religion, and culture. Here the idea of peoplehood transcends the contemporary political organizations and speaks to generations of people, people past and people yet to come.

Ethnic Indians and tribal officials look directly at the federal government. They understand its operation on a fairly sophisticated basis;

they know the politics of American society and see Indians as another ethnic group that needs to assert itself continuously if it is to have any share in the rights and privileges of that society. These people understand the economics of modern life and some but not all of the economic forces that have historically operated to shrink the Indian land base and use the reservation resources for their own enrichment. Tribal officials see the solution to this problem in getting involved in American domestic politics, in litigation, legislation, and other forms of political action to ensure that the laws of the United States will be applied to the reservations in the least harmful manner. One might say the tribals are concerned with the substance of Indian life while the ethnics look to the process.

The Future
of Indian Nations

Self-determination and self-government are not equivalent terms, yet they can describe the same social reality, simply in different contexts. Neither the federal government nor the tribes have spent much time and energy distinguishing between these two concepts, and this failure to speak precisely has produced many misunderstandings and much confusion. Both terms speak of the survival of Indian people, but they point to entirely different social realities in the future. A study of the idea of self-government would not be complete if it omitted a discussion of the possibilities inherent in this idea for the future. Since Indians of all persuasions will not abandon the idea of governing themselves in communities of their own choosing, the idea will continue to be a point around which people can rally—and plan.

Given the present tribal condition, the adherents of both self-government and self-determination must cooperate if the tribe is finally to reconstitute itself. John Collier's thinking seems incomplete now, but his ideas represented about as much as both he and the Indians could realistically hope to achieve at the time. Looking at the other efforts to realize some form of municipal-national control, it is not difficult to see that in every decade of the twentieth century, given the times and perspectives of the people, the movement toward political independence was fairly successful. Self-government and self-determination were both novelties when they were introduced, hard to understand and harder to implement in a precise manner. We hope this study can make a contribution toward both understanding these concepts and helping to prepare the ground for eventual reconciliation of these divergent viewpoints.

Past efforts, successful and unsuccessful, which we have already discussed, seem to point to specific areas in which some changes can be made that will help Indians reestablish themselves. First, there must be a structural reform of tribal governing institutions that is fundamental but also permits a continuity between past and present. The search for such reform has been a constant theme in every period we have considered. Second, some kind of determined and lasting cultural renewal must take place to help resolve the question of Indian identity in the modern world; here emotional continuity must be recognized and considered seriously. Third, economic stability must be established and maintained if Indians are to survive as distinct and healthy communities; the reservation economy must be recognized as uniquely Indian, but it must also be efficient in today's world. Finally, relations between the tribe and the federal and state governments must be stabilized, and mutual respect and parity in political rights must be established.

Recommendations that attempt to speak to these particular areas of Indian life must necessarily also speak to the two points of view that we have found existing in the Indian communities. Recommendations that do not take into account the changes that occur in natural growth processes often fall into the classification formulas, and in the past the tendency of people to absolutize recommendations has meant the death of reform. Therefore, these recommendations will attempt to identify problem areas and suggest possible alternatives that might be considered, providing the consideration is done in good faith by people determined to find a solution to pressing problems.

Reform of Tribal Governments

When John Collier established the framework for tribal governments, there was little of substance that tribes could do for themselves. Consequently, representation on tribal councils was not seen as a critically important item to be considered when a constitution was adopted. Since the bureau wanted the tribes do work primarily on economic rehabilitation, tribal governments were thought to have powers that enabled them to deal effectively with reservation resources. The sociopolitical dimension of life on the reservation itself was not emphasized.

In the decades since the New Deal, reservation populations have grown considerably. Tribal rolls have increased dramatically, and this rapid increase in population of both reservations and tribal membership has caused many problems not anticipated by the people who adopted tribal constitutions a half century ago. Many tribes restrict their voting membership by requiring some kind of residency so that voting in the tribal election is not equivalent to voting to amend constitutions and to accept or reject claims awards and negotiated settlements. Tribal members are affected by both kinds of issues, but reservation residents are much more deeply affected by elections to determine tribal officers and to operate reservation programs. The difference in kinds of elections must be reconciled so that tribal members, whether living on or living off the reservation, feel they have a stake in the outcome and participate as responsible tribal citizens.

Present tribal councils are relatively small and are organized by districts. The origin of some districts goes back to the division of the reservation by agricultural agents and boss farmers, who were charged with teaching the white man's kind of agriculture to tribal members who had received allotments. Recent litigation dealing with representation on the tribal council has moved toward an equality of voting districts in much the same way that *Reynolds v. Sims*[1] redistricted state legislatures. In some instances tribes have argued against redistricting by appeal to tradition, but courts have been reluctant to recognize a tradition that has arisen so recently.

John Collier originally wanted a considerable amount of self-government given to smaller units on reservations, to villages and settlements where there was a somewhat homogenous and historically identifiable group, such as a band or clan. When Senator Wheeler eliminated title I of Collier's original proposal and he and Margold had to rely upon case law to identify tribal powers, there was not much precedent for the recognition of political and municipal powers at the level below that of the tribal entity. So one of the critical elements of tribal government—which would have helped to clarify the national status of tribes from the very beginning of self-government—was missing and could not easily be inserted in tribal constitutions without an uproar from Congress and the Indians.

As tribes increasingly call themselves nations, partially in response to traditional arguments and partially as a means of emphasizing sovereignty against state and federal government, some form of national government must be devised. After the Five Civilized Tribes moved to Oklahoma from the South, they were able to organize themselves in a national fashion, vesting powers in the town structure, which most of them brought intact when they moved. Hence the constitutional precedent is already established for tribes and reservations to adopt a different form of government that emphasizes the identification and separation of three traditional branches of government—legislative, executive, and judicial. The old council forms can also be seen as parliamentary systems in which a failure of confidence in leadership meant a replacement of executive officers and legislators and a reformation of the government. In wholly ethnic Indian terms, tribal governments must soon consider expansion of their forms of political institution.

Another argument exists, however, that relies more heavily upon the older prereservation traditions and may be suitable for consideration from the tribal point of view. Indian tribes in their original setting never attempted to govern a large number of people. Subgroupings in bands and clans was almost always a feature of the larger tribes, and apart from the difficulty of feeding a large number of people, there was another good reason for such subdividing. Indians realized that it was not good government to have leaders and representatives who did not have some kind of personal acquaintance with the people they led. If leaders were remote, people felt alienated, and it was much more difficult for a community to function. Most Indian groups did not exceed several hundred people, and a goodly number were less than a hundred people. This close correlation between the people and the leadership positions in the tribe ensured that the council represented all points of view that were regarded as important within the community.

Tribal governments should consider substantially expanding their council membership to ensure that a more intimate ratio of people to elected officials exists. At a minimum most tribal councils should be doubled—and some tripled—so that each council member represents a much smaller number of people for whom each can accept some well-defined responsibilities. An expanded council would then approach the size of a small legislature, giving the tribal government an aspect of nationhood and allowing it to perform typical legislative functions. Expansion of the council would also assist in distinguishing the executive branch from the legislative function and help to identify areas of responsibility. A much larger legislative body would provide some badly needed protection to the tribal judiciary, which is presently subjected to immense political pressure from tribal council members whenever it begins to exercise important judicial functions.

The standard response to an expanded number of elected tribal officials by the Bureau of Indian Affairs and outside agencies has been that large tribal councils cannot make decisions that need to be made if the tribe is to function. But this point is not as relevant as it might seem.

A small tribal council can easily be controlled by the bureau. When its decision-making process is short-circuited, with little time allowed for discussion and formal action expected to take place at every session of the council, the federal government can manipulate a few members of the council and force them to do its bidding. Hence, it is the tribal government's pliability that the bureau desires, not its efficiency or an understanding of its actions. A much larger tribal council would be more difficult to intimidate, and council members would tend to think more about their responsibilities to their constituents than about their standing with government bureaucrats.

The recent admission by tribal court judges of the importance and validity of traditional customs in determining cases brought in tribal courts is, as we have noted, a progressive move that suggests a process of reconciliation occurring on the reservations. More extensive development of tribal customs as the basis for a tribal court's decision will enable these institutions to draw even closer to the people. Part of the structural change necessary for tribal governments to become more independent is for the various branches of government to have their own identities. A court of elders, either approved by the tribal council or acknowledged by it, which would help to resolve domestic disputes before they become matters for tribal courts, could be a positive innovation. Much of the activity of tribal courts is the handling of domestic disputes, and courts cannot really solve family problems. A council of community elders, on the other hand, who are related to the parties in controversy and might apply other kinds of social pressures, might prove irresistible to the parties in conflict.

The old traditional ways of governing the people relied upon individual self-discipline for enforcement. Today a person is expected to know a bewildering number of rules and regulations and prudently to avoid violating standards based upon an abstract citizen who always seems to manage to obey the law. Tribal courts are being led down the road of the "reasonably prudent man" in adopting non-Indian juridical procedures, and at times this tendency is irritating to tribal peoples. Insofar as law and order can be deinstitutionalized and public behavior made a personal responsibility, a good compromise between old and new ways can be effected. This task cannot be accomplished by the federal government but only by the people on the reservations who see the practical value of such an approach.

In traditional, prereservation society the various clans and warrior societies acted as community policemen to enforce rules made for traveling, hunting, harvesting, and other activities in which the whole band or village was involved. To prevent unequal treatment of the people by the police, some tribes alternated the groups in the role of policemen. Thus, a society would not be unjust or unduly harsh in its enforcement of the rules because they would not be policemen during the next event and there might be retaliation against them. The role of tribal policemen in most tribal groups was that of peacemaker, not law enforcer. Since the Indian Reorganization Act tribal police forces have been understood as law enforcement officers. This image suggests a mistrust of the individuals living in a community and predetermines in the police officer's mind an expectation that the individuals in a community and its institutions are antagonists.

The troubles on the Pine Ridge Indian Reservation before and during the occupation of Wounded Knee give vivid evidence of the products of the law enforcement mentality. Since Wounded Knee, the emphasis of the federal presence in many of the tribes has been on the creation of SWAT teams, additional weaponry, and development of the police force toward a more paramilitary posture. At Pine Ridge itself the tribe has taken another approach. They now designate their policemen as "peace officers" and instruct them to look at their job as one of keeping the peace in the reservation communities, not in compiling impressive crime statistics. Structural recasting of the police function on reservations would significantly enhance the role of tribal government in the lives of the people and help to develop a more cooperative attitude toward both law and government. In view of the rapidly increasing costs of maintaining a modern police force, which virtually occupies a reservation community instead of policing it, this change might bear significant fruits.

The Indian Reorganization Act allowed tribes to create subsidiary institutions to conduct certain kinds of activities on the reservation. During the War on Poverty additional entities such as school boards, development corporations, housing programs, and recreation commissions were established. The degree to which tribes now have institutions that must be managed is astounding to many people. Frequently these tribal subsidiaries are more responsive to outside funding agencies and accreditation organizations than to the tribe or tribal council. By the same token, some of the agencies created by the tribal council are subject to the political whims of council members to the point where administration of programs is simply a matter of patronage distribution. Tribal governments have to find a middle ground between these two extremes. Collier thought the charter would control the creation of these groups and relied upon the sophistication of the tribal leaders to limit their scope and power. Chartering such groups by a national council instead of a smaller tribal council might provide them with a more appropriate image and status. It would not be surrendering any tribal sovereignty but exercising it in a more comprehensive manner.

Cultural Renewal

Culture is a most difficult subject to discuss. It is also the single factor that distinguishes Indians from non-Indians in the minds of both groups. John Collier appreciated Indian culture abstractly, but had a difficult time coming to practical grips with it. He fought to protect Indian religious freedom and believed self-government was a positive step toward preserving and reviving the better elements of tribal cultures. Yet he ensured the passage of the Indian Arts and Crafts Board,[2] which for most of its existence has been a sinecure for non-Indian art hobbyists and buffs and has encouraged both Indians and non-Indians to think of culture as primarily the artifacts produced by the ancestors of today's Indians. Until Indians can get a more comprehensive idea of their own regarding the content of their cultures, resolution of conflicts with the larger society will be almost impossible.

Reviewing the efforts of the federal government in the field of Indian education over the past century, we find an unmistakable trend toward public school education and the belief that education will eventually extinguish tribal cultures, assimilating Indians into the American social and cultural mainstream. Whenever the question of "Indian" education has been raised, federal representatives have suggested that courses in Indian culture be taught in public and federal schools. John Collier saw to it that some courses on Indian traditions were included in the bureau curriculum, and in the 1972 Indian Education Act there were provisions for teaching Indian culture and history. Even the best efforts in Indian education have been directed toward reducing the respective tribal traditions to an academic subject for student consumption.

Indians must begin to understand that a living culture is so much a part of a people that it is virtually incapable of recognition and formal academic transmission. Expecting schools to do the task formerly assumed spontaneously by parents, friends, relatives, and the community in concert is only to reduce tribal culture to a textbook phenomenon. Until Indians accept responsibility for preserving and enhancing their own knowledge of themselves, no institution can enable them to remain as Indians. A glance at the fate of bilingual programs on reservations offers a hopeful approach for the future of Indian education. When bilingual education was first proposed, it was assumed that there were so many Indian children speaking their native tongue as a first language that learning English as a second language was the key to improving the performance of the students.

Proposals for bilingual education were difficult to fund in Congress because most senators and congressmen held to the old idea of the melting pot. To instruct children in the language of the home was thought to be a severe handicap in helping them to adjust to the requirements of modern American life. During these years on the reservations tribal housing programs were initiated and country Indians were encouraged to move into new houses in the few settlements on the reservations. The result was that a new generation of Indian children grew up in these rural slums and learned English as a first language. When the bilingual programs were finally authorized and funded, many of them became vehicles for teaching the native language to children who had been denied the opportunity to learn it because of the location of their homes. Indians hence made a positive program that enhanced their traditions out of a program designed to further erode them. But it was a fortunate circumstance, not a deliberate effort.

Language is the first glue that links peoples together, and the major emphasis in self-determination and ultimately in self-government should be the preservation of language where it still exists and the cultivation of it where it has eroded or fallen into disuse. Although tribal peoples are hospitable, they also have an aspect of exclusivity, and language can help keep these important links alive and useful. Finally language can help to remind people working in Indian-created institutions of the heritage they possess. The nuances of meaning that the old traditions contain and the sacredness of experience can both be expressed in the native language in more comprehensible terms for tribe members than in English. Language is the key to cultural survival and cannot be considered in isolation; it is and must be the substance of self-determination.

In today's stories of mythical old Indians, one fact stands out sharply: The old Indians were in considerably better health than the Indians of today, yet they had no modern medical facilities available to them. Religious healing and proper natural diet enabled them to meet and overcome physical weaknesses and illnesses except those of a contagious nature for which they had no immunity and no period of time in which to gain an immunity. Today certain identifiable diseases, in particular diabetes, are rampant in Indian communities. With the poverty conditions existing on many reservations, junk food has become the major source of nutrition. Cultural revival would seem to include using traditional foods and medicines wherever possible. Restoration of a traditional diet might well enable the people to regain some of their natural strength in warding off diseases.

The U.S. Public Health Service, and earlier the Indian Health Service operating under the Bureau of Indian Affairs, were designed to supplant traditional health practices. During the sixties there was a concerted effort by the Public Health Service to use the traditional medicine men and healers in conjunction with their own services. In some instances, however, the Indian holy man was seen in the same role as the Protestant minister or Catholic priest—a formal religious figure called to comfort the dying and hear any words. People did not understand that it was the particular healing gifts of the holy man that were necessary, not merely his presence at the sickbed. If tribal culture is relevant to today's world, it must be seen as a vital element in the crisis situation, not as an exotic adjunct to the white man's science and knowledge.

The Indian Civil Rights Act does not guarantee religious freedom because of the objections of the Pueblos. Many tribal governments have, nevertheless, included freedom of religion in their constitutions because there are so many different religious traditions now extant on the reservation that it would be absurd to attempt to support the tribal religion as an established religion. Indeed, in some tribes the official tribal religion might well become Presbyterian, Catholic, or Baptist. Traditional tribal religions differ from the Christian denominations that have come to the reservations and gathered converts in one important aspect: The religious ceremonies of some tribes have taken on the guise of a tourist attraction. The Sun Dance at the Sioux reservations today resembles a pageant more than a religious ritual.

The waters of religious freedom became muddied, indeed troubled, in 1990 when the Supreme Court once again addressed First Amendment freedoms. Two members of the Native American Church were fired by a drug treatment organization because they had used peyote during religious ceremonies. When they applied for unemployment compensation from the Oregon Department of Human Resources, they were denied benefits because their employment had been terminated for "work-related misconduct." Peyote is classified as a Schedule 1 controlled substance, and its use is thereby prohibited.

Claiming their First Amendment rights had been violated, the two members of the Native American Church took their case to the U.S. Supreme Court (*Department of Human Resources of Oregon v. Smith*, 1990).[3] In past religious freedom cases, the Court has focused attention on a threefold test in determining what was permissible under the Free Exercise Clause of the First Amendment. First, the objective of the law had to be predicated on a *valid secular purpose*. Second, the state had to demonstrate a *compelling state interest*. And third, the law had to be *nondiscriminatory* in its application. In a 6-3 decision, the Supreme Court in *Smith* upheld the action of the Department of Human Resources in denying benefits to the members of the Native American Church. Unfortunately, the several opinions in the case clouded not only the law but the Court's approach to future decisions. Justice Scalia, who delivered the principal opinion, ignored the traditional tests outlined above; instead, he validated the actions of the state agency by noting that a "neutral law of general applicability" which is nondiscriminatory may take precedence over a religiously motivated ritual. Scalia ignored the "compelling state interest" test. Justice O'Connor, with whom three other Justices concurred in part, used the traditional "compelling state interest" test, but still concluded that Oregon could encroach into the zone of the First Amendment based on its policy of preventing physical harm from the use of a Schedule 1 drug. Justice Blackmun, along with Justices Brennan and Marshall, dissented, indicating that the use of peyote in this instance was not of a recreational nature but was used in a religious context and therefore was protected by the First Amendment.

The Court's decision in the *Smith* case provoked controversy among both Indian and non-Indian religious communities. Two determined efforts were launched to remedy the Court's approach to religious freedom, particularly that of Justice Scalia. One of these efforts, a joint venture by Indian and non-Indian groups, was designed to pressure Congress into passing broad legislation to deal with the issue. Dissenting voices were raised among some of the Christian supporters regarding the inclusion of "peyote use" among protected religious rituals, however, and it was necessary for Native Americans to approach Congress separately on this issue. Success was in the offing, and in 1994 Congress passed the American Indian Religious Freedom Act Amendments[4] legalizing the use of peyote as long as it was connected to a traditional Indian religious ritual.

Even prior to the passage of this important piece of Indian legislation, Congress in 1993, responding to pressure, enacted the Religious Freedom Restoration Act.[5] Under this new statute, no level of government could enforce a law that "substantially burdened" religious observance without demonstrating a "compelling state" need to do so and without using the "least restrictive" means available. Through this enactment, Congress indicated its clear intention to abandon Justice Scalia's approach to religious freedom. The 1993 law has not been without controversy, however. For instance, prison officials claim that the law has been invoked to exempt prison inmates from eating certain foods and from wearing religious articles, despite prohibitions on the wearing of jewelry. Additionally, prisoners have demanded the opportunity to hold certain religious rituals deemed improper by the prison authorities. These and other nontraditional religious exercises inevitably led to a challenge of the law's constitutionality. The ruling finally came in 1997 in the city of Boerne, Texas, where St. Peter's Roman Catholic Church invoked the Religious Freedom Restoration Act in an attempt to demolish most of its building and expand into an area zoned by the city for historic preservation. The City of Boerne denied the church a permit, and St. Peter's took the city to court, alleging it had illegally placed a "substantial burden" on the free exercise of religion. The Supreme Court turned the church down, only adding to the confusion about the place of religion in the American social fabric.

Freedom of religion on reservations today does not simply mean the right to practice a traditional religion. It also must include the right to practice the tribal religion seriously without the expectation by the tribal government that the ceremonies can be used for income-generating purposes. Too many tribes today use their religious traditions in the same manner as do whites—to bless sporting events and powwows and to endorse the actions to the tribal government. For a long time the exotic nature of the tribal religion was about all that could attract white tourists. Those days are declining rapidly. Since Indian Christians are not expected to hold church services as a tourist attraction, traditional Indians should not believe that they are required to do so.

Accountability is the other side of cultural integrity, and in the open society we have in America today accountability is rarely practiced in cultural matters by any group, especially by Indians. The power and viability of a culture is largely determined by the willingness of its practitioners to take themselves seriously. A parade of white imposters pretending to be Indians has become a common phenomenon in many tribes. Articulation of tribal traditions can be the province of almost anyone willing to put himself forward as an expert on these matters. Consequently, the younger generation is never certain what is acceptable tribal behavior and what is not. The majority of adult Indians feel that they have no right to ask questions of people posing as Indians or to call obvious fakes to account. Hence the tradition of many tribes has become what the most aggressive people say it is.

Self-government and self-determination are not possible in a society in which there is no set of criteria defining what behavior and beliefs constitute acceptable expressions of the tribal heritage. Traditional Indians have tended to prostitute their own knowledge by making it available to the wandering scholar, the excited groupie, and the curious filmmaker and writer. The cultural landscape is now so littered with erroneous information that it is extremely difficult for the serious Indian youngster to learn the truth about his past. If Indians are going to govern themselves with any degree of confidence, they must begin to define what is acceptable behavior and invoke the conscience of the community to maintain these standards. Otherwise, the internal substance of the tribal community will become solely those people who have been able to get themselves listed on the tribal roll as federally recognized Indians.

In the decades before and shortly after the Second World War, racial minorities were plagued by the burden of acting in certain predetermined ways. An individual who was a member of a minority community was expected to behave with a degree of humility and submissiveness because he or she was regarded as a representative of the racial group, and antisocial behavior was believed to be the source of derogatory stereotypes of the group. During the sixties racial minorities attacked the more vicious and degrading stereotypes that the white majority had created purporting to explain their behavior, and everyone made great effort to overcome old stereotypes. Though a great deal was accomplished, the fact nevertheless remains that irresponsible behavior by individuals of a racial minority casts aspersions on the whole group.

Part of the problem with the Indian power slogans and protests was that the movement rapidly became antiwhite instead of pro-Indian. The same was true in the other major racial minorities. As a consequence dialogue between the white majority and the various minorities became one of accusation and bitterness, which generated the backlash against all minorities. Self-determination involves having a responsible group that has pride in itself but does not generate this pride by pointing out the shortcomings of other groups.

In this particular respect a great difference exists between the tribal Indians and the ethnic Indians. Tribal Indians maintain a great respect for their own traditions and accord to others a measure of respect for their traditions and beliefs. Ethnic Indians, on the other hand, continuously use the shortcomings of the majority to gain leverage with that majority for items on their own agenda. The Kennedy Report spent a good deal of its energy on guilt-provoking accusations against past misdeeds of the Bureau of Indian Affairs and therefore was very popular with ethnic Indians. Such internal quarrels are dangerous because individuals really do represent their group to others, and racial minorities in particular cannot spend their time helping to create derogatory stereotypes of themselves.

Almost everything that can be recommended in terms of cultural revival and consolidation involves the fundamental problem of determining a contemporary expression of tribal identity and behaving according to its dictates. Obviously, the federal government cannot perform this function, nor can the American public. The cultural revival and integrity of the

American Indian community depends on the cultivation of a responsible attitude and behavior patterns in the communities themselves. Collier did not seem to understand this dimension of human relations and seemed to assume that Indian culture had such obvious strengths as to be immediately attractive to everyone in the same manner as he had been attracted to it. Collier could not have changed the Indian posture toward the rest of American society, nor could any of the subsequent commissioners of Indian affairs or chairmen of the two Indian subcommittees in Congress. Inevitably, cultural self-government and cultural self-determination must precede their political and economic counterparts if developments in these latter areas are to have any substance and significance.

Economic Stability

Finding the solution to Indian economic problems is a desperate task. During the past century economic policy regarding Indians has fluctuated between developing communal assets and encouraging individual Indians to seek their fortune alone in American society. Collier's emphasis on economic development places the reforms of the New Deal squarely within the pendulum swing and enables us to equate his term as commissioner with the sixties as times when the corporate nature of economic enterprise was fostered. As far back as we can take American history, the non-Indian has been fascinated with Indian lands and resources and has demanded that they be used in the same manner as he uses his property. Since Indians have generally resisted this alternative, unless a radical change is made in the manner in which non-Indians perceive land, no lasting economic peace can ever be achieved between Indians and the rest of American society.

Land ownership has been the central legal issue involving Indians, and this century has seen the drastic erosion of the land base of the tribes. Collier's major concern while a private citizen and later as commissioner was to halt the loss of reservation lands and allotments and begin to rebuild the landholdings of the tribes. During the sixties, because there was still a feeling that termination might remain a viable solution of the Indian problem, Congress did little to assist tribes in consolidating their lands. The heirship problem continued to get worse, and the response of the Bureau of Indian Affairs was to purchase a computer to keep track of the Indian owners of allotments.

Indian reservations with allotments have a multitude of problems that unallotted reservations do not have. It is exceedingly difficult to create economic grazing or farming units on allotted reservations because quite often there are not enough allotments contiguous to one another to make up an economically feasible block of land for leasing or tribal use. Questions of ownership of the underlying minerals have plagued some tribes with allotments, and there is good precedent for the proposition that the tribe and the individual Indian owner have ownership of minerals. Water rights for allotments sometimes preclude the tribal water right in the sense that they represent the irrigable acreage on the reservation, and the tribe has to overcome previous allocations of water by the courts in order to begin new developments using their *Winters* water rights. Indians frequently sell their allotments to non-Indians and make it difficult for the tribe to consolidate tracts for its own use. Though tribes have the right to meet high bids, tribes do not always have the funds to make the purchase.

Land consolidation remains the major unsolved economic problem of Indian tribes. Until tribes are able to own their lands in one solid block, they cannot reasonably make plans for use or development of their resources. But consolidation has other implications that make it important. Civil and criminal jurisdiction depend upon the existence of trust lands. Whenever an allotment goes out of trust, the tribe loses jurisdiction over that area and must rely upon negotiated agreements with state and county governments in order to exercise jurisdiction over the area. Zoning for economic development and housing and enforcement of hunting and fishing codes is exceedingly difficult when the area under consideration is not wholly trust land.

Tribes do not have access to funds for land purchase for consolidation purposes because of a number of factors. Interest rates make investment in land prohibitive; income does not enable tribes to repay loans. Administrative costs in maintaining records of ownership on heirship lands continue to escalate, leaving less money for land purchase. Most important, the Reagan administration, in its massive reductions in domestic social programs, forced the tribes to use their income to meet the immediate social needs of their people, foregoing any investments in activities that would help to stabilize the reservation economy. The Indian land situation is therefore becoming increasingly more serious, with no prospect of relief.

During the late sixties the bureau began to emphasize the great mineral wealth that underlay Indian reservations. Its idea was to attract large corporations for long-term leasing of the resources, thereby developing an increased income for tribes, which could be used in meeting matching requirements of federal grants and development projects. Following the Arab oil boycott, when the emphasis shifted to making America free of foreign energy sources, Indians were made to believe that they were the Arabs of the North American continent, possessing coal, oil, natural gas, and uranium in quantities sufficient to hold the American economy at ransom in exchange for considerably higher royalties on their minerals. Some tribal chairmen visualized themselves as the equals of the Saudis and began to demand respect they had not earned and did not merit.

After much debate and considerable rhetoric about Indian energy resources, a new national organization was founded—the Coalition of Energy Resource Tribes (CERT). With large grants from several federal agencies, CERT began operations as technical advisor and representative of the energy-rich Indian tribes. In the formative years of this organization refugees from Iran began to fill positions within the staff of CERT and act as consultants to the group. The men who had helped lead the Shah to disaster were now in the business of counseling the Indians on how to get the same deal for themselves. By 1983 CERT had overspent its budget and was doing drastic staff reductions. Its accomplishments were sparse to nonexistent, but it was the favorite of both the Carter and the Reagan administrations because it preached economic self-sufficiency for the reservations based upon astute use of their energy resources.

One problem with CERT was that very few Indian reservations actually had the energy resources on which it was concentrating. On some of the reservations there was a clear choice between leasing grazing and farming lands to get at the minerals underneath or keeping the lands intact for use by tribal members for agricultural purposes. Hence energy development was not a supplement to existing reservation development; rather, it threatened to supplant existing activities and exchange economic self-sufficiency on the part of many tribal members for an expanded cash income available for programming by the tribal government. Some tribal governments therefore adopted the very methods of exploitation that had destroyed the resources of other parts of the country and made their coal and other energy mineral valuable, at least for the moment.

The economy of many reservations is a microcosm of the national economy. Large welfare rolls exist and large tracts of reservation lands have been set aside for energy development. A massive tribal bureaucracy is attempting to meet the social needs of the people, not realizing that many of these needs have been generated by the leasing of lands for mineral exploitation purposes. Generally the lands abandoned after uranium mining and strip mining of coal are not being restored to useful condition, and consequently injurious slag heaps of discarded refuse are found in many areas that were once free of contamination. The reservation has become a resource to be used and discarded, not a homeland for the tribe. The old combination of subsistence agriculture supplemented by social welfare programs and seasonal work has vanished in some areas, to be replaced by a welfare-cash economy that cannot sustain itself without massive federal assistance. Under the Reagan administration the Indians received only strong admonitions to try harder to develop their private sector and the accusations of James Watt about federal socialism on the reservations.

John Collier saw Indian tribal members as stockholders in a unique form of corporate enterprise. They had an expectation that as the tribal economy began to make progress, they would share in its benefits. But shifts in the federal budget deprived tribal members of the benefits they had been expecting. The development programs of the sixties in most instances created a rural slum that was as dependent upon its connections to the outside world as any suburban or urban area in the country. Housing programs clustered Indians together in small projects on many reservations, depriving them of living on and using their lands. The reservation economic structure became wholly artificial and was totally dependent upon an ever-increasing federal subsidy. Then, when it seemed there was no way to return to the old subsistence economy, and indeed inflation had made that possibility very remote, the Reagan administration simply reduced federal support, but in such absolute terms as to reduce the tribes to near bankruptcy.

Self-government is probably a farce without some steady form of tribal income to support it, and this argument prevails whenever the question is raised about leasing of Indian resources. But equally absurd are the tremendous costs of welfare and social programs that a tribe must bear when it removes its people from intimate and subsistence use of their lands and forces them to become recipients of public largess. The reservation economy of most tribes today is wholly artificial and could not survive but a few weeks without a transfusion from outside the reservation. Many Indians speak of this condition as colonialism, but it is considerably more devastating than simple colonialism. It is the final and systematic and perhaps even ruthlessly efficient destruction of Indian society.

Tribal Indians have fought back against the exploitation of tribal resources by outside non-Indian corporations. But they have not been able to articulate in comprehensible terms the implications they see in the developments that are occurring around them. Instead of raising questions about the practicality of rapid exploitation of reservation resources, they have generally phrased their opposition to projects with religious arguments and appeals to the religious mission of the tribe to protect the land— a worthy and moral stance to be certain, but unlikely to be convincing to tribal accountants charged with keeping the government solvent. They have not yet advocated a return to a natural economy derived from the sophisticated and self-sufficient use of the land, although their speeches clearly forecast the articulation of such beliefs.

The fundamental question of economic stability on the reservations revolves about the dilemma of whether the land is to be exploited, and therefore simply another corporate form of property, or to be a homeland, in which case it assumes a mystical focal point for other activities that support the economic stability of the reservation society. The Bureau of Indian Affairs naturally sees the reservation as valuable property and encourages Indians to view it in the same manner. Federal granting agencies provide funds primarily for development and use purposes, and private foundations also see the reservation as property to be used primarily for economic gain. Therefore, traditional, tribal Indians are at a severe disadvantage in articulating their point of view.

Economic stability depends at least in part on the feeling of familiarity of the people with their means of making a living. Where employment has a substantial relationship with previous activities, the people feel more comfortable and at ease with themselves and are willing to make accommodations to enable them to continue working. Thus fishing, ranching, and agriculture are all familiar and traditional in the sense of being activities in which the people have been engaged for most of this century. Industrial wage work and energy exploitation do not have roots in tribal society and produce a sense of alienation in the people. Even some forms of recreation and resort management seem strange and out of place for many Indians whose tribe has developed this kind of economic activity.

The critical factor in achieving economic stability seems to be in encouraging tribal officials to develop programs that are perceived by the people as natural extensions of things they are already doing. A natural economy maximizes the use of the land in as constructive a manner as possible, almost becoming a modern version of hunting and gathering in the sense that people have the assurance that this kind of activity will always be available to them. Some forms of industrial and wage work can take on the aura of natural economy. The Iroquois, for example, have become specialists in high steel work to the degree that it seems a natural part of their tradition, even though they must live in urban areas away from the reservation in order to engage in it. The Lummis and some of the other tribes have developed sophisticated aquacultures, and this kind of development relates directly to the tribal traditions, even though it is today expressed by and based on highly technical skills.

The Carter administration cut back economic opportunities for Indians rather drastically, but it did not articulate an economic philosophy that had sociological and cultural overtones. The Reagan administration emphasized elitism and uncontrolled exploitation under the aegis of private enterprise, thereby creating a new divisiveness within the Indian reservation community. Further, Reagan's gospel of reliance on the private

sector is absurd when applied to reservations, where the only private enterprise has been the non-Indian trader and the mixed-blood rancher or store-
keeper. With the budget cutbacks it is not possible to have anything except
instant misery on the reservations. Since the reservation economy can only
maintain stability under the present conditions by the infusion of outside
capital, the prospects, both long- and short-term, for Indian economic stability are exceedingly remote. Unfortunately, the Bush and Clinton administrations neither examined the milieu established by the Reagan administration nor offered anything that could serve as a path out of economic chaos
brought about by declining federal support.

An Indian reservation was once defined by an Indian Service official
as a "tract of land surrounded by thieves." In some places today it could
be described as a "small tract of land inhabited by gamblers." The modern
origins of gaming on Indian lands are obscure; some people say the Florida
Seminoles first had the idea, while others feel the California tribes were
initiators of the movement. Actually, gaming was one of those topics never
discussed because it was assumed that the Indian lands were subject to the
nebulous rules that governed federally held lands. Thus it was a surprise to
many people that Republican administrations encouraged the tribes to initiate gaming activities to supplement cuts in their federal monies for services provided by the United States.

Two major areas of concern with the introduction of gaming on
reservations have been jurisdiction and taxation. Particularly on reservations where a significant amount of land has gone out of trust, and where
the lines between tribal and state jurisdiction have often been blurred over
the years, questions have arisen whether the tracts of land proposed for
gaming activities were under state or tribal—and therefore federal—control. Both state and federal courts have been rigorous in applying the criteria for "Indian country" to lands still held in Indian ownership. This
trend has enabled tribal governments to get in the door and become active
players in gaming.

Tribes have resisted the idea that states could tax any activities on Indian lands and therefore, to forestall efforts by the states, have made voluntary grants of gaming income to certain state programs and activities. They
have also argued that gaming has provided much-needed jobs and has taken
people, both Indian and white, off unemployment, reducing the burden
of the state. Certainly gaming has increased jobs as well as spurring large
construction projects, housing developments, and peripheral small business
activities. So the stimulation of local economic activities has not only bal-
anced the loss of taxes, but in some places has far outweighed whatever
benefits direct taxing might have provided.

Indian gaming has produced a new area of litigation based in part on the interpretation of the Indian Gaming Regulatory Act and regulations and the definitions adopted to administer it. Under this federal statute, states and tribes must make compacts to make certain that the Indian gaming produces a minimum disruption to a state's regulation of gaming by its own citizens and corporations. In *Seminole Tribe of Florida v. Florida*,[6] the Supreme Court decided that the Indian Gaming Act, insofar as it could be interpreted to force a state government to negotiate a gaming compact with an Indian tribe, was an unnecessary intrusion on state sovereignty.

The success stories of Indian gaming generally revolve around the programs initiated by those tribes that have invested their gaming income in community projects. The Pequots of Connecticut, for example, have provided for all of their members and in addition have contributed $10 million toward the building of a national Indian museum in Washington, D.C. The Oneidas of Wisconsin have invested heavily in social welfare programs, especially programs that serve the elderly. The Oklahoma tribes have upgraded their tribal court system and have made wise investments to provide employment for tribal members.

Collier—or indeed, Lyndon Johnson—could not have foreseen the radical changes that gaming income would bring to Indian country. From the small, almost informal, poverty-stricken governments of the 1930s through the 1950s, many tribal governments have evolved into multi-million-dollar operations requiring their own attorneys, economic and housing planners, and investment counselors. The wiser tribes understand that gaming cannot last forever, since many states are expanding their own gaming activities as means of generating income and reducing taxes. Perhaps the lesson of gaming for Indians is that sovereignty is much easier to exercise when the treasury has a steady source of income.

Federal-State Relations

Beginning with the militant rhetoric used by the Abourezk Commission to describe the status of tribal governments, the popular slogan among tribal officials is to insist on a "government-to-government relationship" with the federal government. Considering that tribal governments are closely controlled by the federal government and obtain a good deal of their administrative overhead from the federal government, this phrase has less substance than people would like to admit. If we use it to describe the *status* of tribal governments when compared with the United States and in some instances its constituent states, we have a more accurate characterization of the goal of Indians in clarifying their relationship with the United States. They believe that with some understanding and with a steady policy of support and development, there could be a more comprehensible working arrangement with other political entities that would respect the idea and practice of self-government.

Although the treaty recommendations of the Twenty Points did not receive the attention they deserved, they still remain good descriptions of the proper ongoing treaty process that would be most useful for Indian tribes. There has been some indication that among traditional people the idea of arbitration and mediation is favored in disputes with state governments and might be encouraged in the case of federal involvement. The ideology too often embraced by administrations, however, makes Indians wards of the government and emphasizes the idea that Indians are citizens. Treaties are therefore anathema because they provide evidence of the fact of continuing federal responsibility to and for Indians.

Tribal courts and tribal governments have been working toward achieving a full faith and credit relationship with the states, and in view of the expectation that Indian reservations will continue into the future, this is an important area for consideration. It demands a recognition of the basic treaty relationship without making it distasteful to local legislators who often chafe at the idea of accepting tribal governments as equal political entities. There are two ways that full faith and credit can be achieved. A tribe can completely adopt the laws and procedures of a state and become virtually identical to the state in numerous areas of activity. Hunting and fishing regulations can be the same, tax policy can be similar, the tribe carefully avoiding any conflict with the state, and domestic relations laws can be made identical. Cross-deputization can be achieved, making the tribal police and the state police a nearly identical force in the reservation areas. This approach basically surrenders the flexibility of the tribal government to meet the unique needs of the people in exchange for peaceful relations with the state and its agency.

A much more difficult approach, and one favored by tribal Indians, would be comparable with the status of the Amish settlements. Reservations would develop their social relations to a degree where they earned the respect and envy of the non–Indian world. Stories abound of the old days when it was not necessary to have locks on doors on the reservation and where honesty and truthfulness was an outstanding characteristic of Indian society. In the speeches of traditional leaders in recent years, this visionary picture of a society of justice is painted in most vivid terms. The problem with the manner in which traditional people articulate this idea today is that almost all of the blame is placed on the white man for destroying this paradise and little responsibility is taken by Indians for abandoning it. In view of the present state of the reservations, this alternative remains a goal to achieve rather than an immediate condition that can be accomplished.

A middle ground between these two extremes can be found and may indeed be what both tribal leaders and traditional people have in mind as they adopt more of the ideology of self-determination and focus less on self-government. Assuming responsibility for education and various aspects of social welfare, adopting the use of customary law in tribal courts, and refusing development schemes that would injure lands beyond repair all seem to be steps toward creating a better reservation society that hints at the idyllic vision of the traditional people. As more and more individuals make conscious decisions to accept the self-discipline that traditional life imposes, we may well see a substantial change in reservation social conditions, pointing toward an internal integrity that must surely underlie a full faith and credit relationship.

A continuing problem that John Collier could not handle and subsequent generations have not solved with any degree of sophistication is claims against the federal government. Tribes have had a continuing problem getting their claims heard in court. The Indian Claims Commission did not finish its work by any means. It made the process of claims resolution so tedious and placed the tribes and federal government in an adversary position so that reasonable compromises could not be worked out and finally just exhausted the patience of Congress, which terminated it in 1978. Since the expiration of the claims commission, tribes have had to take their cases to the U.S. Court of Claims for resolution.

In recent years a new kind of claim has arisen, partially from the dereliction of the Indian Claims Commission and Bureau of Indian Affairs in fulfilling their duties under the Indian Claims Commission Act. Every Indian tribe or community was supposed to receive notice of its right to file against the federal government under the provisions of the act. Hardly any Indian tribes in the eastern United States were so notified, and it was not until the early seventies that the land claims of eastern Indians began to attract attention. The Maine tribes successfully pursued their claims and were awarded both land and money in a negotiated settlement. Other eastern Indian tribes have been pursuing their claims and are in the process of getting them resolved in agreements of a similar nature. Many Indian claims are still outstanding.

The importance of claims is that until the tribe feels it has received both justice and an accounting for its past relationship with the United States, claims prove to be a disruptive political issue within the tribe. Tribal leaders can be attacked by their opponents on the flimsy ground that they have not pursued the claim with sufficient vigor. Additionally many Indians do not want to embark on any kind of development for themselves until they get their claims money. The Sioux for almost a generation were stymied because many people thought that claims were about to be settled and refused to consider other kinds of developments and activities until the claims were finalized. Claims are both satisfying in terms of fulfilling ancient promises and disruptive in that they take an inordinate amount of time and energy away from other reservation activities that would be more profitable in the long run.

Prompt settlement of outstanding tribal claims against the United States would help to lay the past to rest with some sense of finality and enable tribes to devote their time to other things. Negotiated settlements could be effected that would involve the resolution of other problems, such as heirship lands, capital for development projects, and special funding of certain kinds of projects that would need a sustained financial support system for a period of years. The structural change that resolution of claims would involve would be the elimination of the adversarial, judicial proceeding in favor of negotiated settlements specifying the duration of leases and the exchange of particular rights and privileges.

One of John Collier's most cherished goals was the establishment of a Court of Indian Affairs. As we have already noted, he had to sacrifice this title of his omnibus reform bill in order to get Senate support for self-government. The idea of a national court to handle Indian matters should be revived and made a regular part of the federal judiciary. We already have various federal courts that deal with specific subject matter, and the justification of each of them is that they require a special knowledge and deal with a special body of law and hence relieve the regular federal courts from having to deal with technical subjects with which they might not have expertise.

No area of federal law is more complicated or requires more expertise than federal Indian law. Hundreds of treaties, thousands of statutes, and hundreds of thousands of administrative rulings and actions are involved in federal Indian law. Over six hundred separate Indian communities are dependent in some manner on the vagaries of interpretation of federal Indian law, and literally billions of dollars and the lives of over a million people are at stake in Indian cases. There is sufficient justification for such an institution in both the scope of subject matter and in the amount of money presently spent in litigation on Indian matters by the federal and state governments and Indian tribal governments.

Indians have not traditionally supported this proposal, and with good reason. Appointments to the federal judiciary have generally been regarded as political rewards to the party faithful, and so there is a danger that the Court of Indian Affairs would become dominated by individuals antagonistic to Indians. The Indian position has generally been to demand that the tribes appoint some of the judges or at least have a hand in the selection of the people who would serve in such a court. A variety of ways could be found to ensure impartiality in the decisions of the court, and we cannot take the time to elaborate the complex alternatives that might be considered. The fact remains that this court would provide a focus to litigation dealing with Indian issues and attempt to bring a consistent source of expert knowledge to the solution of issues affecting Indians.

The idea of self-government for Indians began almost as soon as Indians had fairly continuous contact with non-Indians. It has been the subject of wholly arbitrary bureaucratic action and very spontaneous Indian militant activities. Generally, the structure put in place to achieve Indian self-government is premised upon a deep mistrust by the government of the actual process of self-government. Federal officials fear a loss of control over the decisions that Indian communities might make, and therefore, although federal policy several times has declared self-government for tribes, it has not been realized to any great extent.

Indians have preserved the idea of nationhood or peoplehood throughout their period of contact with the non-Indian world but have had great difficulty communicating the essence of what they believe to the larger society. In many respects during the postwar period Indians have acted like other racial minorities in their approach to problems and in their efforts to get the attention of the federal government. But this movement to be a recognized minority group within American society has spawned an Indian traditional backlash, which seems to have directed Indian attention to a deeper appreciation of the old ways.

Apart from some structural changes, there is no good solution to the question of self-government today. Indians have few viable options open to them because they lack the substantial economic and social freedom to experiment with alternative ways of doing things. Self-government is in large part social and community growth, and this growth takes both time and realizations about the world that are not capable of being programmed. A change in perception by both Indians and federal and state officials who deal with Indians is imperative if any substantial progress is to be achieved in the future. Until Indians resolve for themselves a comfortable modern identity that can be used to energize reservation institutions, radical changes will not be of much assistance but will only serve to confuse people.

Self-government is basically a political idea, and it has been superseded in our generation by the demand for self-determination. Indian affairs have thus moved beyond political institutions into an arena primarily cultural, religious, and sociological and there are no good guidelines for either policy or programs in this new area of activity. The old scholarship that treated political and economic activities as separate from the rest of human experience can no longer describe political and economic developments in Indian tribes without reference to the profound cultural and emotional energies that are influencing Indians today. It is probably too late to put the Indian genie back into the bottle. John Collier planned too well in his efforts to give Indians self-government. In setting the theoretical framework for reconstituting an ancient feeling of sovereignty, he prepared the ground for an entirely new expression of Indian communal and corporate existence. We are just beginning to recognize the nature of this expression.

Appendix:
A Comparison of the Wheeler-Howard Act and the Original Collier Bill

Self-Government Provisions

Collier Bill	*Wheeler-Howard (Indian Reorganization) Act*
Power of self-government Adopt constitution and bylaws (ratified by ⅗ vote)	**Power of self-government (section 16)** Adopt constitution and by laws (ratified by majority vote)
Tribal powers To be advised of appropriation estimates, bill, or amendments before being sent to Congress To exercise all existing powers possessed by tribe	**Tribal powers (section 16)** Prevent sale, lease, encumbrance of tribal property and assets without its consent To negotiate with federal, state, and local governments To be advised of appropriation estimates To exercise all existing powers possessed by tribal governments
Powers requiring secretary discretion or approval Organize municipal government Elect officers, hire employees, define membership, fix salaries, prescribe voter qualifications Regulate disposition of property, conserve resources, cultivate art and culture, protect health, safety and welfare of tribal members Establish local court system Accept assets of persons and incompetents, administer tribal funds Maintain public improvements, condemnation power, levy taxes Acquire and manage property, make contracts, perform corporate functions, employ counsel, and pay fees Compel transfer of local BIA employees, regulate trade, exclude undesirables from reservation	**Powers requiring secretary discretion or approval (section 16)** Employment of legal counsel (including fees)

Collier Bill	*Wheeler-Howard* *(Indian Reorganization) Act*
Negotiate and contract with federal, state, and local governments Exercise powers necessary to fulfill governmental functions Secretary enter into agreements with tribe to have tribe perform local services Secretary may establish a system for gradual transfer of certain BIA functions to tribe	
Authorizes appropriation of $5,000,000 for economic development (added as an additional section early in the House hearings)	Authorizes appropriation of $250,000 annually to assist in tribal organization (section 9) Authorizes appropriation of $10,000,000 for loans to tribal corporations for economic development—revolving credit fund (section 10) Authorizes tribes to create a tribal corporation with a charter issued by secretary (initiated by ⅓; ratified by majority vote of tribal members) (section 17) Permits tribe to engage in business, obtain loans, acquire property, issue certificates of interest, transfer land, and all other things necessary for conduct of business Authorizes the election of officers, drafting of bylaws, payment of dividends, etc. Prohibits mortgage or sale of tribal land or lease for more than 10 years

Education and Employment Provisions

Collier Bill	*Wheeler-Howard (Indian Reorganization) Act*
Commissioner to provide training for Indians of ¼ blood for service in bureau and community (may use boarding schools or colleges and professional schools to accomplish this)	Authorizes an appropriation of not more than $250,000 for loans to Indians for vocational and trade schools (section 11); not more than $50,000 may go to high school and college students
Authorizes an appropriation of not more than $50,000 annually for this training; $15,000 may be authorized for outright grants	Secretary shall establish standards of eligibility, without regard to the Civil Service, for positions in the Indian Bureau (section 12)
Declares it to be a policy of Congress to promote and preserve Indian arts, crafts, and culture; Commissioner may employ persons and use existing facilities to achieve this	Qualified Indians shall be extended preference to vacancies that open in the Indian Bureau (section 12)
No separate monies shall be spent for this purpose; they must come from existing school funds	

Indian-Lands Provisions

Collier Bill	*Wheeler-Howard* *(Indian Reorganization) Act*
Terminates policy of allotment	Terminates policy of allotment (section 1)
Extends trust period on allotted lands until otherwise directed by Congress Terminates secretary's power to issue fee patents or certificates of competency No tribal lands shall be voluntarily alienated	Extends trust period on allotted lands until otherwise directed by Congress (section 2)
Withdraws surplus lands that have been open for sale and returns them to tribal control	Withdraws surplus lands that have been open for sale and returns them to tribal control (section 3)
Forbids sale, devise, or transfer of reservation allotted land except to Indian tribe	
Secretary may acquire land for landless Indians—can be for adding to existing reservation or to create new reservation—also for land consolidation Authorizes an appropriation of not more than $2,000,000 annually for this	Secretary may acquire land, water rights, and surface rights for Indians—may be for landless Indians or to add to reservation, such as white-owned checkerboard parcels (section 5) Authorizes an appropriation of not more than $2,000,000 annually for this (section 5)

Collier Bill	Wheeler-Howard (Indian Reorganization) Act
Secretary is authorized to transfer to a tribe any member's interest in farming, grazing, or timber land in exchange for certificates, if such is necessary for consolidation purposes	No sale, devise, or transfer of restricted Indian lands may be made except in the following three ways (section 4):
Title to restricted land passes to tribe upon death of tribal member, not to heir (mandatory)	1. Restricted land may be transferred by owner to a tribe or tribal corporation with secretary's approval—this is voluntary (section 4)
Heir receives equitable certificate	2. Restricted lands may be exchanged for other lands of equal value with secretary's approval, if they do not interfere with consolidation program—this is voluntary (section 4)
No will disposing of land other than in this manner will be approved	
Heir may retain use and occupancy	3. Restricted land may be inherited by tribal member or other heirs, Indian or white (section 4)
	Wills disposing of restricted Indian land must be approved by secretary, and secretary may approve only if heirs are members of deceased's same tribe
Secretary may classify and divide tribal lands into economic units for farming, grazing, forestry	
May lease for economic gain	
May delegate this power to tribe	
Secretary may make rules for timber and grazing conservation and to attain sustained yields	Secretary may make rules for timber and grazing conservation and to attain sustained yield (section 6)
Secretary may proclaim new Indian reservations on land acquired under this act	Secretary may proclaim new Indian reservations on land acquired under this act (section 7)
Indian holdings in the public domain are exempt from this act	Indian holdings in the public domain are exempt from this act (section 8)

Notes

1. A Status Higher Than States

1. U.S., *Constitution*, Art. 1, sec. 8, clause 3.
2. U.S., *Statutes at Large*, 43:253.
3. Ibid., 23:362.
4. Ibid., 86:334.
5. Ibid., 88:2203.
6. Ibid., 1910.

2. Domestic Dependent Nations

1. Cherokee Nation v. Georgia, 30 U.S. (5 Pet.) 1, 20 (1831).
2. Ibid., 17.
3. Worcester v. Georgia, 31 U.S. (6 Pet.) 515, 559 (1832).
4. Ibid., 560–61.
5. Reginald G. Fisher, "An Outline of Pueblo Government," in *So Live the Works of Man*, eds. Donald D. Brand, and Fred E. Harvey, (Albuquerque: University of New Mexico Press, 1939), pp. 153–154.
6. Ibid., p. 147.
7. 2 Kapp. 918, 921. Art. 4 is an example.
8. U.S., *Statutes at Large*, 24:388.
9. Ibid., 30:495.
10. Ibid., 34:267.
11. Ibid., 822.
12. *Ex parte Crow Dog*, 109 U.S. 556, 571 (1883).

3. The Organization of the Reservations

1. U.S., Department of the Interior, Bureau of Indian Affairs, *Annual Report of the Commissioner of Indian Affairs for the Year 1885*, p. 300.
2. U.S., *Statutes at Large*, 23:385.
3. U.S., Department of the Interior, Bureau of Indian Affairs, *Regulations of the Indian Office*, sec. 486, 1884.
4. *Annual Report of the Commissioner of Indian Affairs for the Year 1885*, p. 204.
5. Ibid.
6. Ibid., p. 375.
7. U.S., Congress, House, *Hearings on H.R. 25242, Right of Indians to Nominate Their Agent*, 62d. Cong., 2d sess., 1912, p. 5
8. U.S., Congress, Senate, *Hearings on S. 3904, Granting Indians the Right to Select Agents and Superintendents*, 64th Cong., 1st sess., 1916, p. 30.
9. U.S., Congress, Senate, *Hearings on S. 5335, Recall of Agents or Superintendents by Indian Tribes*, 64th Cong., 1st sess., 1916, pp. 1–2.

4. The Movement for Reform

1. Francis E. Leupp, *The Indian and His Problem* (New York: Charles Scribner's Sons, 1910), p. vii.
2. U.S., *Statutes at Large*, 36:855.
3. 224 U.S. 665 (1912).
4. 231 U.S. 28 (1913).
5. U.S., Department of the Interior, *Lake Mohonk Proceedings*, 1914, p. 76.
6. H.R. 2614, 65th Cong., 2d sess., 1917.
7. H.R. 9852, 67th Cong., 2d sess., 1922.
8. John Collier, *From Every Zenith* (Denver: Sage Books, 1963), p. 126.
9. Collier has now become the subject of many scholarly books, and an extensive review of his career can be found in his own works and in an excellent biography of his active years by Kenneth R. Philp, *John Collier's Crusade for Indian Reform: 1920–1954* (Tucson: University of Arizona Press, 1977).
10. U.S., *Statutes at Large*, 43:253, 636.
11. U.S., *Statutes at Large*, 63:536.
12. U.S., Congress, Senate, *Hearings Pursuant to Senate Resolution 79 and Senate Resolution 308, Survey of Conditions of the Indians in the United States*, pt. 3, 70th Cong., 2d sess., 1928, pp. 954–1017.
13. U.S., Congress, House, *Hearings on H.R. 7826, Reservation Courts of Indian Offenses*, 69th Cong., 1st sess., 1926.
14. Ibid.
15. Lewis Meriam, *The Problem of Indian Administration* (Baltimore: Johns Hopkins Press, 1928), p. 3.
16. Ibid., p. 7.
17. Ibid., p. 21.
18. *Hearings Pursuant to Senate Resolution 79 and Senate Resolution 308*, pt. 6, 71st Cong., 1st sess., 1928, pp. 2725–38.
19. Ibid., p. 14139.
20. Ibid., 14142.
21. Ibid., pt. 22, 71st Cong., 2d. sess., 1932.
22. Ibid., pt. 3, 70th Cong., 2d sess., 1928.
23. Ibid., pt. 17, 71st Cong., 3d sess., 1931.
24. S. 5753, 70th Cong., 1st sess., 1928.
25. U.S., Congress, Senate, *Hearings on S. 4165, Incorporation of the Klamath Indian Corporation*, 71st Cong., 1st sess., 1929; U.S., Congress, Senate, *Hearings on S. 2142*.

26. *Hearings on S. 4165,* 71st Cong., 1st sess. 1929.
27. *Hearings on S. 4165 Incorporation of the Klamath Indian Corporation,* 1930, p. 16.
28. Ibid., 17.
29. Ibid., 32.
30. U.S., *Statutes at Large,* 47:564.

5. The Vision of the Red Atlantis

1. Lawrence Kelly, "The Indian Reorganization Act: Dream or Reality?" *Pacific Historical Review* 44 (1976):291.
2. Philp, *John Collier's Crusade for Indian Reform,* p. 94.
3. U.S., Congress, Senate, *Congressional Record,* 70th Cong., 1st sess., December 21, 1929, p. 1051.
4. Ibid., p. 1052.
5. Ibid.
6. Ibid., p. 1053.
7. Ibid.
8. Philp, *John Collier's Crusade for Indian Reform,* p. 101.
9. Meriam, *The Problem of Indian Administration,* p. 15.
10. Ibid., p. 88.
11. Lawrence Kelly, "John Collier and the Indian New Deal: An Assessment," mimeographed (n.d.), p. 7.
12. John Collier, *Indians of America* (New York: W. W. Norton, 1947), pp. 261–62.
13. Collier, *From Every Zenith,* p. 172.
14. Kelly, "John Collier and the Indian New Deal," p. 10.
15. U.S., *Statutes at Large,* 48:108.
16. Kelly, "John Collier and the Indian New Deal," p. 10.
17. Philp, *John Collier's Crusade for Indian Reform,* p. 135.
18. Ibid., pp. 135–136.
19. Ibid., pp. 137–38.

6. The Collier Bill

1. U.S., Congress, House, *Hearings on H.R. 7902, Readjustment of Indian Affairs,* 73d Cong., 2d sess., 1934, p. 1.
2. Ibid., p. 2.
3. U.S., *Statutes at Large,* 34:1221.
4. Talton v. Mayes, 163 U.S. 376 (1896).
5. *Hearings on H.R. 7902,* 73d Cong., 2d sess., 1934, p. 2.
6. Ibid., p. 7.
7. U.S., *Statutes at Large,* 34:182.
8. This provision is found in sec. 4.
9. U.S., *Statutes at Large,* 34:325, 326.
10. This provision is found in sec. 8.
11. This provision is found in sec. 11.
12. This provision is found in sec. 14.
13. This provision is found in sec. 15.
14. Collier, *From Every Zenith,* p. 241.
15. This provision is found in sec. 2.
16. This provision is found in sec. 9.
17. This provision is found in sec. 10.
18. This provision is found in sec. 11.
19. This provision is found in sec. 7.
20. This provision is found in sec. 5.

21.   This provision is found in sec. 6.

7. *The House Hearings*

1.   Philp, *John Collier's Crusade for Indian Reform*, p. 157.
2.   Ibid., p. 157.
3.   Graham D. Taylor, *The New Deal and American Indian Tribalism: The Administration of the Indian Reorganization Act, 1934–45* (Lincoln: University of Nebraska Press, 1980), p. 23.
4.   *Hearings on 7902*, 73d Cong., 2d sess., 1934, p. 63.
5.   Ibid., p. 64.
6.   Ibid., pp. 64–65.
7.   Ibid., p. 22.
8.   Ibid.
9.   Ibid., p. 47.
10.   Ibid., p. 43.
11.   Ibid., p. 95.
12.   Ibid., p. 96.
13.   Ibid., p. 102.
14.   Ibid., p. 109.
15.   Ibid., p. 52.
16.   Taylor, *The New Deal and Indian Tribalism*, p. 24.
17.   *Hearings on H.R. 7902*, 73d Cong., 2d sess., 1934, p. 70.
18.   Ibid., p. 111.
19.   Sec. 8 of Title III.
20.   *Hearings on H.R. 7902*, 73d Cong., 2d sess., 1934, p. 119.
21.   Ibid., p. 30.
22.   Ibid., p. 35.
23.   Ibid., p. 310.
24.   Ibid., p. 188.
25.   Ibid., p. 133.
26.   Ibid., p. 38.
27.   Ibid., p. 27.
28.   Ibid., p. 491.
29.   Ibid., p. 315.
30.   Ibid., p. 324.
31.   Ibid., pp. 338–40.
32.   Ibid., pp. 170–71.
33.   Ibid., pp. 167–68.
34.   Ibid., p. 304.
35.   Ibid., p. 134.
36.   Ibid., p. 135.
37.   Ibid., p. 235.
38.   Ibid., p. 135.
39.   Ibid., p. 237.
40.   Ibid., p. 299.
41.   Ibid., p. 300.
42.   Ibid., p. 151.
43.   Ibid., pp. 262–71.
44.   Ibid., pp. 272–76.
45.   Ibid., p. 276.
46.   Ibid., p. 205.
47.   Ibid., p. 490.
48.   Ibid., p. 397.

49. Ibid.
50. Ibid., p. 425.
51. Ibid., p. 240.
52. Ibid., p. 244.
53. Ibid., p. 238.
54. Ibid., p. 250.
55. Ibid., p. 249.
56. Ibid., p. 253.
57. Ibid., p. 254.
58. Sec. 8.
59. *Hearings on H.R. 7902*, 73d Cong., 2d sess., 1934, p. 186.
60. Sec. 11.
61. *Hearings on H.R. 7902*, 73d Cong., 2d sess., 1934, p. 187.
62. Ibid., p. 189.
63. Ibid., p. 76.
64. Ibid., p. 193.
65. Ibid., p. 195.
66. Ibid.
67. Ibid.
68. Ibid., p. 492.
69. Ibid., p. 493.
70. Ibid.
71. Ibid., p. 494.
72. Ibid., p. 502.
73. Ibid., p. 493.

8. The Indian Congresses

1. U.S., *Statutes at Large*, 7:13.
2. Theodore H. Haas, *Ten Years of Tribal Government Under the I.R.A.* (Chicago: Haskell Institute Printing Service, 1947), p. 1.
3. Philp, *John Collier's Crusade for Indian Reform*, p. 146.
4. Collier, *From Every Zenith*, p. 174.
5. U.S., Department of Interior, *Rapid City Indian Congress*, mimeographed minutes, March 2–5, 1934, p. 7.
6. Ibid., p. 7.
7. Ibid., pp. 67–68.
8. Ibid., p. 71.
9. Philp, *John Collier's Crusade for Indian Reform*, p. 148.
10. *Rapid City Indian Congress*, p. 78.
11. Kenneth R. Philp, "John Collier and the New Deal: An American Indian Renaissance" (paper presented at the American Historian's Conference, Chicago, 1973), p. 8.
12. *Rapid City Indian Congress*, p. 73.
13. Ibid., p. 104.
14. Ibid., p. 92.
15. Ibid., p. 93.
16. Ibid., p. 126.
17. Ibid., p. 99.
18. Ibid., pp. 105–106.
19. Ibid., p. 127.
20. Philp, "John Collier and the New Deal," p. 8.
21. Philp, *John Collier's Crusade for Indian Reform*, p. 151.
22. Collier, *From Every Zenith*, p. 252.

NOTES

23. U.S., Department of Interior, *Fort Defiance Indian Congress*, mimeographed minutes, March 12–13, 1934, p. 4.
24. Philp, *John Collier's Crusade for Indian Reform*, p. 151.
25. *Fort Defiance Indian Congress*, p. 6.
26. Ibid., p. 19.
27. Philp, *John Collier's Crusade for Indian Reform*, p. 151.
28. *Fort Defiance Indian Congress*, p. 151.
29. Philp, *John Collier's Crusade for Indian Reform*, p. 152.
30. U.S., Department of Interior, *Phoenix Indian Congress*, mimeographed minutes, March 16, 1934, p. 4.
31. Ibid., p. 8.
32. Ibid., p. 9.
33. Philp, *John Collier's Crusade for Indian Reform*, p. 152.
34. *Phoenix Indian Congress*, p. 24.
35. Ibid., p. 27.
36. Ibid., p. 28.
37. Ibid., p. 12.
38. Ibid., p. 19.
39. John Collier, "Opposition to the I.R.A. Bill," mimeographed statement, n.d., p. 3.
40. Ibid., p. 14.
41. Michael T. Smith, "The Wheeler-Howard Act of 1934: 'The Indian New Deal,' " *Journal of the West* 10 (July 1971):527.
42. U.S., Department of Interior, *Anadarko Indian Congress*, mimeographed minutes, March 20, 1934, p. 2.
43. Ibid., pp. 7–8.
44. Ibid., p. 57.
45. Ibid., p. 11.
46. Ibid., p. 51.
47. Ibid., p. 53.
48. Ibid., p. 55.
49. Ibid., p. 56.
50. Ibid., pp. 57–61.
51. Ibid., p. 65.
52. U.S., Department of Interior, *Muskogee Indian Congress*, mimeographed minutes, March 22–23, 1934, p. 12.
53. Ibid., p. 43.
54. Ibid., p. 39.
55. Ibid., p. 45.
56. Philp, *John Collier's Crusade for Indian Reform*, p. 154.
57. Ibid.
58. U.S., Department of Interior, *Chemawa Indian Congress*, mimeographed minutes, March 8–9, 1934, p. 17.
59. Ibid., p. 54.
60. Ibid., p. 63.
61. Ibid., p. 66.
62. Ibid., p. 62.
63. Ibid., p. 72.
64. Ibid., p. 68.
65. Ibid., p. 84.
66. U.S., Department of Interior, *Riverside Indian Congress*, mimeographed minutes, March 17–18, 1934, p. 29.

67. Ibid.
68. Ibid., p. 25.
69. Ibid., p. 36.
70. Ibid., p. 35.
71. Ibid., p. 37.
72. U.S., Department of Interior, *Hayward Indian Congress,* mimeographed minutes, April 23–24, 1934, p. 42.
73. Ibid., p. 49.
74. Ibid., p. 51.
75. Ibid., p. 53.
76. Ibid., p. 61.
77. Ibid., p. 64.
78. U.S., Department of Interior, *Bureau of Indian Affairs Documents,* 1934, p. 1.

9. Political Conflict in the Upper House

1. Joseph S. Clark, *The Senate Establishment* (New York: Hill & Wang, 1963), p. 22.
2. U.S., Congress, Senate, *Hearings on S. 2755, To Grant Indians Living Under Federal Tutelage the Freedom to Organize for Purposes of Local Self-Government and Economic Enterprise,* 73d Cong., 2d sess., 1934, p. 1.
3. Ibid., p. 34.
4. Philp, *John Collier's Crusade for Indian Reform,* p. 144.
5. Ibid.
6. Ibid., p. 145.
7. *Hearings on S. 2755,* 73d Cong., 2d sess., 1934, p. 88.
8. Ibid.
9. Ibid., p. 86.
10. Philp, *John Collier's Crusade for Indian Reform,* p. 156.
11. *Hearings on S. 2755,* 73d Cong., 2d sess., 1934, pp. 66–77.
12. Ibid., p. 94.
13. Ibid.
14. Ibid., p. 96.
15. Ibid., p. 97.
16. Ibid., p. 98.
17. Ibid., p. 64.
18. Ibid., p. 65.
19. Ibid., p. 68.
20. Ibid.
21. Ibid., p. 69.
22. Ibid., p. 148.
23. Ibid., p. 151.
24. Ibid., p. 58.
25. Ibid., p. 59.
26. Ibid., p. 62.
27. 187 U.S. 553 (1903).
28. *Hearings on S. 2755,* 73d Cong., 2d sess., 1934, p. 87.
29. Ibid., p. 192.
30. Ibid., pp. 71–72.
31. Ibid., p. 73.
32. Ibid., p. 74.
33. Ibid., p. 76.
34. Ibid., p. 95.
35. Ibid., pp. 95–96.
36. Ibid., pp. 256–57.

37. Ibid., p. 257.
38. Ibid., p. 259.
39. Ibid.
40. Ibid., p. 69.
41. Ibid., p. 201.
42. Ibid., p. 202.
43. Ibid.
44. Ibid., p. 208.
45. M. K. Sniffen, "The Future of the Indians," *Indian Truth* 11 (March 1934): 3.
46. Ibid.
47. Philp, *John Collier's Crusade for Indian Reform*, p. 155.
48. Ibid., p. 172.
49. *Senate Hearings on S. 2755*, 73d Cong., 2d sess., 1934, p. 310.
50. Ibid.
51. Ibid., p. 324.
52. Ibid., p. 333.
53. Ibid., p. 220.
54. Ibid., p. 173.
55. Ibid., p. 174.
56. Ibid., p. 110.
57. Ibid., p. 112.
58. Ibid., p. 118.
59. Ibid., p. 132.
60. Ibid., pp. 132–33.
61. Ibid., p. 227.
62. Ibid., p. 224.
63. Ibid., p. 225.
64. Ibid., p. 226.
65. Philp, p. 158.
66. Taylor, *The New Deal and Indian Tribalism*, p. 25.
67. *Senate Hearings on S. 2755*, 73d Cong., 2d sess., 1934, p. 237.
68. Ibid., p. 248.
69. Ibid., p. 250.
70. Sec. 17.
71. *Hearings on S. 2755*, 73d Cong., 2d sess., 1934, p. 264.
72. Ibid., p. 303.
73. Taylor, *The New Deal and Indian Tribalism*, p. 27.
74. Ibid.

10. The Indian Reorganization Act of 1934 versus the Collier Bill

1. U.S., *Statutes at Large*, 48: 984.
2. Sec. 16.
3. Sec. 17.
4. Sec. 10.
5. Sec. 12.
6. Sec. 2.
7. Sec. 3.
8. Ibid.
9. Sec. 7.
10. Sec. 5.
11. Sec. 6.
12. Sec. 8.

13. Sec. 3.
14. Sec. 15.

11. *Bringing the Law to Life*

1. U.S., *Statutes at Large*, 48: 984.
2. U.S., Department of Interior, *Opinions of the Solicitor: Indian Affairs* (Washington: U.S. Government Printing Office, 1946), p. 410.
3. Ibid., p. 447.
4. Ibid., p. 471.
5. Ibid., p. 477.
6. Ibid., p. 814.
7. Ibid., p. 613.
8. Ibid., p. 668.
9. U.S., *Statutes at Large*, 18: 420.
10. *Opinions of the Solicitor*, p. 486.
11. Ibid., p. 487.
12. Ibid.
13. Ibid., p. 533.
14. Ibid., p. 536.
15. Ibid.
16. Ibid., p. 896.
17. U.S., *Statutes at Large*, 4: 731.

12. *Ratification and Its Aftermath*

1. Philp, "John Collier and the New Deal," p. 11.
2. Philp, *John Collier's Crusade for Indian Reform*, p. 163.
3. U.S., Congress, House, *Hearings on H.R. 7781, Indian Conditions and Affairs*, 74th Cong., 1st sess., 1935, p. 59.
4. U.S., *Statutes at Large*, XLIX, 378.
5. Philp, *John Collier's Crusade for Indian Reform*, p. 163.
6. Ibid.
7. Philp, "John Collier and the New Deal," p. 29.
8. Taylor, *The New Deal and Indian Tribalism*, p. 37.
9. Ibid.
10. Philp, *John Collier's Crusade for Indian Reform*, p. 173.
11. Philp, "John Collier and the New Deal," p. 14.
12. Theodore H. Haas, "The Indian Reorganization Act in Historical Perspective," in *Indian Affairs and the Indian Reorganization Act: The Twenty-Year Record*, ed. William H. Kelly (Tucson: University of Arizona Press, 1954), p. 12.
13. Ibid., p. 18.
14. Haas, *Tribal Government Under the I.R.A.*, p. 12.
15. Kelly, "John Collier and the Indian New Deal," p. 4.
16. Peter Wright, "John Collier and the Oklahoma Indian Welfare Act of 1936," *Chronicles of Oklahoma* (1972), p. 362.
17. Ibid., pp. 363–64.
18. Philp, *John Collier's Crusade for Indian Reform*, p. 180.
19. Wright, "John Collier and the Oklahoma Indian Welfare Act," p. 363.
20. Ibid., p. 367.
21. Taylor, *The New Deal and Indian Tribalism*, p. 36.
22. U.S., *Statutes at Large*, XLIX, 1967.
23. Wright, "John Collier and the Oklahoma Indian Welfare Act," p. 370.

24. Felix Cohen, *Handbook of Federal Indian Law* (Albuquerque: University of New Mexico Press, 1942), p. 455.
25. Philp, *John Collier's Crusade for Indian Reform*, p. 182.
26. Haas, "The Indian Reorganization Act in Historical Perspective," pp. 12–18.
27. Philp, *John Collier's Crusade for Indian Reform*, pp. 182–83.
28. U.S., *Statutes at Large*, XLIX, 1250.
29. Haas, "The Indian Reorganization Act in Historical Perspective," pp. 12–18.
30. Philp, *John Collier's Crusade for Indian Reform*, p. 200.
31. U.S., Congress, House, *Hearings on H.R. 5878, Yankton Tribe: Amend Wheeler-Howard Act*, 76th Cong., 1st sess., 1939, p. 1.
32. Ibid., pp. 2–3.
33. Ibid., p. 20.
34. Ibid., p. 21.
35. Ibid., p. 70.
36. Ibid., p. 72.
37. Ibid., p. 96.
38. Philp, *John Collier's Crusade for Indian Reform*, p. 200.
39. Ibid., p. 202.
40. U.S., Congress, Senate, *Hearings on S. 1218, Repealing the So-Called Wheeler-Howard Act*, 78th Cong., 2d sess., 1944, p. 1.
41. Ibid., p. 16.

13. The Barren Years

1. Harold E. Fey, "Our National Indian Policy," *The Christian Century* (March 30, 1955), p. 396.
2. *Hearings on S. 1218*, 78th Cong., 2d sess., 1944, p. 160.
3. Harold E. Fey and D'Arcy McNickle, *Indians and Other Americans* (New York: Harper & Brothers, 1959), p. 10.
4. Philp, "John Collier and the New Deal," p. 31.
5. Jay B. Nash, Oliver LaFarge, and W. Carson Ryan, *The New Day for the Indians: A Survey of the Workings of the Indian Reorganization Act* (New York: Academy Press, 1938), p. 30.
6. Collier, *From Every Zenith*, p. 272.
7. Haas, *Tribal Government Under the I.R.A.*, p. 8.
8. Ibid., p. 9.
9. Fey and McNickle, *Indians and Other Americans*, p. 10.
10. Lawrence Kelly, "The Indian Reorganization Act: Dream or Reality?" *Pacific Historical Review* 44 (1976), p. 311.
11. *Hearings on S. 1218*, 78th Cong., 2d sess., 1944, p. 17.
12. Kelly, "Indian Reorganization Act," p. 301.
13. Taylor, *The New Deal and Indian Tribalism*, p. xii.
14. Ibid., p. 66.
15. Ibid., p. 68.
16. Collier, *From Every Zenith*, p. 346.
17. U.S., *Statutes at Large*, 60: 1049.
18. Public Law 280, U.S., *Statutes at Large*, 67:588.
19. U.S., *Statutes at Large*, 69:539.
20. Ibid., 75:47.
21. Ibid., 79:552.
22. Ibid., 78:508.
23. Ibid., 67:588.
24. Ibid., 82:73.

14. *The Indian Civil Rights Act*

1. See for example Cohen, *Handbook of Federal Indian Law*, pp. 427–28.
2. U.S., *Statutes at Large*, 30:495.
3. 163 U.S. 376 (1896).
4. Ibid., 381.
5. Ibid., 382–83.
6. Ibid., 384.
7. 151 F. Supp. 476 (1957).
8. Ibid., 480.
9. 249 F.2d 915, 919 (1966).
10. Ibid.
11. 272 F.2d 131, 134 (1959).
12. 342 F.2d 369, 378–79 (1965).
13. U.S., *Statutes at Large*, 82:77.
14. Note "The Indian Bill of Rights and the Constitutional Status of Tribal Governments," *Harvard Law Review* 82 (1969): 1343.

15. *The Cry for Self-Determination*

1. U.S., Congress, Senate, *Indian Education: A National Tragedy—A National Challenge*, 91st Cong., 1st sess., 1969, S. Rept. 91-501, p. xi.
2. U.S., *Statutes at Large*, 86:327.
3. Ibid., 88:2204.
4. U.S., Congress, House, *Hearings on S. 1017 and Related Bills, Indian Self-Determination and Education Assistance Act*, 93d Cong., 2d sess., 1974.
5. Ibid., p. 33.
6. U.S., *Statutes at Large*, 36:855.
7. Ibid., 4:735, 738.
8. *Hearings on S. 1017*, 93d Cong., 2d sess., 1974, p. 35.
9. U.S., *Statutes at Large*, 86:919.
10. Ibid., 88:77.
11. Ibid., 1910.
12. U.S., American Indian Policy Review Commission, *Final Report, May 17, 1977* (Washington: U.S. Government Printing Office, 1977), p. 4.
13. Ibid., p. 15.

17. *The Future of Indian Nations*

1. 377 U.S. 533 (1964).
2. U.S., *Statutes at Large*, 48:891.
3. 494 U.S. 872 (1990).
4. U.S., *Statutes at Large*, 108:3125.
5. U.S., *Statutes at Large*, 107:1488.
6. 116 Sup. Ct. 1114 (1996).

Bibliography

Books and Articles

Clark, Joseph S. *The Senate Establishment*. New York: Hill & Wang, 1963.

Cohen, Felix. *Handbook of Federal Indian Law*. Albuquerque: University of New Mexico Press, 1942.

Collier, John. *From Every Zenith*. Denver: Sage Books, 1963.

———. "The Genesis and Philosophy of the Indian Reorganization Act." In *Indian Affairs and the Indian Reorganization Act: The Twenty Year Record,* edited by William H. Kelly. Tucson: University of Arizona Press, 1954.

———. *Indians of America*. New York: W. W. Norton, 1947.

———. "Opposition to the I.R.A. Bill." Mimeographed statement. N.d.

Fey, Harold E., and McNickle, D'Arcy. *Indians and Other Americans: Two Ways of Life Meet*. New York: Harper & Brothers, 1959.

———. "Our National Indian Policy." *The Christian Century* (March 30, 1955), pp. 395–97.

Fisher, Reginald G. "An Outline of Pueblo Government," in *So Live the Works of Man*. Edited by Donald D. Brand and Fred E. Harvey. Albuquerque: University of New Mexico Press, 1939.

Haas, Theodore H. "The Indian Reorganization Act in Historical Perspective." In *Indian Affairs and the Indian Reorganization Act: The Twenty-Year Record,* edited by William H. Kelly. Tucson: University of Arizona Press, 1954.

———. *Ten Years of Tribal Government Under the I.R.A.* Chicago: Haskell Institute Printing Service, 1947.

"The Indian Bill of Rights and the Constitutional Status of Tribal Governments" (Note). *Harvard Law Review* 82 (1969): 1343.

Jackson, Helen Hunt. *A Century of Dishonor*. New York: Harper & Brothers, 1881.

Kelly, Lawrence. "The Indian Reorganization Act: Dream or Reality?" *Pacific Historical Review* 44 (1976): 291–312.

———. "John Collier and the Indian New Deal: An Assessment." Mimeographed. N.d.

Leupp, Francis E. *The Indian and His Problem.* New York: Charles Scribner's Sons, 1910.

Mekeel, Scudder. "An Appraisal of the Indian Reorganization Act." *American Anthropology* 46 (1944): 209–17.

Meriam, Lewis. *The Problem of Indian Administration.* Baltimore: Johns Hopkins Press, 1928.

Nash, Jay B., LaFarge, Oliver and Ryan, W. Carson. *The New Day for the Indians: A Survey of the Workings of the Indian Reorganization Act.* New York: Academy Press, 1938.

Parman, Donald, *The Navajo Indian and the New Deal.* New Haven, Conn.: Yale University Press, 1976.

Philp, Kenneth R. "John Collier and the New Deal: An American Indian Renaissance." Paper presented at the American Historian's Conference in Chicago, 1973.

———. "John Collier, 1933–1945." In *The Commissioners of Indian Affairs,* edited by Robert Kvasnicka and Herman J. Viola. Lincoln: University of Nebraska Press, 1979.

———. *John Collier's Crusade for Indian Reform: 1920–1954.* Tucson: University of Arizona Press, 1977.

Smith, Michael T. "The Wheeler-Howard Act of 1934: 'The Indian New Deal.' " *Journal of the West* 10 (July 1971): 521–34.

Sniffen, M. K. "The Future of the Indians." *Indian Truth* 11 (May 1934): 1–7.

———. "Stop, Look, and Consider." *Indian Truth* 11 (March 1934): 1–3.

Taylor, Graham D. *The New Deal and American Indian Tribalism: The Administration of the Indian Reorganization Act, 1934–45.* Lincoln: University of Nebraska Press, 1980.

Wright, Peter. "John Collier and the Oklahoma Indian Welfare Act of 1936." *Chronicles of Oklahoma* (1972), pp. 347–71.

Government Documents

Public Papers of the President, Harry S. Truman. Washington: U.S. Government Printing Office, 1946.

U.S., American Indian Policy Review Commission. *Final Report, May 17, 1977.* Washington: U.S. Government Printing Office, 1977.

U.S. Congress, House. Subcommittee on Indian Affairs. *Hearings on S. 1017 and Related Bills, Indian Self-Determination and Educational Assistance Act.* 93d Cong., 2d sess., 1974.

———. *Hearings on H.R. 5878, Yankton Tribe: Amend Wheeler-Howard Act.* 76th Cong., 1st sess., 1944.

———. *Hearings on H.R. 7781, Indian Conditions and Affairs.* 74th Cong., 1st sess., 1935.

———. *Hearings on H.R. 7826, Reservation Courts of Indian Offenses.* 69th Cong., 1st sess., 1926.

———. *Hearings on H.R. 7902, Readjustment of Indian Affairs.* 73d Cong., 2d sess., 1934.

———. *Hearings on H.R. 25242, Right of Indians to Nominate Their Agent.* 62d Cong., 2d sess., 1912.

———. *Hearings on H.R. 25663, Right of Indians to Nominate Agent: A Supplemental Hearing.* 63d Cong., 2d sess., 1913.

U.S., Congress, Senate. *Congressional Record.* 70th Cong., 1st sess., December 21, 1929, p. 1051.

BIBLIOGRAPHY

_____ . *Hearings Pursuant to Senate Resolution 79 and Senate Resolution 308, Survey of Conditions of the Indians in the United States.* Pt. 6, January 21, 1930. Pt. 17, April–May 1931. Pt. 22, January 21, 22, February 4, 1932. Pt. 26, January 31, December 5, 10, 1930.

_____ . Subcommittee on Indian Affairs. *Hearings on S. 1218, Repealing the So-Called Wheeler-Howard Act.* 78th Cong., 2d sess., 1944.

_____ . *Hearings on S. 2047, A Bill to Promote the General Welfare of the Indians in the State of Oklahoma and for Other Purposes.* 74th Cong., 1st sess., 1935.

_____ . *Hearings on S. 2755, To Grant Indians Living under Federal Tutelage the Freedom to Organize for Purposes of Local Self-Government and Economic Enterprise.* 73d Cong., 2d sess., 1934.

_____ . *Hearings on S. 3588, Klamath Indian Corporation.* 71st Cong., 2d sess., 1930.

_____ . *Hearings on S. 3904, Granting Indians the Right to Select Agents and Superintendents.* 64th Cong., 1st sess., 1916.

_____ . *Hearings on S. 4165, Incorporation of the Klamath Indian Corporation.* 71st Cong., 2d sess., 1930.

_____ . *Hearings on S. 5335, Recall of Agents or Superintendents by Indian Tribes.* 64th Cong., 1st sess., 1916.

U.S., Department of the Interior. Indian Congresses, mimeographed minutes, 1934. Anadarko, Oklahoma, March 20, 1934; Chemawa, Oregon, March 8–9, 1934; Fort Defiance, Arizona, March 12–13, 1934; Hayward, Wisconsin, April 23–24, 1934; Miami, Oklahoma, March 24, 1934; Muskogee, Oklahoma, March 22–23, 1934; Phoenix, Arizona, March 16, 1934; Rapid City, South Dakota, March 2–5, 1934; Riverside, California, March 17–18, 1934; Santo Domingo, New Mexico, March 15, 1934.

_____ . *Opinions of the Solicitor: Indian Affairs.* Washington: U.S. Government Printing Office, 1946.

U.S., Department of the Interior, Bureau of Indian Affairs. "Analysis of Official Vote of Indian Tribes on Wheeler-Howard Bill." Unpublished memo, June 6, 1934.

_____ . *Annual Report of the Commissioner of Indian Affairs for the Year 1885.*

_____ . *Regulations of the Indian Office, 1884.*

Index

Aaron, Reverend C., 120
Abourezk, James, 226, 228, 230
Abourezk Commission, 6, 227–31, 239, 259
Agriculture, Department of, 85
AIM. *See* American Indian Movement
Alaskan Indian Welfare Act, 177
Alaskan Indians, 99, 175, 176, 186
Alcatraz Island invasion, 236, 237
Alford, Thomas, 113
allotment, termination of, 146
American Civil Liberties Union, 63, 134, 173
American Indian Association, 133
American Indian Civil Rights Act, 199
American Indian Defense Association, 45, 50, 56, 61–62, 63, 134, 153
American Indian Federation, 174, 180
American Indian Movement, 199, 237, 239
American Indian Policy Review Commission, 6, 227, 231

American Indian Religion Freedom Act Amendments, 253
American Indian Tribal Court, 211, 214
American Red Cross, 43
Amish settlements, 263
Anadarko Indian Congress, 112
Anderson, Clinton, 195
Anti Saloon League of America, 39
Applied Anthropology Staff, 173
appropriation, tribal awareness, 142
ARA. *See* Area Redevelopment Administration
Arapaho Indians, 4, 113
Area Redevelopment Administration (ARA), 196
Arts and Crafts Board, 250
Ashley, Edward, 39
Ashurst, Henry, 123, 138, 147, 149
Aspinall Wayne, 210
assimilation, 125
Atwood, Stella, 40
Ayers, Roy, 96

Baruch, Bernard M., 41
Bellville, Oliver, 111
Bennett, Robert, 216
Bentley, Martin J., 34
bilateral agreements, 101
bilingual education, 251
Bill of Rights, 194, 209, 213
Blackfeet Indians, 28, 96, 97, 106, 125
Blackmun, Harry A., 253
Board of Indian Commissioners, 62,
  111
boarding schools, 62, 220
Bozeman Trail, 8, 236
Brande, Martin, 235
Brennan, William J., Jr., 253
Brookings Institute, 43, 45
Brosius, S. R., 40
Brown, Joseph W., 97–98
Brown v. Board of Education, 206
Brule Sioux Indians, 4
Bruner, Joseph, 114, 132, 133, 178, 180
Bryan, William Jennings, 41
Burdick, Usher, 180
Bureau of Catholic Missions, 39
Bureau of Indian Affairs, 5, 6, 26, 31,
  37–38, 184, 198
  attacks by Collier, 85–86
  Courts of Indian Offenses, 43, 204
  decentralizing power, 143
  implementation of IRA, 175, 188, 196
  move to Chicago, 190
  occupation of, 226
  paternalism, 126
  Pueblo lands, 39
Burke, Charles, 43, 81
Burke Act, 62, 72
Bursum, Holm, 40
Bursum bill, 40, 41, 109
Bush, George, 7, 261
Butler, Nicholas Murray, 41

Carroll, John, 207, 221
Carter, Jimmy, 7, 230, 260
Castillo, Adam, 94
Catholic Church, 19, 105
Cawker, Harvey, 111
Celler, Emanuel, 210
CERT. *See* Coalition of Energy Resource
  Tribes
Chapman, Henry, 113
charter of incorporation, 57–59
Chavez, Dennis, 86
checkerboard lands, 148

Chemawa Indian Congress, 115
Cherokee Indian cases, 203
Cherokee Indians, 4, 11, 16, 17, 58, 187,
  201, 202
Cheyenne-Arapaho tribe, 93
Cheyenne Indians, 4, 113
Chickasaw Indians, 4, 38
chiefs, Indian, 9–10
Chippewa Indians, 51, 162
Choat v. Trapp, 38
Choctaw Indians, 4, 162
Christian Reform Church, 174
Christian, Theodore, 84
Church, Frank, 195
Citizenship Act of 1924, 3
civil rights, 200, 206
Civil Service, 32, 37–38, 90, 130, 145
Civil War, 22, 23
Civilian Conservation Corps, 62, 63,
  179, 184
Clark, Joseph S., 122
Cleveland, Grover, 32
Clinton, Bill, 7, 261
Coalition of Energy Resource Tribes,
  258
Cohen, Felix S., 61, 103
Coolidge, Calvin, 43
Coolidge, Sherman, 41, 42
Collier bill. *See* Indian reorganization bill
Collier, John:
  adopted by Blackfeet, 106
  American Indian Defense Organiza-
    tion, 45
  appointment as Indian Commissioner,
    61
  Bursum bill, 40, 41
  Court of Indian Affairs, 132
  early Indian activity, 40
  Indian Commissioner, 18, 56
  Indian congresses, 102
  Iron Man, 107
  Joseph Bruner dispute, 133
  Klamath bill, 50, 51
  letters to Congress on Indian reform,
    56–58
  quoted, on indirect rule, 188–89
  ratification of IRA role, 171
  reform, 55, 244, 245
  relations with Burton K. Wheeler, 122
  Tribal Council's bill, 60
  Yankton Sioux repeal efforts, 178
Collier-Margold administrative interpre-
  tations of IRA, 158
Collier-Wheeler Compromise, 136, 137

Colliflower, Madeline, 209, 210
Colville Reservation, 232
Committee of One Hundred, 41, 43, 227
Communism, 111, 116–18, 132
Community Action Program, 6
competency, 127
Confederate states, 24
Congresses, Indian, 102, 115, 119–20, 198
constitution, drafting of, 141
Cosmos Club, 63, 64, 79, 132, 153
Crawford, Wade, 49, 51
credit, 96
credit fund, 144–45
Creek Confederacy, 20, 22
Creek Indians, 4, 20–23, 187
cross-deputization, 263
Crow Dog, 4, 26, 29, 68, 167, 202, 203
Crow Indians, 4, 52, 92, 93, 172
Court of Claims, 153, 264
Court of Indian Affairs, 66, 76–78, 91–
    92, 97, 99, 131, 141, 156, 265, 266
Court of Indian Offenses, 166, 167, 168
culture, 250–56
Curtis Act, 25
customs, Indian, 18
Custer Battlefield, National Cemetery, 52

Dancing Rabbit Creek, Treaty of, 162
Dann, Joe, 133
Dawes, Henry, 42
Dawes Act. See General Allotment Act
Delaware Nations, 101
Department of Human Resources of Oregon v.
    Smith, 252–53
De Priest, Oscar, 82, 100
Dimond, Anthony, 99
Discovery, Doctrine of, 2
Disney, Wesley E., 176
Dodge, Mabel, 40
Domesday Report, 192
domestic dependent nations, 16, 142, 228
Duncan, Isadora, 132

Eastman, Charles, 41
Economic Development Administration
    (EDA), 196
economics, 256, 260
EDA. See Economic Development Ad-
    ministration
education, 42, 71–72, 90, 130, 145, 218,
    219–23, 250–51
Education, Department of, 222, 223

elastic clause, 155
elective, 232
Emergency Conservation Work program,
    62
employment, 145–46
Ervin, Sam, 207, 208, 209
espionage acts, 62
ethnic Indians, 235, 242
Euchee language, 20

Fahey, Charles, 61, 91, 128
Fair Housing Act, 210
Fall, Albert, 39, 40
Farm Security Administration, 184
Federal Emergency Relief Administra-
    tion, 184
federal-state relations, 262–67
fee patenting, 73
Fey, Harold, 184
Fire Thunder, 106
First Amendment, 205, 252–53
fish-ins, 198, 235
Five Civilized Tribes, 4, 23–25, 108,
    114, 167, 177, 202
Fond du Lac Indians, 120
Fools Crow, Frank, 240
Fort Belknap Reservation, 161–62
Fort Defiance Congress, 108, 109
Fort Lawton, 236
Fort Peck Reservation, 125
Fortas, Abe, 182
Fourteenth Amendment, 3, 205
Frazier, Lynn, 46, 47, 56, 59
Fredenberg, Ralph, 96, 134
full-bloods, 105, 151, 165
full faith and credit, 263

Galler, Christine, 117
Gandy bill, 39
General Allotment Act, 5, 14, 25, 38, 42,
    56, 66, 112, 117, 129, 151
General Federation of Women's Clubs,
    40, 63, 134
Generous Woman, Chief, 29
Gilner, George C., 16
Goldman, Emma, 132
Gorman, Howard, 109
Great Lakes Indian Congress, 119–20
Great Society, 5
"Greater Indian America," 198
Greenway, Isabella, 82–83, 89, 99–100
Gregory, Dick, 235

Gros Ventres Indians, 8
guardianship theory, 84–85, 127

Haas, Theodore, 102
Haley, James, 196, 197
Harding, Warren, 41
Harland, Elwood, 135
Haskell Institute, 112
Hastings, William, 138
Hawkins, Kish, 113
Hayden, Carl, 39
Hayden bill, 39
Hayes, Joseph, 115
Hayward Indian Congress, 119–20
Haywood, Bill, 132
Head Start, 217
heirship, 88–89, 128, 148, 256
heneha, 21
Hitchiti language, 20
Hodge, Frederick C., 41
Holtzoff, Alexander, 131
homerule, 152
Hoover, Herbert, 56, 122
Hoover Commission, 192
Hopi Indians, 19
House of Kings, 22
House of Warriors, 22
Howard, Edgar, 59, 82, 100, 136
Hoy-koy-bitty, 113

Ickes, Harold, 61, 62, 83, 136, 158
ICRA. *See* Indian Civil Rights Act
imala labotskalgis, 21
imala lakalgix, 21
Indian agents, 32, 33–36
Indian blood, degree of, 137
Indian Citizenship Act, 42
Indian Civil Rights Act (ICRA), 210–14, 252
Indian Claims Commission, 57, 58, 153, 264
Indian Claims Commission Act, 191
Indian Congress votes, 120
Indian Definition, 150, 151
Indian Education, Office of, 223
Indian Education Act of 1972, 6, 219, 220, 250
Indian Financing Act, 225
Indian Gaming Regulatory Act, 262
Indian Health Service, 251
Indian nationalism, 231
Indian Reorganization Act (IRA), 5, 34

business corporations, 144
education, 145, 188, 196
heirship, 148
Indian lands, 146–48, 194–95, 196–97
passage of, 140
ratification of, 151, 152, 163–66, 171–73, 232
repeal attempts, 178–81
revolving credit fund, 144–45
self-government, 141, 143, 188, 194–95, 196–97
terminated allotment, 146, 188, 194–95, 196–97
tribal powers, 142, 188, 194
Indian Reorganization bill (Collier bill):
amendments to, 98
becomes law, 140
charter of incorporation, 78–79
college loans, 72
conservation, 75, 88
Court of Indian Affairs, 76–78, 91–92
education, 71–72, 90, 130
establishes new reservations, 74
heirship, 88–89
Indian lands, 72–76, 127
introduction of, 66
land consolidation, opposition to, 82
preferential employment, 90
promotes Indian culture, 72
self-government, 67–71
surplus land, 73, 129
terminates allotment, 73
tribal courts, 69
See also Indian Reorganization Act
Indian Reservation Act, 56
Indian Rights Association, 32, 39, 40, 41, 62, 63, 92, 219, 220
Indian Service, 38, 164
Indian Truth, 132
Indians of All Tribes, 237
inherent tribal powers, 158, 160, 167, 168
Interior, Department of, 39, 185, 216
International Treaty Council, 241
IRA. *See* Indian Reorganization Act
Iron Man, 107
Iroquois Federation, 192
Irving, Joe, 106

Jackson, Henry, 195, 216, 220, 226
Job Corps, 217
Johnson, Edwin, 35

Johnson, Jed, 174
Johnson, Lyndon, 184, 217, 262
Johnson–O'Malley Act, 220, 222
Joseph, Chief, 52

Keetowah Society, 114
Kelly, Lawrence, 55, 186
Kennedy, John F., 195
Kennedy, Robert, 21, 219
Kennedy Report, 218, 255
Kickapoo Indians, 34
King, Martin Luther, 206, 210, 218
Kiowa Council, 113
Kirgis, Frederic, 167
Kirkland, Ray, 111, 112
Klamath Indians, 48, 49, 50–52, 144,
    150, 157, 172, 184, 205
Koasati language, 20
Kroeber, Alfred L., 41

La Farge, Oliver, 134
La Follette, Robert, Jr., 46
Laguna Pueblo, 224
Lake Mohonk Conference, 39
La Pointe, Sam, 107, 135–36
leadership, Indian, 9–10
Leavitt Act, 53, 56, 59
Leupp, Francis, 38
Light Horse, 22
Lindquist, G. E. E., 42, 110–12
Little Plume, 29
livestock cooperatives, 185
Lone Wolf v. *Hitchcock,* 128

Major Crimes Act, 4, 29, 77, 201
March on Washington, 237, 240
Margold, Nathan, 105, 142, 158, 159,
    160, 162, 163, 164, 166, 168, 228,
    246
Marshall, John, 16, 17, 142, 203
Marshall, Thurgood, 253
Martinez v. *Southern Ute Tribe,* 204, 205
Matthews, Justice, 26
Mc Carren, Pat, 138
Mc Gillivray, Alexander, 21
Mc Gillycuddy, Agent, 30, 31
Mc Nary, Charles, 48, 49
Medicine Men, 240
Meeds, Lloyd, 6, 221, 222, 229
Mekeel, H. Scudder, 173
Melis, P. E., 46

Menominee Indians, 51, 134, 135, 193, 205
Meriam, Lewis B., 44, 61
Meriam Report, 44, 53, 58–59, 63–64,
    221, 227
Meritt, Edgar B., 61
Merriam, C. Hart, 43
Mescalaro Apache Indians, 40
Mexican government, 19–20
micco aptotka, 21
miccos, 21, 22
Miguel, Robert, 118
Miles, Nelson A., 52
Mille Lac Indians, 120
Milroy, R. H., 20, 30
mining disputes, 94–95
Minneapolis, 199
Mission Indians Federation, 94
Mitke, Charles A., 94–95
mixed-bloods, 105, 137–38, 163
Monohan, A. C., 109
Montgomery bus boycott, 240
Morgan, Jacob, 173
Mormons, 84
Motcum, Peter, 116
Muck, Lee, 46
Muskogee Confederacy, 20, 22
Muskogee Indian Congress, 114
Muskrat, Ruth, 43

NCAI. *See* National Congress of Ameri-
    can Indians
Nahma and Beaver Island Indians, 162
Nash, Philleo, 195, 196
National Advisory Council on Indian
    Education, 219
National Association of Indian Affairs,
    63, 134
National Congress of American Indians
    (NCAI), 194, 198, 206, 207, 216,
    237
National Congress of Mothers and
    Parent-Teacher Association, 39
National Council of American Indians,
    63
National Federation of Federal Employ-
    ees, 130
National Indian Confederacy, 114, 132
National Indian Youth Council, 198–99,
    236
National Research Council, 42
National Women's Christian Temperance
    Union, 39
nationhood, 13, 266

Native American Church, 39, 187, 205, 252
Navajo Indians, 4, 99, 108, 172–73, 184–85, 224
Navajo stock reduction, 108, 185
Nazi organizations, 180
Neighborhood Youth Corps, 217
New Deal, 12, 18, 19, 171, 183, 186, 188, 191, 196, 246, 256
New Frontier, 5, 195
New York *Herald Tribune,* 111
Nez Percé Indians, 8
Nixon, Richard, 222, 226
Nooksack Indians, 163
Norbeck, Peter, 130
Nye, G. M., 46

O'Connor, James, 180
O'Connor, Sandra Day, 253
Office of Economic Opportunity, 197, 234
Officer, James, 195
Oklahoma Indian Congress, 111–15
Oklahoma Indian Credit Corporation, 176, 177
Oklahoma Indian Welfare Act, 176, 177
Old Testament, 27
Olney, Nealty, 117
Omaha Indians, 94
O'Malley, Thomas, 82, 97, 98, 137
Omnibus Act of 1910, 34, 38
oral tradition, 234

Papago Indians, 95, 109, 123, 138, 147, 149
Papago mineral dispute, 123, 138, 149
Parent-Teacher Association, 39
Parker, Arthur C., 41
Peavey, Hubert, 90, 100, 138
peoplehood, 12, 266
Pershing, John J., 41
Philp, Kenneth, 56, 58, 61
Phoenix Indian Congress, 109
Pine, W. B., 46
Pine Ridge Indian Reservation, 213, 239, 240, 249
Plains Indians, 104
"Powers of Indian Tribes," 158, 160
Prairie Island Sioux, 161
preferential employment, 90, 145–46
Preston, Porter, 45
Preston-Eagle Report, 45

Price, Hiram, 29
Price, Oliver, 106
private property, 129
Public Health Service, 252
Public Law 280, 199, 207, 208
Pueblo Indians, 19, 20, 38, 39, 62, 69, 109, 126, 184, 187, 208, 210
Pueblo lands, 40, 41, 42
Pueblo Lands Board Act, 42
Pueblo Relief Act, 62

Quapaw Indians, 92, 224
Quinault Indians, 108

Rapid City Indian Congress, 103–107, 164
ratification, 151, 152, 163–66, 171–73
Reagan, Ronald, 7, 191, 260, 261
Reclamation, Bureau of, 45, 58
"red-baiting," 112
Red Cloud, 8, 30, 236, 237
Red Cloud, Mitchell, 120
Red Deer dance, 40
Red Tomahawk, Francis, 106
red towns, 20
reform, 37, 38, 55, 245
Reifel, Ben, 210
religion, 39, 252–54
Religious Freedom Restoration Act, 253–54
Resettlement Administration, 184
revenue-sharing, 224–25
revolving credit fund, 144–45, 186
Reynolds v. *Sims,* 246
Rhoads, Charles, 45, 56, 61, 62
Riverside Indian Congress, 118
Robinson, Joseph T., 61
Rocky Boy Reservation, 97
Roe Cloud, Henry, 4, 95, 112
Rogers, Will, 83, 98, 175, 178, 179, 180
Roosevelt, Franklin Delano, 54, 60, 62, 112, 124, 136, 138, 170, 180
Rosebud Sioux Indians, 94
Russia, 106

Saice, Gabriel, 119
St. Pierre, John, 179
Saluskin, James, 93
Sam, Thomas, 117
San Carlos Apache Indians, 110
Santa Domingo Congress, 109

Santa Ysabel Reservation, 172
Santee Sioux Indians, 94
Scalia, Antonin, 253
Schmeckebier, Laurence F., 43
secretary discretion, 94, 104, 130, 142–43
self-determination, 215, 216, 217, 231, 237, 244, 245, 254, 264
Self Determination and Education Act, 6, 220, 226
self-government, 13, 14, 15, 19, 26, 64, 170, 190, 244–46, 254, 259, 264, 266–67
Sells, Cato, 39
Seltica, 116
Selwyn, Llewelyn, 180
Seminole Tribe of Florida v. *Florida,* 262
Seven Major Crimes Act. *See* Major Crimes Act
Seymour, Flora Warren, 112, 132
Shawnee language, 20
Shepard, Ward, 63, 103, 110, 127
Siegel, Melvin, 103, 110, 115, 119
Sioux Benefits, 99, 106, 107, 137, 149
Sioux Indians, 4, 8, 13, 265
Sloan, Thomas, 34, 41, 94, 135
Smith, Clement, 178
Sniffen, Matthew K., 132
socialism, 111
Society of American Indians, 39
Soil Conservation Service, 184
Soldier, George Whirlwind, 95
solicitor, 154, 171
Southwest Indian Congress, 107–11
Spotted Eagle, 107
Stephens, John, 32, 34, 56
Steward, Luther, 130
Stiewer, Frederick, 128
surplus Indian lands, 147

Talton v. *Mayes,* 201–202, 204, 205, 211, 212
Taos, Pueblo, 40
Taylor, Graham, 186, 187
Teapot Dome scandal, 41
territory, Indian, 55
Thom, Melvin, 236
Thomas, Elmer, 46, 123, 124–26, 129, 132–35, 150, 175
Thomas-Rogers bill, 175, 176
Thompson, Morris, 221
Thompson, William, 129, 135
Towner, Elwood A., 180

traditional Indians, 233–36, 240–42
treaties, 4, 7–8
tribal business corporations, 144
tribal concept, 186–87
tribal councils, 248
Tribal Councils bill, 60, 79
tribal courts, 30, 159, 248
Tribal Government Tax Status Act, 225
tribal membership, 205
Twenty Points, 238, 239, 263

Udall, Stewart, 216, 224, 227
United Nation Americans, 237
United Nations, 241
United Nations Commission on Human Rights, 242
United States v. *Sandoval,* 38
United Traders Association, 109
University of Chicago, 198
Ute Indians, 4

Vice President's Council on Indian Opportunity, 217
Villard, Oswald Garrison, 41

Wallace, Henry, 136
War on Poverty, 6, 184, 197, 249
Watkins, Arthur, 5, 193, 194
Werner, Theodore, 82, 84, 89, 93, 97, 100
West Coast Indian Conferences, 115–19
Wheeler, Burton K., 122, 124–25, 128–31, 136, 137, 150–52, 155–56, 169, 177–78, 180, 246
Wheeler-Howard Act, 137, 141, 158, 177, 178, 181. *See also* Indian Reorganization Act
Wheeler-Howard bill, 93, 102. *See also* Indian Reorganization bill
White, William Allen, 41
White Bull, George, 105
White Calf, 29
White Crow, Jack, 227
white towns, 20–21
Wilbur, Lyman, 41, 123
William the Conqueror, 192
Willis, Paul, 94
Wilson, Edward, 119
Wilson, Richard, 239
Winnebago Indians, 94, 163
Wissler, Clark, 41

Woehlke, Walter, 97, 103, 107, 109–11, 114–16, 118
Wooldridge, Earl, 97, 98
Work Projects Administration, 179
Wounded Knee, 12–13, 14, 199, 216, 226, 231, 239–40, 249

Yakima Indians, 92, 116–17, 133, 224
Yankton Sioux Indians, 94, 178–79, 180
Yellowtail, Robert, 92

Zimmerman, William, 61, 115, 136, 189, 193